ODD MAN
RUSH

A HARVARD KID'S HOCKEY ODYSSEY FROM CENTRAL PARK TO SOMEWHERE IN SWEDEN—WITH STOPS ALONG THE WAY

BILL KEENAN

Foreword by Adam Graves

SPORTS
PUBLISHING

Sports Publishing books may be purchased in bulk at special discounts for sales promotion, corporate gifts, fund-raising, or educational purposes. Special editions can also be created to specifications. For details, contact the Special Sales Department, Sports Publishing, 307 West 36th Street, 11th Floor, New York, NY 10018 or sportspubbooks@ skyhorsepublishing.com.

Sports Publishing® is a registered trademark of Skyhorse Publishing, Inc.®, a Delaware corporation.

Visit our website at www.sportspubbooks.com.

10 9 8 7 6 5 4 3 2

Library of Congress Cataloging-in-Publication Data is available on file.

Cover design by Tom Lau
Cover photo credits: Left, David Silverman; center, Magnus de Wall; right, Jonny Dahlgren

ISBN: 978-1-61321-817-4
Ebook ISBN: 978-1-61321-861-7

Printed in the United States of America

TABLE OF CONTENTS

5391

Author's note:

I have changed some names in order to protect the innocent—and more importantly, the guilty. Also, although some characters are composites and the narrative has been compressed in places to keep the story moving, the events portrayed in the book are accurate to the best of my recollection. Finally, in instances where foreign languages appear, if grammatically or otherwise incorrect, sorry—I'm still working on English.

In any event, if you want the truth, as I saw it when I wrote it, you're in luck. If it weren't the truth, I'd still be playing hockey, not writing about it.

Foreword

by Adam Graves

I FIRST MET Billy at my summer hockey camp in Windsor, Ontario, in 1993. He even has a Polaroid picture to prove it. I can vividly remember the young, eager, smiling kid from New York City. He was a mere seven years old, and I was twenty-five having just finished my second season with the Rangers. My career has been an open book: I played sixteen seasons in the National Hockey League and was lucky enough to win two Stanley Cups—with the Edmonton Oilers in 1990 and the NY Rangers in 1994. Hockey has given me the opportunity to meet incredible people throughout my journey and I firmly believe that meeting individuals like Billy is truly the highlight of my career. I know you will enjoy his stories and how he lived for the game of hockey.

Hockey took me from a small town in Canada to New York City and the bright lights of Madison Square Garden; it took Billy from an apartment on Manhattan's Upper East Side to small towns in the European countryside. We are living proof that no matter where you come from, or where you are going, our great sport is the same, and so are the characters you are lucky enough to play with along the way.

Hockey is more than just a game. Hockey is its own culture— a lifestyle, which brings people together from every walk of life. It crosses barriers and transcends social, geographic, and economic boundaries like few other things can. When people ask me what I miss most about the game, the answer is always the same: the friendships, the unique teammates and coaches in the locker room, and the moments away from the ice.

Billy and I have something else in common. He not only came to the rink early but he always lingered late. I recognize this quality in myself, as I never wanted to miss a thing either. Unfortunately, there comes a time for every player when you have to say goodbye. Billy has found a way to preserve his experiences and have them live on. His perseverance was evident, as he continued to pursue his passion for hockey through adversity. If you want to hear about the real characters of the game with no punches pulled and understand the true grit that keeps us coming back to the rink day after day, keep reading. That's what Billy's story is all about.

Odd Man Rush

1. When a hockey team enters the offensive zone and outnumbers the players on the opposing team by one or more players, e.g., two-on-one, three-on-two, three-on-one, etc.

2. When a young American hockey player from New York City skates around Europe, trying to figure out what the hell he's doing with his life.

Prologue

Released from the penalty box, I haul ass across the ice as the chanting grows louder.

"*KEE-NAN DU ARSCH-LOCH!*" Clap, clap, clap-clap-clap. "*KEE-NAN DU ARSCH-LOCH!*" Clap, clap, clap-clap-clap.

The last time a crowd chanted my name, I was six. And dreaming.

"*KEE-NAN DU ARSCH-LOCH!*" Clap, clap, clap-clap-clap. "*KEE-NAN DU ARSCH-LOCH!*" Clap, clap, clap-clap-clap.

Everyone on the bench cheeks to the right to make room. "What're they saying?" I shout to our hulking Russian centerman over the roar of the 2,000 shitfaced fans, a swell of bright green and black punctuated by waving flags and glowing sparklers. The safest place during Herford games is on the ice.

"Nothing. Zey chant nothing," Oleg replies devoid of emotion.

"They're chanting *something*. I hear my name."

"You not hear your name."

"Yeah I do. Hear it? *Keenan dooo something.*"

"Fine. Zey say something. But I not hear Keenan."

"Oleg, they're saying Keenan. *Keenan dooo something.*" I remove my helmet, spray some water on my head, and run my hand through my hair as I gaze into the crowd.

Oleg sighs. "Fine. Zey are yelling, like, *Keenan sucks. Keenan sucks. Keenan . . .*"

"Okay, okay," I interrupt him, quickly strapping my helmet back on my head. "I got it."

"Wait," Oleg says. "Zis is not *sucks* zey chant. Zis is something more worse zan *suck*. I don't know which word zis is in English." Grinning evilly, he looks up at the ceiling of the arena. "*Behind*, maybe? *Behind circle*? Keenan is a *behind circle*? But something more worse."

"You mean *asshole*?"

He bangs his stick on the boards. "*Asshole*! Right." Still grinning, he adds, "Zey don't like you, buddy."

"Thanks for the clarification." I pick up a water bottle, spewing a stream of water on a Herford player as he skates by before squirting a few pumps into my mouth and spitting it onto the ice.

The final five minutes of the game are chaos. Still leading 1–0, we exchange breakaway chances with Herford but no one scores. In the last minute, with their goalie pulled for an extra attacker, they blitz our goaltender, Hans, with an onslaught of shots. Hans uses every inch of both his pliable body and his sure stick to deny them. On the bench, even more chaos ensues. Word has it that some of the more hammered Herford fans are in the midst of breaking into our locker room in an attempt to steal our clothes, one of their charming traditions. Making the trip back to Neuwied in my jockstrap—in a bus permanently pumping at meat locker—is not something I'm excited about, but our veterans, having seen this before, assure us that our fans will counter with a strong defense.

Traditionally, after the final buzzer, both teams line up for a civil post-game handshake, but there's no chance that's happening tonight because our opponents are a bunch of *arschlochs*. More importantly, the participants in the Westphalia Regional Figure Skating Qualifier are already lining up to take the ice. We mob Hans in his goal crease and skate towards the Neuwied section of the arena to give our loyal, rabid fans a well-deserved stick salute while a few remaining Herford fans fire empty beer cans at us.

Moments later in the locker room, while my teammates peel off their sweat-drenched equipment—and as Oleg, Mother Russia himself, makes a show of scraping the ice from his skate blades—our goalie receives a big round of applause and a few celebratory tape balls rocketed at his face. Hans nods in appreciation with a wave and a few curses.

Like every other goalie, Hans has his idiosyncrasies. Between periods he takes three bags of gummy bears from his locker, dumps the candies onto the bench, piling the oranges, greens, and yellows into one mound and the reds into another. Then, very gently, with his thumb and index finger, he picks up a single red one, stares at it lovingly, and pops it into his mouth, savoring every chew—must have something to do with red being a power color, like Tiger Woods always wearing red on Sundays.

"Worked again, huh?" I say eyeing the empty gummy bear wrappers.

"What?"

"The gummy bear bullshit you do between periods."

He shrugs. "I like the way the red ones taste. The green ones and the yellow ones and the orange ones, not so much."

I stare at him. "That's it?"

"That's it."

"So it's not like you think the red ones give you good luck or something?"

He gives me a funny look. "Of course not. That would be weird."

I linger a few seconds, wondering if Henrik Lundqvist eats Hershey bars or bananas or smokes a pack of Marlboro Reds during intermissions, then I tap Hans on his leg pads. "Great game."

Returning to my locker, I join in the celebration: "Atta way, fellas," I yell. "Great fuckin' win tonight! We owed those fuckers after that shitshow against them last month. Fuckin' great team win, boys! Great fuckin' win!" As I finish my soliloquy, Willi, with a bag of ice taped to his shoulder, downs his beer, tosses it off the side of the trash can, and tries to fire up the boom box but there's no outlet in the locker room. There rarely is.

As I pull my jersey off, something cold and round hits me in the nose. Wiping the ice from my face, I make out Oleg's grin from across the room.

"Nice shot, jackass."

"*Заткнись, иди на хуй.*"

I can't tell if he likes me or not. I can't tell if I like him.

After a road win, the long bus trips home can be more fun than the game. Victories bring a team together. Also, rumor has it we're stopping at McDonald's. The players who tend to keep to themselves in the front of the bus will roam towards the rear where the loud guys rule. Even at Harvard, where the fun times were rare, some of those Saturday night bus trips home to Cambridge from the North Country of upstate New York bordered on fun.

Coach Donato would sit up front laughing like a half-wit watching *Family Guy* on his portable DVD player, though we wondered which jokes he found funny. Our designated team impressionist would grab the mic and imitate Ervin, our team hypnotist (you read that right). Finally, in the back of the bus, it was all about the "would you rather" game, your typical Harvard intellectual meeting of the minds, most often led by our captain and future Arizona Coyotes defenseman, Dylan "Dicer" Reese: "Would you rather make out with a dude for five minutes or have him suck your dick for one minute?" "Ricky couldn't last a minute!" someone would shout. "Especially if Stevie was givin' him the gummer!" another would add.

"Who shit themselves?" Coach Donato would yell from the front row, turning his head and peering towards the back of the bus. "Probably you, Donuts," the guy sitting in the row behind me would say just loud enough for the surrounding players to hear. "Head's usually up his ass . . . shouldn't be hard for him to crack the case," another player would add from an unidentifiable seat a few rows back.

After wins, pretty much everything is funny.

"*Dumme ziege!*" someone yells. It means "dumb goat," I think, and there's one in every story. A few guys smile at me so I nod and laugh. It'd be nice to know what's going on. But for now, I remain on the periphery, not yet in on the jokes and possibly the butt of them.

All that said, at twenty-two, there's no place I'd rather be than on this bus returning home with my teammates. But that's the way it works with me and hockey. Even when it's horrible, it's wonderful.

PART ONE

FIRST PERIOD

CHAPTER ONE

Canuck to the Core

It DIDN'T START in a small Canadian town on a frozen pond in a backyard, but rather at Lasker Rink, an outdoor swimming pool located on the northern end of Central Park in New York City. On my fifth birthday, and after a year of pleading, Mom and Dad bought me a pair of skates and a hockey stick, and we ventured a mile up Fifth Avenue to give it a go.

When I set foot on that frozen-over pool, I was gone. It was love at first stride. Skating mostly on my ankles, I chased the puck all over the rink except the corners, not because I was scared to get hit, but because I was afraid I'd get my foot caught in the six-inch rut that separated the boards from the ice surface. The undulations on the non-hazardous portions of the ice rivaled the Augusta National greens, though I bet Augusta is higher on the Stimpmeter.

By the time I was five and three-quarters, I watched all the New York Rangers games on television, and in elementary school, all my writing assignments, regardless of the topic assigned by the teacher, revolved around my favorite Ranger, Adam Graves.

Graves could do it all: score goals, pester opponents, stick up for his teammates, and come through when his teammates and the entire city of New York were counting on him. What he lacked in skill, he made up for with grit. He played each shift with absolutely no regard for the well-being of his body. His on-ice accomplishments, however, were equaled, if not surpassed, by his generosity of spirit and commitment towards helping people off the ice. He was just as likely to be found visiting children at hospitals as he was working on his game at the rink.

Adam Graves was a god. And he had holy hockey hair.[1]

Once I got my footing on the ice with the help of a few hard wraps of tape around my ankles, I emulated Graves on every level, from his skating style, to his manner of celebrating his goals, to his mullet.[1] I decided to adopt Graves's Canadian accent and spent hours repeating "abooot" and "ooot" in my bathroom mirror. My mom sewed Canadian flags on all my jackets. I paraded around my first grade classroom with Loonies and Toonies jingling in my pockets, proudly displaying the large maple leaf patch. I even insisted that my teachers call me Guy. It didn't stick but my first grade teacher, Ms. Rhodie, a native Swede, convinced me that Sweden was probably just as worthy of my allegiance as my native Canada. Ms. Rhodie understood hockey was my favorite sport and didn't mind that I spelled it favourite.

Yeah, I was abooot as obsessed as you could get.

I was so enamored with Graves that I wanted to share his pain. Whenever he was injured or got dinged up in a fight, I'd ice my hands, or my face, or, in one bizarre instance, my balls to get the imaginary swelling down before his next shift. It's a wonder my parents entrusted my life to that kid.

There wasn't anything to wonder though. I was Bill Keenan from Windsor, Ontario, the hockey player who was going to play for the New York Rangers. What was so hard to understand about that?

---

1   "Hockey hair" isn't quite a mullet. It takes on many forms but the common theme is long flowing locks. Synonyms include salad, sal, bucket, lid, and flow. Graves had sick flow. Early '90s Jagr had something else that might very well account for the break-up of Czechoslovakia.

I was six when I played in my first organized hockey game as a member of the North Park Mini Mites—an away game starting at 6:30 a.m. against Beaver Dam (the name warrants applause)—and to say I was excited would have been the understatement of the decade. Instead of scrambling in the morning to put on my hockey gear at the rink, Dad helped me suit up the previous night—we're talking elbow pads, shin pads, shoulder pads, and neckguard[2]—pretty much everything. In the morning, we laced up my skates, strapped on my helmet, popped a few hand warmers in my hockey gloves, and off we went, Dad hoping like hell he had the rink directions right.

Someone once said it's not whether you win or lose, it's how you play the game. Well, that person didn't know shit.

In the locker room before we took the ice for our game, I could already tell my teammates weren't as into it as I was—only six other kids showed up for starters. On top of that, simply buckling their helmets was a major accomplishment for them and their parents who snapped fifty photos of the feat. I stared, appalled, as none of these kids even knew how to hold their sticks properly.

There were a couple guys who at least appeared to like hockey. Winston had almost every Rangers player's rookie card and his dad had season tickets. But on the ice, Winston was scared shitless of the puck. He'd scurry away whenever it came near him, usually tumbling to his face within the first two strides. It was remarkable he could even see the black disc considering his Rec-Specs fogged up right after his last gulp of hot chocolate before we hit the ice. Winston was our goalie.

Our second game at Lasker had a better turnout of nine kids, including one girl. I thought it was embarrassing that my right-winger had on double runners until I found out my left-winger was wearing figure skates. Neither one was the girl.

Before the game, Coach Randall gave us the first, and still one of the worst pep talks of my life, the highlight being his declaration that, "Winning doesn't matter. Good sportsmanship and having fun are what matter. Besides, none of you are going to play in the NHL."

2　Looked like a neck brace.

I stared at his hangdog face and thought, *Sportsmanship? Fun without winning? What drug was this guy on? Why can't I play in the NHL? Somebody has to be on the Rangers in fifteen years. Why not me?*

The November air was crisp that Saturday morning as snowflakes seemed to hover weightlessly in the air much like the pungent smell of pot that originated from the group of hooded guys huddled on a Central Park North bench. The game was delayed due to yet another Zamboni malfunction so opening faceoff was just before sunrise around 6:23 a.m. Winston was stellar in net, playing mainly on his back, a highly unorthodox and ineffective style. After his mom laced up his skates and wiped his nose, he had an uncanny ability to avoid the protective rubber mats and stomp solely on the pavement from the locker room to the ice surface.

Coach Randall's next piece of wisdom for the team came after the first period. "Play till you hear the whistle." Sound advice, I admit, but with both rinks at Lasker hosting games simultaneously, it was damn near impossible to decipher which ref (re: over-involved dad holding onto the boards) was blowing his whistle to enforce whatever rules he decided to invent.

After the game, I approached Coach Randall and asked if he was ever going to assemble a power play unit instead of just sending out the next line. It's not like I was suggesting we run the umbrella PP with me quarterbacking it. But when half your team uses masking tape on their stick blades, I probably should have known better. "Bill, I know you want to win, but remember, there is no 'I' in team," he told me following our 7–0 loss. *No "I" in team,* I thought as Coach Randall went around congratulating us for our effort. *He's right, but there's definitely a "you" in dumb.*

Once out of my gear, I sulked down Fifth Avenue with Dad as I watched my two linemates skip together, hand-in-hand, a block ahead of me. "I don't want to play on this team," I told him.

"What?" he responded, certain he'd misheard me.

"Coach said winning doesn't matter, and that I'll never play in the NHL, and that he doesn't want to do anything too complicated because he doesn't want to confuse us, and that we shouldn't go too hard because he doesn't want to be responsible for us getting hurt, and that girls can play hockey with boys and . . ."

"Okay, okay," Dad said. "Understood." He couldn't have been too shocked though. Just the other day, a mother had confronted him because she was concerned about me always yelling for passes without saying "please."

When we got back to the apartment, we started researching higher-level youth leagues in New Jersey and Long Island. Unfortunately, by that point, the rosters for all those teams had been finalized, so I was left to play the season with the North Park Mini Mites, and all I can say is it's a good thing winning didn't matter to Coach Randall, as our 1–14 record was good for last in the league. We were bad—probably would've gotten spanked by the original District 5 Mighty Ducks team. Christ, Winston had a bottle of Perrier on top of his net.

But despite our abysmal performance, it wasn't a total loss for me. According to the Elias Sports Bureau, I scored 23 goals (only two on my own net) and notched a couple of assists, both of which were shots that deflected off one of my teammates who was doing snow angels. Admittedly, I wasn't much of a passer, but that wasn't because I didn't want to share the puck. I didn't pass because most of my teammates collapsed to the ice, inexplicably, within moments of coming into contact with the puck, or even the thought of it.[3]

Our season concluded with a pizza party during which Coach Randall doled out team awards. One kid got the sportsmanship trophy, one kid got the most improved player trophy, and every kid got a participation trophy (which was more about parents participating by writing checks than it was about the kid participating in any practices or games.)

Anyway, I threw mine out when I got home.

Following my season with the North Park Mini Mites, I landed a spot with one of the top youth travel teams in the area, the New Jersey Rockets.

---

3   Any youth hockey forward who claims he cares about assists is lying.

The anticipation built all summer. NHL stars like Jeremy Roenick and the Mullen brothers had played their youth hockey for the Rockets. The team played in the Atlantic District Minor Hockey League, not one of those scam leagues where every player gets a trophy at the end of the season.

The organization took the game seriously: All teams had home *and* away jerseys; plus, each jersey had a fighting strap and the player's last name stitched to the back—*stitched*, not iron-on. And according to team rules, game jerseys were never to be stuffed in our hockey bags but instead always placed on hangers. And no player was allowed to wear 66 or 99. It was like a mini-pro team if you saw us skating around in our game uniforms. You'd never even know our starting goalie's mother pawned her engagement ring to pay for her son's equipment and travel expenses.

But my excitement soon turned to anxiety after my first practice. At St. Bernard's School, we got dismissed from second grade at 4:00 p.m., giving Mom an hour and a half to make the two-hour trip to central Jersey. As I raced into the locker room still dressed in my school uniform (khakis, collared shirt, and loafers), the room fell silent. No one talked to me that day, or that week. I made the embarrassing trip to the coaches' room to get my skates tied (the only guy who couldn't do it himself), and returned to find the three rolls of black hockey tape in my hockey bag gone. I might not have contributed to the team on the ice that day but at least I did in the locker room.

Back at Lasker I was the big fish in a small frozen over pool, but those days were over and not being The Man took some adjustment. I wasn't an outcast but I never quite felt at home. In the locker room, there were no figure skates, girls, bottles of Perrier, or Rec-Specs but there was a lot of cursing and spitting. This was a *real* hockey team.

On the ice, everyone could skate forwards *and* backwards; do hockey stops in *both* directions; and everyone, even the goalies, could lift the puck all the way to the crossbar. On top of that, the Rockets played at Bridgewater Sports Arena which had two regulation-sized rinks; Lasker, on the other hand, had two separate ice surfaces (re: two pools), but combined, they weren't half the size of a real hockey rink. At North Park, there was a buzzer sounding every minute-and-a-half (even on breakaways) to signal a line change. On the Rockets, shifts were forty-five seconds and changes were on the fly.

Winning mattered to the Rockets—a lot. That meant I spent most games at the end of the bench, handing guys water bottles and opening the gate. But while I didn't receive much ice time in games, practices were a different deal. Our head coach, a recent Princeton graduate who had captained the Tigers hockey team his senior year, showed me a whole new part of the game I had never learned while playing with North Park—it was called defense. While it wasn't much fun learning to back-check, I felt an allegiance to work hard for Coach Scowby. After all, he was from Saskatchewan and I didn't want to let down a fellow Canuck.

But it wasn't just the players and coaches on the Rockets who took the game seriously. The North Park mothers wore mink coats and sipped coffee from thermoses, offering plenty of encouragement to their sons (and daughters) regardless of play. Meanwhile, the fathers would spend their time shaking the hell out of each other's hands, exchanging business cards, and talking about country houses and the stock market. Hockey's a physical sport, but the only body contact at Lasker was that of a mother's consoling arm after her kid got a bloody nose from "dry air" or a father's tap on the helmet after a game. Rockets parents were more into it. One group spent games leaning precariously over the balcony, hands cupped around their mouths, barking instructions at their kids (and other kids) like "Pick it up, Joey!" "Move the puck, Bobby!" "Play the damn body, Billy!" The other group was quieter but just as intense. They stood by the glass wearing their leather Rockets jackets with their kid's number pinned to their Rockets hat. One hand held a stopwatch timing their kid's shifts and the other hand held a whiskey nip.

Coach Sowby always told us to play hungry.

"I gotta score today," said our chunky but skilled centerman, Joey, as he reached in my bag to get some black tape for his stick.

"Me too," I replied, hoping he wouldn't use the last of my tape again since I needed some too.

"Nah, you don't understand. I *need* to score today. My pops said no dinner for me if I don't get a goal." Big Joe, a retired Jersey cop living off disability payments, took eating as seriously as he took his son's hockey. Big Joe must have been three bills easy. One game when Joey got a ten-minute misconduct, Big Joe brought him a sub to eat in the penalty box.

I knew from watching Gravey that toughness was a key part of hockey. I also knew how to deliver a knockout blow to my teachers at school—end a sentence with a preposition. But the hockey world saw body blows differently. Thankfully, I never had to deal with the dinner deprivation technique. That probably wouldn't have worked anyway.

After receiving an inadvertent slash to the wrist in a game against the Philly Junior Flyers—a miniature version of the Broad Street Bullies with rat tails—I fell to the ice and stayed down, clutching my wrist and waiting for a coach. That's the way it worked at North Park. But no coach came this time. I did, however, hear a voice shout some instructions as I writhed on the ice. "Get up, pussy." I turned on my side searching for the Junior Flyers player. "Seriously, get the fuck up. We got a game to finish." It was my teammate, Zandy.

I knew the only way I'd be accepted by my teammates was if I played hard, acted more like them, and learned more bad words. While the St. Bernard's School motto was explicitly stated on our oxford shirts, "*Perge Sed Caute*" (Proceed but with Caution), I had finally learned the implicit motto of the New Jersey Rockets, "*Don't Be a Pussy.*"

By the time my second season with the Rockets rolled around, I had Mom pack a pair of JNCO jeans (with a chain wallet and non-functioning beeper), a No Fear shirt, and some BK Dymacel kicks that I could change into before arriving at practice, leaving my school uniform, or "tuxedo" as my teammates called it, in the car. I could finally tie my own skates and knew how to fuckin' curse.

Before a game at the halfway point of the season, my teammate Zandy yelled across the locker room, "Dilly, gimme some of that black tape."

In hockey circles, adding the letter "Y" to the end of either your first or last name is a rite of passage—Adam Graves's teammates called him Gravey—and even though Zandy (and eventually the rest of the guys and parents) called me Dilly rather than Billy, I knew I had earned my spot. Dilly became my alter ego, the version of myself that I liked the best. I masqueraded as William Howard Keenan III on the Upper East Side. But on the ice, I was Dilly the hockey player. I changed my AOL screen name to Dilly9.

I wasn't even fazed when I found out what Dilly was short for.

CHAPTER TWO

Junior Hockey Circus

THAT SUMMER AFTER my second season with the Rockets, Mom, magician that she was, got me a spot in Adam Graves's summer hockey camp. My head practically exploded. It was a homecoming of sorts. I was going to Windsor, Ontario, Adam's hometown, to learn the game at the feet (or the skates) of the master.

I sat shotgun the entire ten-hour drive, my nose flattened against the passenger side window barely able to stay in my seat, the seatbelt digging into my shoulder, as we crossed the Ambassador Bridge over the Detroit River. I don't think I blinked once when we finally made it onto Canadian soil—farmland as far as the eye could see in every direction. I had never seen this many miles of crops in my life. Hell, I didn't know what a crop was. When we made our first pit stop north of the border to fill up the gas tank, I rushed into the convenience store, found a distinctly Canadian looking candy bar called Caramilk, and finally used the Canadian currency I'd been carrying in my pocket for the past three years. It was abooot time.

It was on this trip that I discovered it—TSN, Canada's version of ESPN. On ESPN, the day pitchers and catchers report for spring training trumps coverage of the Stanley Cup Finals. TSN, however, ran nonstop coverage of NHL pre-training camp stories while MLB scores were relegated to the ticker on the bottom of the screen.

The Sunday night before my first day of camp as I was stickhandling a golf ball in the hotel room racking up damage charges, Mom warned me not to get my hopes up.

"What do you mean?" I got nervous. My hopes were about as up as they could get.

"Well, Adam will show up once in a while, but he's most likely going to be busy getting ready for the season. You might not see him much."

For one of the few times I can remember, Mom was wrong. Adam Graves was there every day.

I knew Graves was big—I had a life-size poster of him in my room at home—but in person, he was massive. It looked like he had his shoulder pads on underneath his white T-shirt. I hung on his every word as he delivered the Gospel of Graves. "Shoot pucks, boys, eh. Any time you have a chance to work on your shot, make the most of it. It's a privilege to play this game. You're all lucky you have the parents you've got. If you want to play this game at a high level, you've got to always be looking to improve. And if you want to score lots of goals, shoot biscuits every day after school. Build yourself a net in shop class if you have to. Whatever it takes."

It was the first time I enjoyed having an older person stand above me and tell me what to do. I took scrupulous notes in my notebook: "Shoot biscuits all day. Find out what shop class is."

"Your driveway, backyard, basement . . . doesn't matter where, boys. Set up a net and fire pucks," Graves instructed.

Driveway? Backyard? Basement? I was going to have to improvise.

Meanwhile, it was also nice to be around other kids who were *actually* Canadian.

CANADIAN KID: How many goals you score last year?

ME: Twenty-three. You?
CANADIAN KID: Twenty-four. You related to Mike Keenan?
ME: He's my uncle.

I wasn't related to New York Rangers coach Mike Keenan but it was nice to be around kids who knew who he was.

The camp concluded with a scrimmage Friday afternoon. Campers were split into two teams and Graves played half the game with one team and half with the other. During my last shift, Gravey, with nine seven-year-olds draped to his back and another half dozen swarming his ankles, deked through the entire opposing team (and a few of the kids who didn't know which team they were on), until a dream I'd had finally became a reality—me and Graves together on an odd man rush. Graves faked the shot and the defenseman fell (not because of the fake, he just tripped on his own stick). The goalie didn't stand a chance—nearly his entire body, all three feet of it, was already well inside the net. As I banged my stick on the ice, Gravey hit me with a perfect pass which I deflected in. I celebrated by grabbing Graves's shin then collapsing to the ice.

After the game, Graves spent some time talking to me and Mom. It took Mom about ten minutes to explain to him that we came to Windsor, Ontario, just for his camp—no Canadian relatives to visit, no cross-country vacation. He gave Mom a look that translated roughly into *you must be nuts*. He then gave me the jersey he wore that day in the scrimmage. It was darkened and heavy from his sweat which came not from the scrimmage but rather the three hours he spent outside in the August heat talking to each camper that afternoon.

On our drive home, Mom suggested I put the jersey in my hockey bag and she could wash it when we got back home. *Wash the jersey Adam Graves took off his back and gave me himself? Maybe Gravey was right. Mom was nuts.*

When I returned home armed with the skills, knowledge, and jersey that I believed I'd take right to the NHL, our apartment was undergoing renovations. Kids who play hockey have an uncanny ability to make any space into some type of rink, whether it's playing knee-hockey in the hallway of a hotel with a group of teammates at a tournament or using the kneehole of a desk as a goal. Most of the time, these games involve mini sticks and a small ball.

Mom and Dad saw the large vacant room with columns and a newly completed fireplace as our future living room. Me, I saw a hockey rink—an actual one. Because my parents supported their children's dreams, and they knew I wouldn't shut up about it, the rink won.

"You're crazy, buddy," our doorman Eugene said as he helped me haul the regulation-sized hockey net to our seventh floor apartment. But I made great use of the net. Every day after school, I strapped on my rollerblades, grabbed my stick, and honed my game. I wore the jersey Graves had given me hoping something would rub off: His goal scoring touch, his intimidating toughness, his incredible hockey hair.

The smell was the only thing that stuck.

After two weeks of errant wrist shots, the inevitable happened. My parents couldn't believe my poor judgment in taking high shots. I couldn't believe my shot was hard enough to break the window. Once all the shards of broken glass were picked up that Monday afternoon, Mom and Dad had double-paned glass installed on all the windows, and I was back at it, firing fluttering low shots into the net.

In my mind, the Rangers announcers, Sam Rosen and John Davidson, narrated every play.

SAM ROSEN: *Keenan steals it from Daneyko, and the Rangers have a two-on-one . . . Keenan streaking in . . . over to Graves—*
MOM: Bill! Time for dinner!
SAM ROSEN: *The crowd is going wild. Graves . . . back to Keenan . . . GOAL! It's a power play goal!*
MOM: Your food's getting cold!
JOHN DAVIDSON: *Keenan and Graves! They do it again! What a play, OH BABY!*
MOM: Bill. Dinnertime. Come on!

After the game, I'd head to the mirror in my room where imaginary Stan Fischler, The Hockey Maven himself, would interview me.

Gravey and I had undeniable chemistry in those games in my living room.

Mom: Bill, Get to the table *NOW!*

Cranky Mrs. Healy, who was a hundred and fifty years old and lived on the floor below us, called Mom one day complaining of a leak in her ceiling that she was convinced was coming from our apartment. She was always complaining about something. The shriek from Mom's mouth when she saw me trying to make ice in the living room rink about broke the new window she'd just replaced. The line had to be drawn somewhere.

At school, I saw life through a hockey prism. Multiplication and division weren't too bad: *The Rangers have four lines and three forwards on each line, so three times four is twelve forwards . . . The Rangers have fourteen total forwards and only twelve play in each game, so that means there are two extra forwards who don't play each game—usually a fighter and a guy just called up from Binghamton in the AHL—so twelve goes into fourteen one time with a remainder of two . . .* And so on.

Anything beyond basic arithmetic though, I was screwed.

The 1994–95 NHL season was marred by a lockout which wiped out the first half of the schedule. What's a lockout? I couldn't figure out why someone couldn't find a key.

But the good part was that the Rangers had won the Stanley Cup the year before, ending a forty-four year drought, which meant they had even longer to parade it around New York City. Mom found an event where fans could to take pictures with Lord Stanley's Cup. When it was my turn to pose for a photo, Mom nudged me forward, "Go ahead, Bill. It's okay. You're allowed to touch it."[4] *I know, Mom,* I thought, *but it's a well-known fact if you touch the Cup before you actually win it, you're jinxed forever. If I put my hands on it, no team I ever play on will win one. Jeez, Mom, don't you know anything?*

---

4   It would be decades before another female would say those words to me.

When I was old enough, I enrolled in a summer hockey camp in Massachusetts called Paul Vincent's Dynamic Skating School. The camp's motto, 100% OR NOTHING, was enforced to the point that if campers weren't trying their hardest, they were escorted off the ice and, periodically, told to go home. (The counselors weren't spared: Paul Vincent was known to throw them off the ice if they did a poor job of demonstrating a drill.) Unparalleled in its approach to teaching hockey, PV's, as I so fondly called it, was the highlight of my summers.

Paul was a New England hockey legend who had helped develop countless college and professional players, and for some reason, he took a liking to me. "Willy, yah're a good kid and a good hockey playah," he'd tell me in his thick Boston accent. "Yah can play as high as yah want in this game. Just keep workin' hahd." He saw something in me that I never saw in myself. "Thanks Mr. V. That means a lot," I'd respond. He'd smile, whack me on the shin pads, and then proceed to skate us campers into the ice for the next five hours with parachutes strapped to our backs.

Hockey is a cold-weather sport for most normal people, but for us obsessive-types, it was a year-round deal. While my classmates at school lived from vacation to vacation, I lived from hockey tournament to hockey tournament. During the fall and winter, I played on the New Jersey Rockets. Then, in the spring and summer, I played on one of the handful of select teams that offered kids an opportunity to stay on the ice for 365 days—a spring team based out of Stamford called the Connecticut Yankees. The Yankees were one of those select teams with nine first line centers, five number one defensemen, and two starting goalies.

One of my linemates, a big forward (and future NHLer), appeared to have two last names.

"Hey Jordy, why's the roster say your last name is Smotherman but your jersey has LaVallée on it?" I asked.

"My dad's last name's Smotherman, but my Mom is French-Canadian and her last name is LaVallée so I wanted to change it for hockey—more Canadian sounding."

Guy Keenan wasn't the only crazy one, eh?

The majority of my Yankee time was spent at tournaments throughout New England and Canada, and the rigorous schedule meant missing more class than St. Bernard's School allowed. My parents thought they had hid all the hand-delivered notes from the school questioning their decision to permit me to miss school, but I saw them. I must have contracted about sixteen different flu viruses and attended nine grandparents' funerals during my elementary school years. Eventually, the school brass accepted they were dealing with a temporarily-insane kid, and did their best to meet me in the middle, or at least what they deemed to be the middle. Mr. Johnson, our headmaster, would sidle over and ask in his affected English accent with one eyebrow raised and his lips pursed, "Feeling better, Mr. Keenan? Another bout of influenza last Friday, I presume?" He rarely strayed from speaking in iambic pentameter.

"Yes sir, feeling good . . . well. Thank you for asking."

"You know, Mr. Keenan, perhaps you could be the team physician for the New York Rangers one day."

"Never thought abooot that," I'd respond in my affected Canadian accent.

"Or, your English teacher, Mr. Austin, mentioned you seemed to enjoy writing. Mr. George Plimpton, a St. Bernard's lad himself, who grew up right across the street from you at 1165 Fifth, experienced great success as a sports journalist. He even wrote that book, *Paper Lion*, where he played for a professional football team. That might be something to consider as you get older."

I'd nod at him, thinking, *Who the hell is Mr. George Plimpton? And why does he always call everyone Mr.? He just doesn't get it. Wayne Gretzky's two sons go to this school. I wish The Great One could knock some sense into him.* I didn't want to be the guy performing surgery on players. And I didn't want to be the guy writing about the players. I just wanted *to be* the player.

The Connecticut Yankees dominated the regional tournaments in New England, but we knew our real competition awaited us north of the border; we ran into problems in Toronto, Montreal, Quebec City, Vancouver, Winnipeg, Edmonton, and Calgary. Not only were these teams intimidating on the ice, but their names alone left us wondering if we could compete—how do you beat the Montreal Viper Outlaw AAA Elites or the Pursuit of Excellence 86's? And then there were the top three Detroit teams with their major sponsors: Honeybaked Ham Selects AAA, Little Caesar's AAA, and Detroit Compuware AAA. That's a lot of "A's."

It was the Saturday night of the weeklong Calgary Stampede tournament in July. It was one of those tournaments where we'd play three games a day, stripping down to our lower half gear in between tilts with just enough time to refuel—players on Tim Hortons, parents on Jack Daniel's.

We had just lost in double overtime to the Minnesota Blades, a game that left me despising their number 27 who scored the game-winner. He was the Adam Banks of their team and had scored against us every time we played. I hated everything about him—his dumb face, his incredible scoring ability, everything. I knew I'd be seeing him again but I didn't anticipate we'd be good friends and college team-mates one day. Despite our overtime loss on Saturday to the Blades, we qualified for Sunday's elimination round.

Our Sunday morning matchup was against the Dartmouth Subways AAA team from Nova Scotia. The night before, a bunch of us decided to take a quick dip in the Flamingo Inn's pool. While we took turns working on our jackknife jumps and scoring each other's under-water handstands, what looked like an army of kid soldiers dressed in black marched into the adjacent workout room. Turned out they weren't soldiers but rather the Subways. Through the glass window, we watched in awe as our opponents ran through an intense workout that had them lifting, jumping, pushing, pulling, sweating, and screaming. Until then, I thought *I'd* taken the game seriously.

Later that evening, one of the parents organized a team dinner at a nearby tavern. Even our first-line centerman, Robbie Schremp, who somehow traveled to all the tournaments without a parent, came along. Robbie was arguably the top 1986-born player in the US at the time, and, physically-speaking, was far more mature and stood head and shoulders above us (and even some of the parents). It was at these

"Triple A" tournaments that Robbie introduced the rest of us players to movies that were *not* Triple A. If there was a youth hockey hall of fame, there would be a statue of Robbie outside. No wonder he went on to be a first round NHL draft pick. At dinner, I ordered a Shirley Temple and Robbie ordered a Labatt Blue. The young waitress asked for ID, after which Robbie, wearing his customary wifebeater and scraggly goatee, lifted his right arm, flexed his bicep, and winked at her. She blushed, brought him a beer . . . and her phone number.

The waitress dropped him off at the rink twenty minutes before the drop of the puck the following day. We were thirteen years old.

The Canadian teams were easy to spot on the ice and the Subways fit the stereotype. They always had at least one player who was 6'5" with a beard. We could never verify birthdates even when we asked the guy's wife and kid who showed up to cheer him on. Canadian teams also had a small red octagon above their jersey numbers with the word "STOP" on it or "ARRÊT" depending on which province they were from. Yet, these same jerseys also had fighting straps. Our Yankee jerseys had neither.

Despite Robbie's three goals, the Subways devoured us, 8–4. We had Robbie but the Subways had an even more dominant center who either scored or assisted on seven of their goals. There had been a lot of hype around the baby-faced playmaker during the tournament—some were calling him "The Next One" in a nod to Gretzky's nickname, "The Great One." Rumor had it there were even a couple NHL scouts in attendance to watch him play. He wasn't particularly big or strong but his speed and skills allowed him to make opposing defensemen, including ours, look completely inept. He knew every player's move—picking off our passes like they were intended for him, darting through gaps only he could see. He didn't anticipate the play; he knew the play. The only time he wasn't a threat was when he was resting on the bench, and unfortunately for us, that wasn't often. I was convinced he was one of those kids who had a forged birth certificate, making him younger than he actually was. After all, not only was he dominant in the '86 division but he was also the standout in the '85 division. He was born in August 1987.

"Boy, that kid could play, huh," Dad said after the game.

"Yeah, he was pretty good," I replied, pretending to be unimpressed. "But I think it's a little early for all this hype. We're thirteen and he's still just twelve, maybe eleven. He's got a long way to go before he'll be as special as everyone says." I rifled through the team rosters in the tournament program until I found him. Hometown: Cole Harbour, Nova Scotia, #87, Sidney Crosby. *Yeah, we'll see how far this little shit makes it*, I thought.

And this is why I'll never be a hockey scout.

The action in the parking lot was often more physical than what took place on the ice, generally taking the form of parent-on-coach violence. After the Subways beatdown, our backup goalie's mother, pissed that her son was left on the bench in the face of the blowout nearly ran over our assistant coach with her Ford pickup. I shouldn't have been surprised; after all, she was the parent of a goalie and a goalie's temperament has to come from *somewhere*. To be fair, she was out of options. She had already tried the opposite approach to no avail, slipping her room key under the assistant coach's door the night before the game.

But our terrific starting goalie, a little blabbermouth named Jonny, had potential and rarely left the ice. Jonny rarely shut up, too, but most of the conversations were about the same thing: Jackie, the daughter of our head coach, Mike Backman, and sister of our teammate, Sean Backman.

JONNY: Holy shit, Billy. You see Backman's sister today? I'm gonna get with her.
ME: She even know you exist?
JONNY (strapping on his goalie pads and finally removing his hat that seems to this day to be perpetually cocked off to the side): Doesn't matter, I'm gonna get with her.
ME: You talk to her? She probably won't get with you until you say stuff to her.
JONNY: I IM with her every night.
RANDOM TEAMMATE SITTING NEXT TO US IN LOCKER ROOM: You should try to cyber with her.

ME: Or talk to her first, in real life. Actually, first shower, *then* talk to her. That's what Schremp does.
JONNY: I know she wants me. I'm gonna nail her someday.

Turned out he was right: A decade-plus later, Jonathan Quick married Jackie and shortly thereafter led the Los Angeles Kings to two Stanley Cups while earning the Conn Smythe Trophy for playoff MVP.

He indeed did nail Jackie, at least twice, as they have two kids now.

* * *

After achieving some decent success in minor hockey, I decided my next goal would be to secure a commitment to a Division 1 college in the US, where I could play hockey and get a degree, a win-win situation for me and my parents. All of which meant I had to figure out where to play junior hockey, but fortunately, the decision was made for me: After my freshman year of high school, I was recruited to play on a Long Island-based Junior B hockey team called the New York Bobcats.

Junior hockey is open to any amateur aged twenty-one and younger; being fifteen, it was little surprise that I was the youngest and skinniest Bobcat. Keeping on weight had always been a problem for me. In training camp that August, during the first weigh-in of the preseason, I slipped a pair of two-and-a-half pound plates into each of my front pockets. At 144 pounds, I was still more than twenty pounds lighter than the next lightest player on the team.

Coach Creatine, our strength and conditioning guru and part-time assistant coach, who I'm pretty sure didn't own a pair of hockey skates, was all about dropping words like "lactic" and "physiological" as well as consulting the numbers: "Gentleman, the results are in from the preseason off-ice testing. As you can tell from these sheets I'm handing out, the majority of you degenerates are carrying too much fat on your frames." The scatter plot of body fat results showed twenty-three dots all situated somewhere between 10 and 20 percent. There were twenty-four players on the team. "And apparently one of you ass-holes had your ugly, anorexic girlfriend mess around with my calipers 'cause we had one reading show four percent body fat. Fuckin' gotta upgrade our technology here and quit runnin' a goddamn Mickey Mouse operation." With the opening presented to us players to give each other shit about the girls we were (or wanted) to be with, a collective laugh ensued in the locker room as I sat there hoping no one would realize the ugly, anorexic girlfriend was their newest fifteen-year-old rookie winger.

"Bonesy, you got some skill, but you're fuckin' skinny as shit," Coach Marshall told me. "Look like fuckin' Bambi on ice out there. We need you to pack on some muscle. Gotta get your legs big." Coach Marshall knew about muscles—his neck was thicker than my quads. "Look at any NHL guy. Check out the guys on the Islanders when they practice here. They all got big legs. We need you up around 165, 170." I wasn't a huge fan of checking out guys' legs, but I knew where he was coming from. Regardless, the only way I was going to get to 165 was if I were weighed with all my equipment on . . . soaking wet . . . on Jupiter.

I knew I wasn't exactly built to be a hockey player, at least not physically. This became clear to me at an early age. It's never a good sign for an aspiring professional hockey player to have his older sister, an aspiring professional ballerina, look in envy at her brother's slender frame and wish she had his body. All I could do was eat lot of pasta and hope for the best.

The majority of the guys on the team had already graduated from high school, so, by default, I hung out with a sixteen-year-old defenseman named Jakub Kubrak. Kubes and I differed drastically in body type: If I was built like a dollar bill, he was built like a bank safe. He soon became my best friend on the team.

Kubes was also from New York City, but a different New York City than the one in which I grew up. The son of Polish immigrants, he was born on the outskirts of Warsaw and raised in the Ridgewood section of Queens. If you don't know where that is, neither did I. All I did know is it was a few blocks from the Brownsville housing projects where Mike Tyson grew up. Whenever we'd drive Kubes home from practice, he'd never let us take him all the way to his neighborhood. Kubes was tough. His head was like a concrete wall, his skin like cracked paint. I only saw him fight on the ice, but he never lost a fight there. Luckily for me, he treated me like a younger brother. He didn't have much growing up, but he always had my back.

Due to my age and the oddball league rules, I wasn't allowed to participate in the off-ice workouts with the rest of the team at the local gym, and since I was also too young to get a gym membership, I turned our laundry room at home into a makeshift sports club, where I could work out at all hours. I loved how the distorted mirror in the laundry room made me appear thick and stocky. There was hope.

Like many young hockey players, my development was aided by an intense sibling rivalry. There were punches thrown, tears shed, and meltdowns displayed nearly every evening. Lillie, my little sister eleven years my junior, helped me develop my toughness, especially when she was still too young to talk and tell Mom the real reason she was crying.

Lil, whose bedroom was adjacent to Bill's 24-Hour Hockey Preparatorium, never complained about the crashing and banging of the five-pound dumbbells, but I can't say the same for some of my perturbed neighbors like the walking mummy Mrs. Healy, who bitched and moaned, even though the next Adam Graves was in her midst. Even at five years old, Lil often joined me in the gym, timing me with her stopwatch, goalie mask on, yelling words of encouragement. To this day, she is the best trainer I ever had.

But all my weight training didn't help me when it came to going up against the rival Connecticut Clippers —the *Slap Shot* team of the Metropolitan Junior B Hockey League. Clad in black from helmet to skates, they spent the final few minutes of warmups standing on the red line, growling and hissing at the other team. Some of their opponents laughed at the theatrics, while others shat their pants.

My first shift, I was shaking in my skates, as I lined up against the Clippers' 6'6" right winger. The goon spat on my skates. Breathing provoked fights with the Clippers.

My face was blue as I bit down hard on my mouthguard and looked out the cage of my helmet. For a moment, I envisioned eating through a straw with a bib around my neck for the rest of my life.

Glaring down at me, with his visor tilted well above his eyes, he said, "I'm gonna rearrange your face, you little bitch. You hear me?" He had dark, thick, steel wool-like scruff—probably hadn't shaved in a couple weeks. I hadn't shaved in fifteen years.

"Our Father, who art in heaven . . ."

As the ref dropped the puck, the goon flung off his gloves, unlatched his helmet, and, with a flick of his wrist, spun it on the ice and motioned for me to join him as he skated slowly backward to center ice.

I had dreamt about this moment—me squaring up against some behemoth. After dodging a wild hook, I deliver an upper cut that renders my opponent unconscious and take a glorious lap around the rink, both arms raised high and fists clenched as the crowd goes fuckin' apeshit. But that was the dream; in reality, I wanted no part of this nutbag.

Kubes had stuck up for me more times than I could count and I knew at some point I had to do it myself. Life is about facing your fears and this was one of my top three, the others being talking to cute girls and using airplane lavatories.

It's Junior Hockey code to remove one's helmet before fighting but I was so nervous that I nearly knocked myself over unsnapping it.

The goon rolled his eyes as he began to salivate and a droplet of drool dribbled down his mouth, hanging momentarily on the whiskers of his scarred up chin. "Jesus Christ, just rip the fuckin' thing off."

"Just a moment, kind sir, but I'm having a spot of trouble with this final strap. By the way, if it's not a problem, would you mind saving at least one of my teeth after you knock them from my mouth, so my parents can identify my body?"

It wasn't the first time I'd dropped my gloves that season though. I dropped my gloves every day after practice but that was to pick up the pucks with the rest of the rookies. This time, it'd be my teeth I'd be looking to collect from the ice.

From the corner of my eye, I could see the referee pulling out his notebook and pen, checking jersey numbers of all the players on the ice. It was the only way to keep track of all the penalties he would inevitably be assessing.

I could hear my teammates on the bench screaming: "Atta boy, Bonesy! Fuckin' light him up!" one guy yelled. "What the fuck are you doing, Keenan?!" shouted Kubes.

It was too late.

I'd seen the fight videos on YouTube and had already decided on my strategy: I charged him, hoping that decreasing the distance his hands had to travel to make contact with my face would lessen their impact. I went in hyperventilating, with both eyes closed voluntarily; my left eye remained shut involuntarily for the next month and I couldn't breathe out of my nose.

The PA announcer earned whatever his salary was in those games: "And finally (gasp), number 17 for the Clippers, two minutes for roughing, five minutes for fighting, and (gasp) a game misconduct for instigating. All penalties were at the nine-second mark of the first period."

After the game, as I iced down my face and contemplated the fortune that the tooth fairy would be leaving under my pillow that night, I felt a whack on my shin pad.

"Bonesy, you showed me two things out there today: One, you got some balls, big fuckin' balls. Good to see 'em finally," Coach Marshall said, grabbing his crotch as spit globules sprayed from his mouth. If I had a nickel every time Coach Marshall called me tough, I would have had five cents by the end of the season. "And second," he continued, holding up two fingers in front of my mangled face, "you got absolute shit for brains. Next time, pick someone in your weight class. I can't have players fuckin' dying mid-season."

The Bobcats were a good Junior B team (well, they were *a* Junior B team) but no colleges took players directly from that league for a couple reasons, the first being there were simply higher level junior leagues with a more talented selection of players, and the other being that scoring goals seemed to be incidental in most games as the main attraction was the fighting. No teams had sirens to play after goals were scored but every team had a recording of a boxing ring bell that they'd play over the loudspeaker when two guys squared off. It was rumored the Clippers had a WWF-replica belt awarded each month to the player who had the best fight. The last belt I earned was a second-degree white one in karate class.

One month into the regular season, the league mandated that two policemen show up to every game. Games were recorded on video, not for teams to use as learning tools but to capture all the line brawls and sucker punches, making it easier to dole out suspensions. I always knew what to do when the benches cleared: Immediately seek out the opposing team's backup goalie and slow dance with him until the refs (and cops) got everything under control.

Even off the ice, there was the constant threat of season-ending injuries. It was the Clippers annual Christmas tournament and everyone was in the holiday spirit including the Connecticut State troopers who were decked out in Santa hats. After getting eliminated in the semis on Saturday night, Coach Marshall stormed into the locker room, flipping over a table resulting in Gatorade flooding the floor. "Why the fuck are you guys getting changed?" he roared. *Well, Coach. We just got eliminated for one, and second, I got a ten-page essay on the meaning of some green light in the* Great Gatsby *due on Monday and I haven't even given Mom the assignment yet.* "I'm sick of watching you play like absolute dogfuck!" Coach Marshall, with nearly all his body's blood in his face, stood in the center of the locker room doing a slow 360 degree turn as guys inconspicuously wiped his flecks of spit from their faces. "You boys don't wanna go? Gimme your equipment. I'll go." If only he had made the offer before the game.

Still enraged by our horseshit effort and the fact that the Gatorade he flipped over had ruined his new suede shoes, Coach Marshall wanted to bag skate us a la Herb Brooks's post-Norway game. But this was a Junior B hockey tournament, not an Olympic tuneup. The ice wasn't free; there was already another game underway. Undeterred, Coach ordered us to take off only our skates, head into the pitch black, icy night, and run four miles. This was a real bitch, especially for the three guys who had been kicked out of the game in the second period and were already showered and in street clothes. Coach had them put back on their freezing cold, wet gear.

One mile into our cross-country punishment, our starting goalie slipped, tore his ACL, and ruined any chance we had of winning the league that season. Coach Marshall had us finish the run.

God Bless Us, Every One!

*   *   *

After surviving my first year of juniors, I knew I had to move up a level if I wanted to attract college scouts. There was the option to head to the Midwest to play, but considering I couldn't do my own laundry or boil water, and lacked all basic survival skills, I needed to stay close  to home so I signed with the New York Apple Core of the Eastern Junior Hockey League.

I know what you're thinking: What marketing expert came up with this intimidating mascot? Luckily for us, mascots don't mean jack, and besides, we had the most original jerseys in the EJHL.

My parents were excited to see me one step closer to reaching Division 1 hockey. Also, they were thrilled that Apple Core had a team locker room at the rink which meant I no longer had to air out my equipment in the front hallway of our apartment.

Comprised primarily of New England teams, the EJHL had a strong reputation for producing D-I players, many of whom went on to play in the professional ranks, but, as is the case in much of the hockey world, we had our fair share of oddballs, including our head coach, Henry Lazar. Nicknamed "The Lizard" for reasons that were never made clear to me, Coach Lazar wore the same outfit day after day after day: Dark green Apple Core jacket, khakis, white socks, and black shoes; his green Apple Core hat, cocked to the side, only came off his head when he spiked it off a player's helmet after an opponent had scored a goal.

The Lizard was by no means a tactical guru. When it came to positioning, his most common insight during games was, "Where the fuck's the right wing?!" (That would be me.) He wasn't exactly the best motivator, either; his signature phrase of encouragement was, "Don't fuck it up!"

The Lizard's first passion was helping his players move onto college hockey programs, and his second passion was watching reruns of *I Love Lucy* and *The Honeymooners*. He sought players who could win games and didn't cause problems. Those were really the only two criteria he had.

There was one guy on the team who never had to worry about The Lizard's incessant yelling—our goalie, Jeff Mansfield, who was deaf. Henry convinced Jeff, a Massachusetts native, to pass up all the opportunities he had to play juniors near home and to play with the Core in Long Beach, Long Island. Jeff had a successful stint with the Core and went on to mind the net at Princeton University.

Henry found our other goalie playing junior hockey in Montana. Relatively unknown and just a year removed from leaving his home in Austria, Mathias Lange signed with the Core after Henry convinced him a college scholarship was a possibility. He was right. Mathias received a full ride to RPI, played professionally in Germany, and then found himself in the net representing Austria at the 2014 Olympic Games.

The Lizard signed another Boston transplant in Al DiPietro. It was either incredible foresight or incredible luck, but signing Rick DiPietro's younger brother the same year as the NHL lockout meant the Islanders supposed franchise goaltender was a regular at the Apple Core practices that year. I must have taken a few hundred shots on him that season in practice and I had one dazzling breakaway goal. I rifled the puck bar down so fast, it's like he didn't even see it. Even though he was on the bench at the time squirting water on his face wondering why our head coach couldn't skate, Rick DiPietro was responsible for that net during that particular drill. The puck is on my mantel at home.

I also played alongside Vito Kirichenko, a Russian behemoth whose January 1 birthday always raised suspicion from opposing teams. Vito looked about as Russian as one could get—might as well have walked in wearing a ushanka and holding a hammer-and-sickle. Although he barely spoke English when he arrived at Long Beach Ice Arena for his first day of practice in August, he was still able to get his point across: "I. Vito. Pass me puck. I score."

It took some time for Vito to adjust to life in the US. Postgame team trips to the local Subway sandwich shop were always interesting—no one, including the Subway employees, had ever seen someone order a meat-ball sub with all the vegetables and sauces including mayo and BBQ. On the ice, Vito had some trouble with his passing at the beginning of the season. It's not that he didn't pass—he did, and they were hard, tape-to-tape passes. Unfortunately, they were usually to players on the other team, defensive zone turnovers that often led to goals against which prompted The Lizard to call him out as being a "Fuckin' Red Agent."

The growing pains would soon dissipate, however. Vito limited his d-zone cough-ups and finally eased up on the condiments at Subway. The Lizard helped him find an English tutor and by the end of the season, the Chelyabinsk native was fluent in English, and, better yet, had finally ditched his blonde rat tail. Now, instead of saying, "I. Vito. Pass me puck. I score," he'd tell me, "Pass me ze fahkin' puck, you fahk. I'm zuperstar."

Our assistant coaches added to the atmosphere. A coach who went by "Happy"—that was his full name according to his business card—always offered tremendous insight in between periods. After The Lizard finished firing water bottles off the walls, Happy chimed in with his words of wisdom: "Fuck, I . . . uh . . . I . . . um . . . y' know . . . I just want to fuckin' win this game. *Fuck!*" Then there was Coach Jackson, dressed in his brown and green plaid suit, who had the Herb Brooks scene from the film *Miracle* memorized down to the silences between sentences. "I'm sick and tired of hearing how great a team the Soviet, er, I mean the Glades have. This is your time, now go out there and take it!"

Vince Lombardis, they weren't.

Despite their quirks—or possibly because of them—the combination of personalities kept everyone sane, and their connections helped a number of the players get into colleges they might otherwise never have been able to attend.

Thanks to a solid first season with the Core and some equally solid grades in school, I began garnering interest from some Ivy League schools. Some scouts[5] even considered me a sure bet NHLer. But, according to The Lizard, all the schools shared the same concern: Was I physically strong enough to compete at the Division 1 college level?

That was a legitimate concern. A number of current professional hockey players are surprisingly small—Patrick Kane, who, as of this writing, is one of the NHL leaders in scoring, is listed at 5'11" and 180, but from where I sit, I'd say it's more like 5'9" and 165. However, given their choice, coaches want size and bulk, so I continued lifting weights whenever I could. If I saw something that looked heavy, I'd try to pick it up: chairs, boxes of cat litter, my little sister, manhole covers, my older sister, whatever. Eating-wise, my motto became "eat until you sweat."

At the beginning of my second season with the Core, I was listed at 6'1" and 180 pounds, which meant I was *maybe* 6'0" and *possibly* 160. However, I wasn't the only bag of bones on the team. Next to me in the locker room sat a tall, lanky guy who, two years out of high school, was hoping to get interest from a Division 1 school before his junior hockey eligibility ran out; he'd passed up a few D-III offers and decided to play one more season to see if any D-I colleges would give him a shot.[6] Matty Gilroy and I became good friends and the chemistry translated well onto the ice. We played on the same line and I always knew where he was, in part because he

---

5   My gramma

6   It turned out to be a good decision for Matt. After a solid final season of junior hockey, he was offered a walk-on spot at Boston University but with no guarantees. The catch was that the roster opening was for a defenseman and Matt had played forward his whole life. Tough transition one would think, right? Fast forward five years, Matt was patrolling the blue line for the New York Rangers after winning the Hobey Baker Award as the nation's top college hockey player. Lesson: Never give up.

constantly lathered his body in Old Spice deodorant spray before, during, and after games, so it was easy for me to pick up the Pure Sport scent.

Colleges, always in the market for good American hockey players, came around, but it was soon apparent that the recruiting process wouldn't be as glamorous as I had envisioned. I half-expected gushing letters from coaches, home visits, and limos filled with scantily clad sorority girls; instead, it was tentative phone calls and semi-hopeful letters.

My high school, Collegiate, which was on the Upper West Side of Manhattan and had only fifty boys per grade, didn't have a hockey team, or for that matter football or lacrosse, but we dominated in debating. Bruce Breimer, my high school guidance counselor, made up for what was lacking in the athletic department.

"Transcript looks good, Bill," he told me, as I tried to get comfortable in the wingback chair in his office. "Good SATs, PSATs, SAT IIs. What major are you considering? Law? Medicine? Business?"

"To be honest, I'm looking to play hockey . . ."

He gave me a look. "Hockey? Ice hockey?"

"Yes, sir. A couple of Division 1 schools have reached out . . ."

"There's no ice hockey in New York City, Bill. Where've you been playing?"

"On a Junior team out in Long Island."

I went on to give him a highly condensed version of my "career." Luckily for me, not only did he not fall asleep, but he was totally on board and in the end, downright helpful.

The Lizard told me that the Harvard hockey team was looking to add another forward; the Core had recently developed two players who went on to play at Harvard so the road had been paved for me. In October, a Harvard assistant coach, Bobby Jay, contacted me to set up a visit. (To that end, hockey teammates were horrible to one another, i.e. posing as a D-I coach, one of the guys would call up an ex-teammate pretending to be, say, Jerry York of Boston College, and offer a scholarship. Some would even set up fake campus visits. Guys were ruthless.)

Harvard invited me for an all-expenses-paid visit to campus to meet with the coaching staff and stay the night with one of the players. After arriving in Cambridge, I parked in the lot near the hockey teams' weight training facility, and through the tinted glass windows, I watched in awe as players snatched, squatted, and pressed massive weights, all the while balancing on one leg. I hated to imagine what the men's off-ice training would be like.

My confidence soon rebounded after an hour meeting with the coaching staff and a big night out in Cambridge with a few guys on the team. They treated me like gold and I felt Big Time.

Now this is what really happened: Wearing my new white unconstructed sport coat with rolled up sleeves, I showed up, drank too much, tried to fit in, threw up twice, and went home.

Later that week before a game against the Junior Bruins, Coach Jackson (the Herb Brooks wannabe lackey) took me aside.

"Billy, I ever tell you about the time I met Scotty Bowman?"

He had, about a dozen times. "Nah, Coach."

"I was coaching the Macon Whoopee in the old Central League. We're on the last leg of two-week roadie and I'd probably had eight of my last nine meals at Old Country Buffet. I'm finishing up another round in the crapper and in walks Scotty Bowman, goddamn Hall of Famer, coach of the Sabres in the National League at the time. I go to shake his hand but he waves me off. We get to shooting the crap, though, and Billy, Scotty offers me a job to scout for his club, right in the men's bathroom at the old Buffalo Coliseum." Coach Jackson paused for a moment, looking up at the fluorescent lights in the locker room, either trying to figure out how he went from being offered a role as an NHL scout to being the assistant coach of Apple Core or possibly taking a moment to remember why the hell he was telling me this story. "Billy, I was just in the pisser and the Harvard coaches are here tonight to watch our game. You see where I'm going with this?"

"I think so, Coach. I gotta be ready to take advantage of opportunities when I get them."

"Right," he replied. "And stay away from Old Country Buffet if at all possible."

I busted my ass to impress the Crimson coaches, but it was tough to look good, as players who had already committed to a school suffered from what was commonly known as Just Committed to College Syndrome, the primary symptom of which was dogging it. No longer feeling the pressure to impress the scouts, committed players were more concerned about impressing their teammates' sisters who stood by the glass.

As an uncommitted player, I felt the burden to perform increase as those teammates of mine who had already committed to school no longer came to the rink every day focused on winning. Committing to college meant bragging rights and a free pass to give half-ass efforts during practices and games for the rest of the season. Trash talk in the EJ consisted of one question: "Oh yeah, where you going to college, bud?"

Now assists might not have been worth a damn in mini-mites, but in junior hockey, they were another way to bump up your all important point total (goals + assists = points) on which scouts judged players. For my classmates at Collegiate School, a solid GPA was their ticket to a good college, but for Apple Core players, it was Gs, As, and Ps that would decide our college dreams.

After each goal, it was all about getting to the referee as soon as possible without seeming like a complete selfish prick. Once within earshot, the ref would be bombarded with players yelling out their numbers repeatedly in hopes of racking up another point. And it wasn't just the guys on the ice; there would be guys on the bench yelling their numbers hoping to get what is known as a "phantom assist."[7] Once the ref reported the official decision to the PA announcer, fingers were crossed inside our hockey gloves as we waited to hear who was awarded the coveted points. And it didn't stop there. There were even instances when a guy (me) would intentionally take a penalty near the end of the game just to get to the penalty box where he would

---

7   Phantoms are assists that clearly were not legitimately earned. See Henrik and Daniel Sedin.

be within earshot of the scorer and could chisel a last minute apple.[8] I might be the only player in the history of hockey to record an assist on a teammate's penalty shot goal.

I was still constantly on edge until receiving a phone call just before Christmas of 2004. "Bill," Mom yelled, "pick up. It's Harvard. *Pick up the phone!*"

I assumed that by "Harvard," Mom meant "Ted Donato," a former NHL journeyman, and the Crimson's head coach. I picked up the phone. "Hello? Coach Donato?" I needed to confirm that it was actually him and not one of my teammates playing a prank.

"Willy, how are ya?" The moment he called me Willy,[9] I knew it was the real deal. He got right to the point: "We've watched you here over the past season or so and we like your game. You need to get stronger on the puck, but that'll come as your body matures. We think you can help this team, and we want you as part of our class of 2009 here in Cambridge."

I covered the mouthpiece and whispered, "*Holy. Shit. Holy. Shit. Holy. Shit.*" then performed nine mental back handsprings through the living room.

"Willy, you still there?"

"Yeah, Coach. I'm here. That's awesome. I can't wait to get to school."

"We'll fax over some paperwork today. Get your application into the admissions office right away and we'll be in touch soon."

"I'm on it."

After Donato hung up, but before I could hang up, a voice came through the phone: "Oh, Bill! I'm so proud of you."

"Thanks, Mom."

"We knew you could make this happen."

"Thanks, Dad."

Man, I thought, *I've gotta start giving these guys my cell number.*

---

8   Apples are assists. No great story behind that. Just deal with it.

9   One of the handful of instances in my life where it was okay to call me Willy.

Later that spring after I overcame a slight bout of Just Committed to College Syndrome, Apple Core was headed to the EJHL semifinals. The night before our match-up, I challenged my sister Lil, who was seven at the time, to a best-of-seven mini sticks series. Most likely upset that I took the first two games in convincing fashion, Lil struck me in the face with her plastic stick (which she still swears was by accident). The cheap shot left me with a nasty black eye. Because I was leading at the time, we agreed it was only fair that she concede the series. Lil went to her room crying because she lost. She always acted like such a girl. I went to my room crying because my eye hurt.

The next day after defeating the Junior Bruins in the semis, The Lizard strolled into the locker room and wandered over to my locker. "Billy, you got someone who wants to speak with you in the hallway. He looks important."

"What do you mean important?" I asked.

The Lizard smirked, shrugged, and slithered away, kicking a few tape balls on his way out. Maybe he was messing with me . . . but maybe not, so I quickly tore off my equipment, threw on my sweats, and hustled into the hallway, where a large man wearing a shiny black leather jacket, holding a matte black clipboard, met me. He stuck out his massive, callused hand. "Dale Evans, how are ya?"

"Bill Keenan. Doing well, Mr. Evans."

"Christ, do I look that fuckin' old? Call me Dale. I'm an east coast scout for the New York Islanders. Good game tonight . . . what happened to your eye there?"

"Caught a high stick the other day in the quarters. Chippy game but that's playoff hockey," I responded.

"Sure is." A grin emerged on his face. "Saw you're headed up to play for Teddy Donato next fall. I played a season with him in Manchester. Asbolute gongshow, that guy is, a real beauty."

He said some other stuff about Harvard but I was having trouble focusing after he mentioned the Islanders. "Sorry," I said, "Can you repeat that last thing?"

"You need to fill out your frame. But you'll put on weight as you get older. Trust me." He grinned, patting his stomach. "So you're actually from New York City. That right?"

"That's right."

"Like right in the City? Manhattan?"

"Yeah."

He nodded. "The wife's been pestering me about moving there since I started working for the Islanders, but we got a five-year-old and I'm worried he won't be able to play. They got fuckin' rinks in Manhattan? Where the hell did you play as a kid?"

"There're a couple of rinks around. Pretty shitty but they're there. Mostly played out in Jersey and Connecticut."

"Must have some good parents. Alright, Billy," he said handing me a couple forms with New York Islanders letterhead. "Fill these out and mail them to us this week. We'll be watching you when you get to Harvard."

I filled out the forms in the locker room that day and affixed six first class stamps. Two months later, it was time for the NHL draft. I parked myself in front of my computer and stared at the screen for hours. Three old Connecticut Yankee teammates were picked that year: Matt Lashoff (first round), Jonny Quick (third round), Jordan LaVallée/Smotherman (fourth round), and Robbie Schremp had been a first round pick in the prior year's draft. They were all big-time pro prospects and I was clasping my hands together, saying some prayers. My heart stopped momentarily before each of the Islanders' selections. After nine rounds, it was over. I wasn't picked. *At least I didn't get my hopes up*, I thought as I removed my brand new New York Islanders hat.

CHAPTER THREE

Crimson Crazed

I'm SURE FOR most of the world, the locker room in Harvard's Bright Hockey Center was just another locker room. But most of the world didn't know any better.

It was the first week of September, a few days before I was to begin my freshman year. I was alone, and I slowly walked by each locker, the strap of my equipment bag digging a groove into my shoulder, the remainder of my luggage clogging up the hallway. When I got to the stall in the far corner of the room, there it was: My nameplate. Above my locker.

Noting how pristine all the upperclassmen's lockers were, I carefully placed each shin pad, elbow pad, and glove in its proper spot. Once everything was in its place, I took a deep breath, knowing this was the last time the air in the room would be breathable.

Eventually, the rest of the team piled in. Some acknowledged me. Some didn't. The freshmen recruiting class included one goalie, two defensemen, and five forwards, and prior to college, most of us had crossed paths at one time or another. Nicky Coskren, a forward from

St. Sebastian's School in Needham, Massachusetts, was a fellow Paul Vincent acolyte. Nick Snow, another forward, played on an EJ rival, the New England Coyotes. Steve Rolecek captained Andover Prep School and we had gone head-to-head in a few summer showcase tournaments. And Stevie Mandes, a junior, was my teammate back on the New Jersey Rockets. Some of the upperclassmen had come from the top American Junior league, the USHL—there was the former captain of the Lincoln Stars and the leading scorer of the Sioux Falls Stampede—and there was a slew of NHL draft picks. My team at Apple Core had some good players, but the competition here was a whole new level.

After exchanging a couple Facebook messages, Steve Rolecek and I met for the first time outside Annenberg Hall.

"Any hot girls in your dorm?" Rolo asked.

"Nah. How 'bout yours?"

"Nope. Wanna go play some *NHL* on my Xbox?"

"Sure."

Aside from a couple conversations, I didn't know too much about the coaching staff. Coach Donato had just finished a successful NHL career. He seemed like most hockey players I'd come across from Boston—he liked the word "fahk" but couldn't pronounce the letter "r."

Due to a bizarre NCAA rule—and, as even casual followers of college sports know, there are a *lot* of bizarre NCAA rules—the coaching staff was prohibited from running practice until October but they could monitor these so-called captains' practices, which were led by the senior class. Three of our coaches, fueled by caffeine and sugar donuts, sat in the stands, where they assessed and judged all the while scribbling in notebooks.

When the coaches got on the ice the following week, I longed for the days of being assessed and judged.

On October 1 at 6:30 a.m. the inappropriately named "skill sessions" began. There was no skill involved in these thirty minute, puke-inducing outings intended to "wake us the fuck up" and weed out the two token guys trying to walk-on the team that year, Sunday Skate and Yard Sale.

The coaches herded us onto the ice in groups of four—usually one guy from each class—and blew the hell out of their whistles. "Summer's over, boys," Coach Donato yelled in between whistles, a huge smile plastered on his round mug as we skated up and down and up and down and up and down. "Time to get to fahkin' work, yah fahks! Let's fahkin' go! Pick it up. Again!" he'd yell as the whistle would sound and we'd take off. Goal line, blue line, goal line, red line, goal line, far blue line, goal line, suck wind, suck wind, vomit (optional), repeat.

As soon as we got pucks involved, a typical practice went something like this: Player loses a tooth from a hit; player skates off ice with tooth in hand; coach calls him selfish because lines are now uneven; player who inflicted the damage has his father who's a dentist fix the tooth; player who inflicted damage enters dental school five years later.[10]

Although he seemed to get off on screaming at us nonstop during practice, Coach Donato's off-ice exchanges were, conversely, to the point and fahk-free. "Willy, keep pushing the older guys," he told me. "You gotta prove to us that you deserve that spot more than they do. You gotta get stronger on the puck. Cornell's forwards are bigger than our defensemen and their defensemen are NHL-sized. You won't be effective if they can knock you around. We need you heavier. Keep working in the weight room and doing what the strength coaches tell you." All I could think at dinner that night as I ate until nausea set in was why the hell was the freshman fifteen only reserved for the girls at Harvard?

There were ten forwards from the previous year's Harvard roster who were regulars in the lineup, which left six or seven guys (depending on injuries) fighting for the last two spots.

The other dynamic was that my teammates, and especially the teammates in my graduating class, were already my best friends, and eventual roommates for the next three years of school. We all knew the pressures one another were under, whether it was with schoolwork

---

10　All true.

or girls or just life. If I had dicked around all semester and needed help, they were the ones who somehow found a study guide. If a girl I liked didn't feel the same way, they were the ones to point out her flaws. If I was sitting alone playing skills competition mode on *NHL 07*, they were the ones who picked up the other controller to play a best-out-of-seven series that I would inevitably lose. Hockey was what mattered most to all of us. It was our shared passion for the game that created a deep understanding of one another's hardships on and off the ice. However, we were each other's greatest competition. If one guy was in the lineup, that meant he took the spot of someone else. It wasn't personal; it was the way things worked. As strong as our bonds were, having success on the ice was always at the expense of someone else.

As the preseason wound down, it was time for our first Kangaroo Court as the team assembled in the locker room on a Sunday afternoon. The seniors were the judges, jury, lead witnesses, and prosecutors. There was no defense.

"Two freshmen left. We got Rolo with a confirmed makeout session with a girl hockey player. That's a flat five dollar fine." Our senior captain tallied the numbers.

"Heard there were two," chimed another senior.

"Ten dollars."

"Three!" said our senior goalie.

"Rolo," our captain turned to face him, "You got anything to say?" Freshmen were banned from talking in court. Rolo shrugged and held up two fingers.

"We'll keep it at ten bucks. Cut the shit with the hockey broads from now on. Moving on, we got Keenan. Can't forget that *Miami Vice* shit he pulled on his visit. Where are you Don Johnson?" He turned to me. "Still got that linen jacket?" I shook my head. I had it, but before I could be sentenced, a cell phone rang. Cell phones were supposed to be switched off upon entering the locker room. As the collective eyes in the room zeroed in on the culprit, Sunday Skate, no one expected him to pick it up and mumble a few words into the receiver. "What can I say," he said to the room, slipping his phone back inside his pocket. "Bitches." Sunday Skate was fined fifty dollars for the five-second crime. He paid later that afternoon, and was officially cut from the team the following day.

* * *

After watching the first three games from the stands, I was ecstatic to see my name on the dry erase board as the third line right wing for our game against Princeton.

As our bus pulled into the Hobey Baker Memorial Rink parking lot that bone-cold October night, I had a sense of confidence; after all, I had good memories from the last time I played at Princeton's Baker Rink. Now I'm not going to sit here and say I was a dominant force that game in '93—that's for you to decide; I'll just tell you the facts. I scored four goals for the North Park Mini Mites in a 4–0 shutout against the Beacon Hill Club—our only win of the season. Granted, the only time I was in my defensive zone that game was during the five-minute warmup and the opposing team's goalie was a shooter tutor. But, hey, four goals are four goals.

Lying on the floor in front of my stall, I draped my legs over my seat and stared up at my Crimson jersey. I must have worked on my three sticks for an hour before that game, tweaking, adjusting, readjusting, and re-tweaking. Like a hunter preparing his weapon, I futzed with and flexed those sticks. As always, each of my stick blades was meticulously taped, but for some reason, even though I'd taped several million blades, I couldn't get it just right. When I finally donned my jersey before warmups, it felt unusually heavy and uncomfortable.

Then it was Donato's turn. "Important youse set the tone early, boys. Straight lines all night. Everybody goes up and back, nobody skating sidewards. These Princeton d-men are real aggressive, pinch every chance they get. Forwards, youse gotta recognize this and look to blow the zone for a stretch pass. D, don't fumble fuck with it—head up and find the forwards. Wingers need to talk, though. Can't have botha youse blowing the zone. Can't blow two guys. Only blow one guy." It was exactly the final thought I needed before my first college hockey game.

I played a quick shift in the first period and another in the second. I tried to stay focused and engaged, but at times it was tough because my role that night was what in hockey circles is called the grocery stick: I was the guy who sat in the spot separating the defenseman from the forwards. I could have been replaced by a bucket of pucks. Or air.

After my token third period shift in which my line generated some offense, I came off the ice feeling confident but knowing I most likely wasn't stepping on the ice again until the final buzzer sounded.

After showering one of the refs with some impressively expletive-laden personal insults, Donato was assessed a bench minor for abuse of officials. I already had one leg over the boards when I felt Donato give me the tap to serve the two-minute penalty. As I glided across the ice to the box, looking up at the scoreboard showing 2:17 remaining in the game with us leading by one goal, my hope for one last shift had materialized assuming we could kill off the penalty.

With the two-minute minor about to expire, I could see Donato, one foot propped on the boards, waving his arms wildly for me to skate right to the bench. With my palms facing up, I plastered a confused look on my face. Despite the thick pane of glass in front of me, I heard his barking clearly, "Get to the bench. To the fuckin' bench!" But he didn't hear the voice in my head, "Fuck off, Donuts."

As I readied to exit the box, the Princeton goalie sprinted to his bench for an extra attacker as a Tiger forward broke the puck into our zone. Then, moments after my penalty expired, the Princeton player turned the puck over to one of our defensemen. Whacking my stick on the ice as I hurried to center ice, I yelled for the puck even louder than Donato was still hollering at me to get off the ice. My teammate snapped a perfect pass on my tape sending me on a breakaway . . . with no goalie. Streaking over the center red line, a thin layer of mist that I could almost taste was all that separated me from the open net. It was like a hockey mirage.

First game as a member of the Harvard Crimson, and I was going to score my first goal on the same rink where I had played as a mini-mite. There was something poetic about it, a coming full-circle moment.

I'd seen clips on YouTube of guys on open-net breakaways being too nonchalant, trying to roof the puck and accidentally shooting it over the net. No chance that would be the fate of this biscuit. I knew where I was shooting—exactly where you're taught *never* to shoot as a kid—center of the net. Approaching the hash marks, I lifted my right leg, took one last look at the middle bar in the net, before leaning into my shot and . . .

SNAP!

If there were a pie chart depicting how a hockey player spends his time, a large sliver would belong to "Stick Maintenance." And now, when I needed it the most, my graphite stick had snapped. I watched helplessly as the puck trickled slowly to the net, only to be stopped by the excess snow just short of the crease. Then the buzzer sounded. The rules state that when a player's stick breaks, he must immediately discard it. Apparently, the referee thought I was trying to score with my stick after it had broken (he was right), and at the sixty-minute mark, with no time remaining, I was assessed a minor penalty.

Things improved the following day when, during the team meal, Coach Donato sidled over and said, "We thought you did good last night, Willy. But penalties are gonna kill us this year. This league is too tight on defense, and when I look at the scoresheet and see Billy Keenan with four PIMS, I need to make a change. You're gonna be scratched tonight but Duzie [the team's first line center] is feeling sick. So you might be going. Be ready."

I dressed for warmups, my heart pounding so hard that the Crimson logo on the front of my jersey was thumping. It was Quinnipiac's inaugural game in the ECAC. TD Bank Sports Center was filled to capacity, and the 8,000-plus fans were on their feet. It was a controlled chaos, much like the new hairstyle I was trying out. And just as those who encountered me for the first time needed a moment to take in the new 'do, I too needed a second to adjust and acclimate to the spectacle now before me.

After the game, my equipment was drenched in sweat—the pads, the helmet, the gloves. Everything felt as if it had been through the hockey game from hell. The reek had a life of its own, so much so that you could practically see it. Unfortunately, it wasn't my sweat.

You see, Duzie, who'd been vomiting and shitting for the past fifteen or so hours, forgot to pack his equipment onto the bus before we left Princeton for Connecticut. As an extra forward on the trip and with him being close in size to me, I was forced to hand over my gear to him (after warmups) when it had been deemed that Duzie—whose health level was at about 18 percent—would be more effective than me at 100 percent. The coaching staff's confidence in me was touching.

After the game, Duzie handed me back my newly infected gear which I handled like radioactive waste. "Thanks for saving my ass, bud. I appreciate it." He then ran to the toilet to throw up. Me, I performed an exorcism on my equipment and then took a six-hour shower in 500-degree water.

* * *

Later that week, it was freshman initiation time for the hockey team. Each of us newbies was assigned a character we were to dress up as and given a list of tasks to perform: I had no idea I was joining Sigma Phi Puck.

After completing our third task of streaming gay porn on all the Widener Library computers, it was off to Annenberg, the freshmen dining hall. We sat down at our usual table during the peak dinner hour. "May I have everyone's attention, please," Nicky Coskren yelled, and he yelled so loudly that he didn't really need the megaphone. (Nicky, it should be noted, was dressed like a prostitute, or actually a "dime store hooker" as our instruction sheet called it, complete with fishnets, thong, and makeup.) "Introducing, for your viewing pleasure, Billy the Ballerina." With that, Snowsy, dressed as Ronald McDonald, hit play on the boom box as I climbed up on the table that would soon become my stage.

Somehow, word had gotten out that I had done a short stint at the School of American Ballet when I was a kid . . . quit laughing. It definitely improved my coordination and body control. Plus, my mom made me do it.

As I pirouetted on the table in front of Harvard's entire freshman class, I wasn't embarrassed because I looked like a fool and danced like an idiot; no, I was embarrassed because I knew the exact steps to the opening act of Balanchine's Nutcracker, and, thanks to my skinny physique, my legs looked pretty good in the pink tights. When the music stopped, I curtsied and officially retired from ballet.

My ballet skills didn't stop my teammates from turning my room into the Official Harvard Crimson Hockey Team Party Room. For reasons that were never made clear, my roommate left school in the middle of first semester.[11] When word got out, it was unilaterally decided Keenan's room was the party room. (Keenan, it bears mentioning, had no say in the matter.) Although the sign outside my door politely instructed those who came in to PLEASE REMOVE YOUR SHOES, well, they didn't.

The first team party was the night of our initiation. Once the team-only part was over, the upperclassmen, in what appeared to be some final ritual, issued an eyepatch to each of us freshmen. "Don't lose 'em, boys," they told us. "You'll need 'em over the next four years." When the first batch of Harvard girls, an eager group of the heavyweight crew team known by the upperclassmen as "the furniture,"[12] arrived at the party, it all became clear. A part of me wished I had two eye patches.

Now I'm no prize, but the first girl I spoke to had the BMI of a non-pulling NFL guard and a face that lets you know God has his off days too. "Can you hold my drink while I use the restroom?" she asked, handing me her red Solo cup. "I don't trust the older guys on your team. I don't want them to roofie me or something." *Don't flatter yourself,* I thought.

"Are they all this bad?" I asked one of our senior defensemen as the beast clomped to the urinal to take a leak.

"They get progressively hotter." He downed his beer. "By spring, you'll be cranking one out to the picture on her student ID card."

"You serious?"

"Relax. We got other broads coming soon."

---

11 All I really knew about him is he liked Obama, *Star Wars*, and could rip out a Rubik's Cube in seconds.

12 On a scale from 1-10, the furniture comprised the null set.

Fortunately, imports from some of the neighboring colleges trickled in and many eye patches soon dangled around our necks. The night climaxed in my room with Nicky Coskren, me, and two girls from Boston College.

"Ashley, let's check out that thing I told you about earlier. It's in my room, right across the yard," said Nicky.

"You're so stubborn. What's your sign?" The Smash, it turned out, was game to check out *any* things in *any* Harvard hockey player's room.

After they stumbled out, it was just me and Cassie MacMillan.

"What's with the eye patches all you guys were wearing?" she asked.

"We had a pirate-themed party earlier so I guess some guys decided to keep them."

"Pirate theme? But you're dressed like a ballerina and your friend was dressed like a hooker, sort of."

"It's complicated," I said, fiddling with my tutu and removing my ballet slippers.

"I know hockey players," she said, bailing me out. "They're not that complicated." She was right about one thing. Easy Mac knew hockey players. But so what if she'd been *friends* with virtually all my upperclassmen teammates and most of BC, BU, and Northeastern's hockey teams. She was cool, sexy, clearly a Beanpot fan, but, most importantly, willing.

"So I heard you have a girl back home," she said, taking a seat in my desk chair. The plan worked just as the upperclassmen had advised us freshmen.

"There're shades of gray." This was black and white though. I didn't have a girlfriend, never did. "We're sort of on and off—pretty hard to stay together now that we're so far away," I said. She smiled and slowly walked to my bed. I started having flashbacks of the Princeton game, hoping I wouldn't botch this open-netter.

Easy Mac pointed to the bag of pretzels on my desk and slurred, "You mind if I have some? Drinking six vodka tonics makes me kinda hungry."

"Help yourself."

She opened the bag of pretzel sticks and salt poured onto my sheets. "Crazy things happen to Ash and I literally every time we're here. It's super random."

"Yeah, there should be a reality show about you two." I took a sip from my water bottle then placed it on a coaster.

"So true," she said twirling a lock of hair around her finger. "So, must be nice having your own room, huh?" Pretzel dust spewed from her mouth.

"Yeah, sure. Great fun. You want a plate or something?"

"That's okay. I'm fine. You're sweet though."

"Thanks. Listen, I'm pretty tired and got practice tomorrow. I might just head to sleep." I could hear Coach Donato's voice in my head, "*Finish your chances! Bear down and fahkin' finish!*" But the pile of crumbs kept growing and eating at me.

"Is that right?" She leaned back on my bed, crossing her tanned legs and thrusting her breasts forward. "No room for me in here?" she whispered, tilting her chin down and pouting her lips.

I was tempted. I mean, it would've been my first college hook up and the locker room reviews on her were incredible.

She then began fellating the pretzel stick, creating a sea of salt in my sheets. "I really should get to bed. I got practice really early." She bit the pretzel. I winced as she blew me a pretzel-filled kiss.

I couldn't take it any longer. "For God's sakes, could you watch where you're eating those things? I changed my sheets last night." After she stormed out of my room, I spent fifteen minutes vacuuming.

After Easy Mac told The Smash about Pretzelfest, she told a bunch of guys on the team, who told everybody else on the team, earning me a new nickname. I also got fined thirty-five dollars.

Move over, Dilly. Welcome, Negative Game.

CHAPTER FOUR

Confessions of a Band-Aid

NEGATIVE GAME WAS an apt nickname, but a more appropriate moniker might've been Healthy Scratch.[13] Being the first guy on at practice and the last guy off the ice didn't matter; results and effectiveness in games were how we were judged, and if I wasn't playing, proving my effectiveness would be impossible.

For players who weren't regulars in the lineup (me), practices *were* our games. "Show us in practice that you deserve to be playing on the weekends. You gotta play desperate, Willy," Donato would instruct me. So, I flew around the ice like a maniac, catapulting my body into anything that moved. "Jesus Christ, Willy, relax with that shit. It's fahkin' practice f'r fucks sakes!" he'd then yell at me twenty minutes later during 3-on-3 down-low battle drills.

I couldn't figure it out.

---

13 Healthy scratch: Not suiting up for the games but rather watching in your suit from the pressbox and trying to avoid eye contact with anyone who might recognize you.

Things were getting worse when I was no longer on the power play or penalty kill—and I'm not talking about the actual PP or PK. I'm talking about the "mock PP" and "mock PK," where the fourth/fifth liners played the role of simulating the upcoming weekend's opponents. Even if it was just practice, I still couldn't crack the lineup.

"Whoa, Willy, have a seat," Coach Donato would say as he reached out with his stick, holding me back while simultaneously hopping over the boards. "I'll take this shift—show all youse the right way to work the point on the powah play." There are different types of coaches, one of which is a player's coach—a guy who can relate to the players. Coach Donato was a breed of his own, a coach who thought he *was* a player.

Daily calls home to Mom to bitch and moan offered little solace.

"Why don't you talk to the coach?" she'd ask.

"I can't talk to him, Mom. He doesn't wanna listen to us whine about playing time." What I wanted to tell her was, *If I complain, he'll tell me to shut the fahk up and quit fahking whining, and play fahking hard during practice, and wait my fahking turn.*

"You're at Harvard, Bill," she'd say, eternally patient and encouraging. "If hockey's not going your way, you need to stay active in other things. Haven't you found any of your classes interesting? Join a club, for God's sakes."

I did join a club—Skate Club. After practice, all the guys who weren't regulars in the lineup remained on the ice for an extra twenty minutes to stay in game shape. These were essentially run like the skill sessions we endured prior to the season. Okay, it wasn't a club, *per se*, but it was something.

College sports are rife with tradition. At Harvard, it was tradition after being swept in a weekend series for the guys who were scratched, who had nothing to do with the back-to-back shellacking, to spend Sunday morning in the gym lifting to make amends for the team's shitty performance. So we did our "sport-specific" lift while across the gym, the women's water polo team performed the same exercises. Someone in a position to effect change might have questioned the efficacy of this solution to losing. I wasn't in that position.

Then there were the pregame skates. Supposedly, if we had class and couldn't attend, the healthy scratches were exempt; therefore, they were deemed "optional" skates. But the only thing that we had as an "option" was to get bag skated over the width of the ice or length (note: Length is better, as it requires fewer stops). Class, no class, test, no test, didn't matter—not showing up as healthy scratch on game day for the hour long bag session gave the coaches all they needed to question your commitment. On the rare occasion that the team (the actual team, not the Skate Club team) had a winning streak going, the coaches were usually in a good mood, so after an abbreviated bag skate, the healthy scratches would scrimmage against the three coaches, just long enough for us to miss lunch at the dining hall. While the coaches were focused on scoring in these scrimmages (after all, scoring goals is a key component to winning), we healthy scratches seized these games as an opportunity to take unnecessarily high shots and engage in nifty stickwork on our coaches who weren't wearing any equipment. If you ever see a college coach sporting a fresh wound on his face while behind the bench during a game, odds are it was inflicted earlier that day by one of the healthy scratches sitting in the press box.

Our assistant coach, Bobby Jay, was a bit more personable and tried to offer some advice: "Billy, you're a guy we see who can bring those intangibles. That's how you can get back in the lineup." Here's the problem—in the hockey circles, "intangibles" refer to the qualities that fighters and ten-year veterans bring to a team. They're great if you're involved in professional hockey like Coach Donato and Coach Jay were two years earlier. But this was college, and there were no fighters or ten-year vets. College lineups were comprised of the players that coaches thought could contribute goals and assists right here, right now. Therefore, the "intangible" talk was pretty much saying, *Billy, you're shit out of luck until someone in the lineup gets hurt.* Coach Jay then would tell me, "Keep pushing and persevering. You gotta stick with it, that's what this game is about for players and coaches."

Coach Jay left the team at the end of the season.

The pressure mounted because opportunities to impress were limited to practice and even there, I couldn't go too hard, because,

God forbid, I injure one of the regulars in the lineup who could contribute to the team. I could feel my every move being scrutinized by the coaching staff (or maybe at that point, they didn't give a shit). Each time I missed the net, I knew it was bad. Each time, I didn't chip the puck out of the zone on a breakout it was worse. According to Donato, there were just two options for wingers on the breakout—chip it out, or fuck off. And don't get me started on how I felt standing in line thinking about trying to receive a cross-ice rocket of a pass on my backhand. Most of those ended up in section *S* of the stands, where I watched the games on weekends.

Winning games meant happy coaches and less bag skating. But as much as I wanted to see us win and have my teammates do well, I found myself performing subtle fist pumps during games after the opposition scored on us. Losing meant lineup changes. It was sad to be actively rooting against my own team, kind of selfish, but true.

Time may be a hockey player's ally on the ice, but for a guy who's not playing, it's the enemy. I had far too much time to think, which is never good for hockey players. Maybe I should change my stick, try a different curve, lie, flex. Maybe fiddle with my skate blades—less hollow and shorter radius. Or even use waxed laces in my skates. Our equipment manager had a heart attack that year. I couldn't help but feel partly responsible.

Off the ice, my classes were fascinating . . . or so I assumed. It was Harvard, after all and Harvard classes *had* to be fascinating, right? But I couldn't vouch for their level of fascination, or lack thereof, because I had no real interest in any of them. Sure, I was taking a class called *History of Science 137: Dogs and How We Know Them*, but I needed something to even out my grade from Intro to Economics. I was always physically present in the classroom—okay, *almost* always . . . okay, I bought some of the textbooks—but the cutest bitch in class was Professor Jansen's golden retriever and mentally, well, my mind was always on the game.

As my earnest, hyperintelligent professors went on about things that might actually help me in the real world someday, I heard Donato's voice: "Keep working, Willy! We need you stronger so you can get to the net! Come in here, cut in like this, back out like that, then slide it over to the far side, simple, simple! That's alls you gotta do!" *Yeah*, I'd think, *simple to you, who'd done it for years in the NHL. If I could do this, that, and the other thing, I wouldn't be playing at the Bright Hockey Center. I'd be a few miles down Memorial Drive playing at the TD Garden for the Bruins.* College was a place to grow and learn, but my focus shrunk every single day. My existence, self-esteem, self-confidence, and self-worth lay in the hands of my coaches. I judged myself on how much I played every Friday or Saturday.

To stay sane, I found other ways to occupy my brain during games. At the annual Beanpot Tournament in February at TD Bank Garden, after finally convincing the security guard outside the rink that I was actually a member of the Harvard team, which involved Googling the team's roster on my phone,[14] I sat in the press box with the other healthy scratches and media personnel and watched my teammates take on a strong Boston University squad, which included my former Apple Core linemate Matty Gilroy. After grabbing a complimentary bag of popcorn, I wandered around until I spotted the cute writer who covered the Boston area for some college hockey publication. I had a quiet thing for her—she had a sultry way about her, plus she knew hockey and was unaware of my Negative Game idiocy—so I moved over to where she was sitting and positioned myself close enough so she could feel my presence, but not too close that she felt the need to pack up and head elsewhere.

Munching on my popcorn, I began my quest for a solid opener. By the third period, three bags of popcorn later, I still had nothing. One of my roommates summed it up eloquently the week before at a party: "You fuckin' battle with broads." Right when I was about to give up, she dropped her pen. Before I could do the gentlemanly thing and pick it up for her, she bent over and snatched it herself. As she leaned over, her shirt hiked up, revealing the tattoo on her lower back, a street sign that said "SLIPPERY WHEN WET."[15]

---

14   This didn't always work. On one road trip my freshman year, I had to buy a ticket to watch Harvard play Clarkson because the security guy didn't believe I was on the team. Yeah, I just show up in a suit two hours before games in Potsdam, New York, for fun.

15   This was the highlight of my freshman year.

Jackpot.

I furiously Googled references to the phrase on my phone trying to figure out something witty to say,[16] reviewing them in my head, deciding to say one[17], un-deciding, re-deciding, but wussing out. I settled for a few incoherent mumbles and a gurgling sound all of which she luckily didn't hear.

Also, we lost to BU, 5-3, but at least I caught Donato with a high stick in the pregame skate to the tune of six stitches.

Our season came to an abrupt end (and some would say merciful end . . . and by "some," I mean "me") at the beginning of March after a first round loss to Maine in the NCAA tournament. Our end of the year awards banquet was scheduled for the following Tuesday at the Harvard Varsity Club in Boston, during which the team's MVP and Most Improved Player would receive their trophies. The real awards, however, were doled out that morning on the players-only trolley ride to Boston. There was the Kenny Sure Shot Award, given to the guy who thinks he's the biggest ladies' man; the Ball and Chain, which is awarded to the player who spends the most time with his girlfriend; the Super Rookie Award, handed to the freshman who displays the most heroic/ass kissing behavior towards the coaching staff through the year; the Stain of the Year Award given to the player who most consistently leaves his teammates hanging out to dry, be it on the ice, in the classroom, or at the bar; and the Creep of the Year Award, which is delivered to the guy who is deemed creepiest around girls. I wasn't expecting to win any awards, either before, during, or after the banquet, but just like that, I was one of the frontrunners in the Creep category.

How would a kind, warm, respectful, suave gentleman like Bill Keenan find himself in that position? Let me explain.

One of the duties as a freshman on the hockey team was to host high school hockey recruits who could help us get to the Frozen Four. "Show the kid a good time," Coach Donato would say, meaning take

---

16 "Bon Jovi fan?"

17 "Rain in the forecast tonight?"

him out, get him shitfaced, and get him laid so he'll want to turn Crimson. I was appointed the duty of hosting TJ Leroux, a highly coveted seventeen-year-old forward from the USHL. The stocky North Dakota native didn't have much exposure to city life.

Now every player on a team has a role—goal scorer, grinder, penalty-killing shot-blocking go-hard, etc. I was hoping that at some point my role on the Crimson would be one of these, pretty much anything defined by my play on the ice. For now though, I had to settle for the role of escorting recruits around on their visits. Couldn't be too hard, right?

Soon after TJ arrived in Cambridge, I called Nikki, a cute freshman at Pine Manor College and a big hockey fan. She knew the drill. TJ, a few of the guys, and I headed out to the Hong Kong bar down the street, where Nikki and her friends from Pine Mattress were waiting. Six hours and seven scorpion bowls later, we were ushered out of the Kong . . . *sans* TJ. I searched the city for him (I texted two other guys on the team and walked down some random streets) with Nikki in tow, but no luck. Then I remembered I'd given TJ a key to my room, just in case something like this happened. So Nikki and I stumbled to my dorm.

TJ wasn't in the room. But Nikki was. And so was Negative Game.

SPOILER ALERT: I fuck it up.
ME (gawking at her body): So d'you, um, d'you mind if I take my shirt off?
NIKKI (smiling seductively and putting her hair in a ponytail): As long as you take mine off too.
ME (gulping): Gulp.
NIKKI (breathing heavily as I put her in a bear hug): Want me to just unhook it myself?
ME (gurgling): Gurgle.
NIKKI (gasping): No. Wait. Stop. Not tonight.
ME (confused): What? Stop what?
NIKKI (still gasping): Your hand. I want to, but I can't . . .
ME (still confused): I'm not touching you.
NIKKI (becoming pissed): Seriously, stop it. Get your hand away from there.

ME (standing up to prove I wasn't touching her): Look! Two hands! Neither of them on you!

NIKKI (noticing an unidentified arm outstretched from underneath the bed): You creep, Bill! What're you two trying to do to me!?

TJ (wasted): Syzzghnape aqqsonata. Mmmmmmmm.

ME (after Nikki slapped the shit out of me): OW!

Cleaning TJ's puke off my floor the next morning was an added bonus.

Go Crimson. I ended up taking home the Creep of the Year award. My acceptance speech was short, as I had to defer most of the credit to TJ who ended up at the University of North Dakota.

As much fun as it was leading unsuspecting young men down the road to perdition, there were still spring lift sessions to be attended five days a week. For the first time in my life, I actually felt like my body was getting stronger. All the weightlifting was finally paying dividends, but it came at the price of sharp pains in my lower back. They only lasted a split second and were fairly infrequent, but they were there. And I was scared.

Our strength coach, however, wasn't particularly fazed. When he finally quit blowing his whistle for no apparent reason, he'd tell me, "This ain't a fuckin' jungle gym, Keenan. Quit swinging around like you're on goddamn monkey bars." I explained I was trying to stretch my back which had been bothering me. "Back spasms," he said, diagnosing my problem with a quick glance. "Grab a foam roller and roll out."

I should have been more wary of his advice. After conducting some preseason strength tests, he put together a packet for each player that apparently ranked us individually by a so-called strength index. He was awfully proud of it, but I'm pretty sure all he did was rank us based on the proximity of our last name's first letter to the letter "A." This guy put more time grooming his pencil-thin goatee than he did learning the basics of hockey. I knew working out was important but I was trying to be the best hockey player I could be, not the best single-leg Romanian deadlifter. Anyway, I got the foam roller out, rolled my back on it, and limped back to the squat rack.

It didn't help. But I soldiered on.

The summer after my freshman year, I headed to LA with a few other guys on the team to train at the LA Kings' facility. The majority of the training took place in the weight room and on the track but twice a week we'd hit the ice, and it was a star-studded cast, with me as one of the extras. As long as I didn't stick out as a complete hack, I decided, there'd be no reason for one of the coaches to kick my ass off the ice. I was probably better suited to be in the stands with the other star-struck fans. Standing in line for drills, I tried to act like it was no big deal with Rangers captain Chris Drury in front of me and future Hall of Famer Rob Blake behind me. I thought about bringing my camera phone on the ice but decided that it'd probably get broken and I wasn't due for an upgrade anytime soon. *Just try not to inadvertently stick one of them in the face and end his career*, I thought. That went double for the scrimmages where most of the guys were pretty laid back, considering it was July and we were in Southern California. There was, however, one nut who treated the whole thing like Game 7 of the Finals. "Let's fuckin' see some effort, boys. Fuck me. Gotta have guys coming back through the neutral zone and f'r fucks sake let's start crashing the net and getting traffic in front of this 'tender. Gotta be crisper. Fuck, boys. Get some chatter goin'. Fuck me!"

That was Sean Avery. I stayed *way* the hell out of his way.

After the ice sessions were over, it was the normal routine, you know, signing autographs for the fans. Even though what I really wanted to do was steal one of the little kid's pens and get some signed memorabilia for myself, I played it cool. I'd sign jerseys and hats, whatever the kids wanted, and with a single flick of my wrists their souvenirs would plummet in value. Sure, none of these kids had a goddamn clue who the hell I was, but I was surrounded by a bunch of big time guys so I must have been someone, right? Boy, were they clueless. It was great.

By August, a new Russian centerman entered the mix, showing up with an entourage at these informal practices. Word was that a couple weeks ago at a tournament in Finland with his KHL team, he snuck away and caught a flight to the US with his agent. Judging by the long, jagged scar on his hip, I had some insight into why he seemed so excited to arrive in America and be on the verge of signing an NHL contract.

Whacking me in the back of the legs after his first practice, the smiling Russian asked me or more like ordered me to stay on the ice. "Pass me puck," he said. (He must have heard all about my crisp, tape-to-tape five footers and the silky, smooth sauce I'd been dishing to Drury all summer.) Unfortunately, "pass me puck" was code for plant your ass on the faceoff dot and feed me one-timers for forty-five minutes, ensuring you miss your ride to the hotel where you're staying and have to call a cab to get back. Two thoughts entered my mind as I stood there trying not to screw up my passes to him: 1) I'm going to remember this for the rest of my life and he'll probably forget this by the end of the day; and 2) this guy is going to score a lot of goals in the NHL. It wasn't the most fun I've had on the ice (it was close though), but at least I can say I helped Evgeni Malkin with his one-t's—must be the reason he won the NHL scoring title twice in his first six seasons.

Geno must have really liked the way I feathered it onto his tape (or he knew this was the highlight of my summer and possibly hockey existence) because it became a regular thing that summer. Now I should also tell you, for the first time ever I was wearing a visor instead of a full cage because, you know, I was a nineteen-year-old dumbass trying to act like a pro. After one drill where I mistakenly intercepted a Sean Avery pass, he offered his thoughts on my new visor: "Nice fuckin' welding shield, bud." Anyway, Malkin had me passing to him from different angles, one of which was just off the side of the net. He would rip shots inches from my face and hit his spot every time . . . except once, when sure enough one of his lasers deflected off the crossbar into my mouth, leaving me doubled over with blood spewing out.

"Sorry, Billy," he said inspecting his handiwork and skating to the bench to grab a used towel to contain the bleeding from my open wound.

As the blood poured from my mouth and I felt two of my teeth wiggle loose, all I could think was, *Holy Shit, Evgeni Malkin knows my name!*

Even though the Kings didn't sign me and Malkin didn't invite me to be his personal assistant in Pittsburgh, just being on the same surface as NHLers got me in shape to maybe, I prayed, have a shot at Harvard my sophomore year.

In September, after once again watching the first three games from the stands, I found myself back in the starting lineup for our clash against St. Lawrence. I was ready. And so was Coach Donato.

"Get youse fahkin' asses in gear tonight, f'r fahks sakes. I hate their fahkin' coach, I hate their fahkin' players, I hate their fahkin' school, I hate their fahkin' fans. Goddammit I hate fahkin' these guys!" *I wouldn't enjoy fucking these guys either, Coach,* I thought. I looked across the locker room and saw one of my teammates mouth "seven" to me. It was a solid effort by Donato but nowhere near his PR of eighteen.

The Harvard Bright Center was packed, compared to our practice attendance. "S-L-U," chanted the crowd. The seven Harvard fans who showed up halfway through the first period, were quick to retaliate, yelling "T." The game itself was a blur save for the announcement by our PA man: "Crimson goal scored by number ten, Bill Keenan. Unassisted. That's Keenan, his first goal as a member of the Crimson, scored unassisted at 10:21 of the 2nd period."

The goal itself was a thing of beauty. According to Coach Donato's scouting report which I inadvertently skimmed prior to the game, the SLU goalie struggled with high shots (every goalie struggled with high shots according to the carbon copy scouting reports Donato prepared for each game) so whenever possible, we should fake the low shot, get him on his knees, then put it upstairs. Now I hadn't had much success faking out anyone onto their knees since arriving at school, but midway through the second period, I found myself one-on-one with the keeper, and with the help of some divine intervention, the 'tender bit on my shoulder fake, providing me with plenty of room over his glove hand to loft a muffin in to the back of the net, which I did, before celebrating like an assjockey.

Donato's postgame speech was almost as well-spoken as its pregame counterpart: "Big fahkin' win tonight, boys! You know where that started? With our dumps! Good dumps, boys! No horseshit dumps tonight. That's what I been tellin' youse all week! Good dumps equal big wins!"[18]

After the postgame speech, our equipment manager handed me the puck I'd rifled into the net and I held onto it the rest of the night. Players remember their first goal like they remember their first kiss—the anticipation leading up to it, the wild celebration after. It's a moment frozen in every player's mind—a time that belongs to that player. The referee blows his whistle, the clock stops, and teammates swarm you. Time stops for a few beats, empowering the goal scorer, reminding him why he spends all that time playing a game.

The following week, we upset the eventual national champions Boston College 4–0, which helped us crack the NCAA Top 15. I was playing often and well and I felt like a rock star, aside from the whole sleeping with girls, making a ton of money, and being famous parts. I was so cheerful about everything that Coach Donato's jokes were actually funny to me—well maybe not, but I fake laughed at them at least. As I crossed the Charles River Bridge, I no longer contemplated jumping but rather the picturesque view of downtown Boston. I also got my own fan club, that is, if you could call a pale, bony kid who had glasses complete with transition lenses and a long, greasy ponytail a fan club. My linemates were always quick to point him out to me during warmups. "Keenan, your fuckin' boyfriend's here again," they'd say as I tried not to make eye contact with the kid who held up his sign that said "GO BILLY KEENAN—REPRESENTIN' NYC!"

Off the ice, I tried to experience other opportunities Harvard had to offer. Sophomore year is when the notorious Final Clubs[19] punch potential members. There were three main clubs that attracted athletes: The Owl (predominantly football players), AD (lacrosse), and Delphic (baseball). Hockey players, for the most part, were distributed among the three of them, but I opted to take a different route when

---

18 Dump: Strategically shooting the puck into the opposition's defensive zone away from the goalie, setting your team up for a quality possession in the opposition's side of the ice.

19 For more about Final Clubs, and punching and all that sort of Harvard crap, see *The Social Network*.

I was punched by the Porcellian Club. Known on campus as the PC, it was the club where those guys who claimed they had the idea for Facebook were members. There's also the rumor that if members don't make their first million by age thirty, the club gives it to them. I'm counting down the days.

In the PC, I found out who that guy Plimpton was that my elementary school principal had been telling me about, as Papa G's picture hung proudly inside the club. It was an eclectic group consisting of many who thought playing hockey involved a grass field, goggles, and a skirt. Sure, there were some guys who draped cashmere sweaters over their shoulders, wore monogrammed Oxford shirts, and used the word "whom" in conversation. But the fact is they didn't really care I played hockey. And I liked that. Hell, I *needed* that. Harvard loves stereotyping its students and groups, a lesson I learned when it became clear that I was viewed as either a spoiled New York City rich boy or a dumb jock. There was no gray area. To the majority of my fellow students, I was either a snob or a meathead. But they were all a bunch of pretentious elitists from the boondocks, trying to come off as cool and hip in the big city, so what did they know?

In mid-November, the tweak in my lower back became more frequent, painful, and disconcerting. It even started radiating down the back of my leg. Like all hockey players are taught, I didn't say a word about it, because keeping quiet about pain was a part of our game, a prerequisite for success, as important to us as hockey hair, cursing, and spitting.[20] What I didn't realize is that there are two types of pain: The type that you can play through because while it might hurt, it won't make it worse, and the type that, without proper care, could cause irreversible damage.

What had started as some periodic discomfort in my lower back had quickly turned into sharp pains that soared down the back of my right leg into my foot—sharp, scary pains.

College hockey gets a bad rap for being soft compared to Canadian Major Junior, so you can imagine that Ivy League hockey has its

---

20 Typical hockey maxim: "If it's not broken, you can play. If it is broken, you can still play."

doubters. From a different angle, however, Ivy League hockey teams have twenty-five revved up twenty-year-olds who are playing half as many games as they did in Juniors, and are now surrounded with an overall mediocre-looking group of girls. To top it off, the players are forced to wear full cages, when in Juniors, most were wearing visors. The result is a lot of pent-up testosterone and some physical hockey. Not surprisingly, the constant banging and bashing continued to take its toll on me. I could hear the voices of my past hockey coaches, *pain is evil leaving your body; pain is just a state of mind.*

It culminated in December of my sophomore year, when I was unable to bend over and tie the laces of my skates. I hung up my equipment that day, unprepared for how long it would remain there untouched.

I missed practice that week for the first time since I'd entered school and my teammates were very understanding: "How's your vagina?" they'd ask as I limped to the training room while they headed out to practice. There was no cast, crutches, or bloody mess. How bad could it hurt?

Like any well-informed hypochondriac, I went straight to the most reliable source to diagnose the problem myself. After typing in my symptoms to WebMD.com, it was clear: I had either herniated discs or syphilis.

The MRI the following week confirmed my hunch—two herniated discs in my lower back. Unlike a broken bone (or syphilis), there was no structured treatment for such an injury. I opted to take a non-invasive approach, embracing physical therapy with the trainers at school, acupuncture with Dr. Wong in Boston, and five epidural shots at Mass General hospital. One of the doctors put me on Neurontin, a drug developed for people with epilepsy that left me constantly woozy. I had a supply of painkillers that could have paid for the psychological counseling I probably needed.

The epidural shots provided the most notable relief but only lasted a day or two. Then I'd lose all sensation in my right foot and shuffle around campus like Kevin Spacey in *The Usual Suspects*. I even received some injections of Toradol, a powerful painkiller now under much scrutiny by the FDA due to claims of fatal heart attacks and organ failure. Toradol gave me relief for about twenty-four hours; the following day, the pain would be back and worse.

While my teammates were on the ice practicing, I spent my time in the training room hooked up to electric stim or ultrasound or whatever other crap they had that appeared useful but rarely did anything except spread MRSA. In an attempt to distract myself, I decided to open my mouth and get to know some of the other student-athletes at the school. Because basketball was the other winter sport, I spent a lot of time on the training tables with some guys on the Crimson hoops team. Most of the time, it was the starting point guard, a tall, scrawny Asian kid from Southern California, who ended up on the table next to me. While he got treatment for his knee and I got some for my back, our conversations invariably always turned to the same subject: Girls. "I just don't want some girl who likes me 'cause I'm a ball player, you know? All I want to find is a cool chick who is fun to be around and likes me for me. It'd be better if she didn't even know I played basketball at all," he'd tell me over and over. My first reaction was that he probably wouldn't be into The Smash or Easy Mac. But I couldn't bring myself to say what I really thought: *Seriously, dude? You're playing basketball at Harvard. It's not exactly like you're on anyone's March Madness Final Four bracket. Don't think you need to worry about any groupies wanting you 'cause they're impressed by your basketball credentials.*

Jeremy Lin was far more prescient than I.

While my treatment in the training room proved pretty much useless, I decided to branch out and try hypnosis. Ervin, a psychiatrist/hypnotist/generally odd individual who had graduated from Harvard in the seventies, had become Coach Donato's lucky charm, and before games, he tried putting the team in a trance that would enable us to win, the exact same game prep that Wayne Gretzky never did. Once Ervin flipped off the lights in the locker room, it was go time. The laughter and farting couldn't have been easy to edit out of the audio recordings he was making to document the sessions. During my solo sessions—where, for some reason, he felt the need to remove his shirt—Ervin droned, "Now imagine your slipped discs are little hockey pucks, sliding their way back into place," as he hovered uncomfortably close to my face, his tuna sandwich breath making me gag and his curly chest hair intermittently grazing my cheek. Unsurprisingly, my hockey puck-like discs didn't do as they were told.

The pain progressively worsened and began to change me as a person. I couldn't sit for more than ten minutes at a time, and when I stood up, I had to think through any movement as even the slightest wrong move would send horrible, sharp pains radiating down my ass, leg, calf, and foot. Sleeping was the only time I found a little relief, but even then, I experienced agonizing pains whenever I'd roll over. I knew eventually the human body breaks down but figured it would be something I could worry about when I was ninety-one, not nineteen.

As much as my family and friends tried to empathize with me, I isolated myself. Hockey had always been the thing that validated me—what made me puff my chest out just a little bit every day when I stepped outside—and now it was gone. It was difficult too, considering my chest didn't have much bulge to begin with.

Some people drink, some do drugs—my antidote was to detach myself from everyone and act like a dickhead.

"Keenan, we're going down to the Square to grab dinner with some of the seniors. Come on."

"Nah."

"Dude, you gotta leave your room once in a while. I mean, you gotta eat at some point."

"I'll order in."

"Alright, man. Hey, those broads from BC said they wanna come over after our game Saturday. That blonde was asking about you."

"I'm all set." Plus, I knew the blonde hadn't been asking about me. She'd still yet to respond to my Facebook friend request . . . or my message . . . or my poke.

"What's with that?" he said pointing to the six-pack on my floor. "You don't even drink Miller Lite . . . or beer really." It was true, but college was about expanding one's horizons and it was time I gave something new a try. "And what's the deal with your closet. You got like two shirts hanging in there. Laundry day?"

"Nah, one for each night I plan on going out this year. Can you shut my door on the way out?" I wanted to finish the book I was reading, *What Does it All Mean?* by Thomas Nagel.

I could feel myself drifting away from the team. On road trips, Coach Donato assigned Ervin as my roommate. Sleeping was difficult for me as it was. Now, it was damn near impossible.

Finally, it became clear I had no more noninvasive options, so at the end of my sophomore year, I underwent back surgery at the Hospital for Special Surgery in New York. I spent the summer at home recovering and hoping to begin rehab by September, but when I returned to school and started my rehab program, the pain slowly returned. My doctors told me this was normal, that every now and then I would feel spurts of pain but it would eventually subside and completely disappear.

It didn't. For that matter, it got worse.

As I started to spiral downwards, I found hope when an unassuming guy began showing up at practice. Off the ice, he looked like the rest of us but on the ice, he was way the hell better. After the infamous 2004 incident in which Todd Bertuzzi had attacked him resulting in a serious concussion and three broken vertebrae, Steve Moore was back at his alma mater to rehab. Watching a former Crimson player quietly work his way back to the NHL and continue fulfilling his dream offered some inspiration at a time when I needed it. But as motivating as it was to see him fight his way back from the devastating injury, I still wasn't getting any better. It did, however, make me feel less sorry for myself, which I'm sure was a relief to my roommates and parents.

One afternoon as I was making my routine walk to the training room from our locker room, I heard a faint voice coming from the coaches' room. Coach Donato had given the team an unusual off-day from practice saying he had to go scout some new recruit. The door of the coaches' room was slightly ajar, just enough that I could hear Coach Donato, "Andreychuk, Hawerchuk, Konowalchuk then Bourque came over . . . I finally felt I belonged." I craned my neck making certain not to utter a sound and saw Donato lying on the leather couch, hands resting at his sides, eyes closed, as a tear began running down his flushed cheek. Then another voice chimed in and I could see a tape recorder just above Donato's head. "Okay, Teddy . . . now when I count back down to one, you're going to slowly open your eyes . . . ten, nine, eight . . ."

And I thought I had issues.

But I couldn't blame Donato for wanting to recapture his playing days. After all, he embodied what all of us players hoped to be some day. After leading Harvard to the Beanpot title and National Championship in 1989 and receiving Frozen Four MVP honors, Donato embarked on a successful thirteen-year NHL career which included a trip to the Olympics. What more could a guy ask for in a career? He even appeared on *The Price is Right* and made it to the Showcase Showdown.

By Christmas of my junior year, I hadn't practiced in almost fifteen months. (If you're unable to bend down to tie your own skates, the trainers don't let you on the ice.) Now one would think being on the ice is what I would have missed most, and believe me, I missed it like hell. But the longer I was away from the game, the more I realized it wasn't about the wins or goals; it was about those times in between that I yearned for. Not being able to participate in practice meant not being part of the shenanigans that took place—like pissing off the goalies by firing pucks off their skates and into the net while in line during drills or enjoying the natural high that ensues after all practices. It's experiencing the ups and downs with your teammates that creates that bond between players unique to hockey teams. Not being able to skate meant I was no longer a part of that process. Like the excess snow that the Zamboni picks up, I was scooped up and dumped out behind the rink. I could hear Mom's voice in the back of my head, urging me on, "Don't be a bitch." But I continued to be one.

I'd find myself moping around the rink during practice, feeling as much like an outsider as our student team manager, Fook Mi. I'd linger in the bowels of the rink, not wanting to watch but unable to leave the rink, listening to the sounds: pucks ringing off posts, skates carving the ice, coaches yelling for no reason. Practices almost always ended with a continuous 2-on-1 drill, a challenge that pitted the defensemen and goalies against the forwards—bragging rights on the line. Freshman year, Coach Donato would cut to the front of one of the lines which somehow always resulted in the two of us being matched up as the forward tandem. I could read Donato's lips when he'd look across the ice only to realize I was his partner: "Fuck me," his lips would say. I was thinking the same thing.

We'd regroup in the neutral zone then dart down the ice on the odd man rush. I'd hightail it to the far post, stick on the ice, and Donato would carry the puck the entire length of the rink until the top of the circles, where he'd unleash a rising slapshot that would whiz by my face and the goalie's, hitting the top corner of the net. "Nice decoy, Willy!" he'd shout, pointing his stick at me before raising it in the air and celebrating his goal.

Standing in the hallways of the rink, listening to my teammates out on the ice, I even missed being Donato's decoy.

The locker room, once my haven, had become a place I no longer felt comfortable. I missed walking into practice after having skipped all my morning classes and staring at the stick rack, deciding which one I'd use that day. I missed loitering around the locker room and interrupting guys' stories or delivering the punch lines of stories I'd already heard, just to be an ass. I missed sitting in my gear listening to pre-practice speeches and making eye contact with certain guys when Donato would say something stupid. I missed that feeling after practice when I'd take off my shoulder pads, steam rising off my red, hairless chest, sweat dripping off my hair, waiting for someone to wipe the ice off his skates and peg me with it. I missed the way the game played with my senses. It's funny, though—that unmistakable odor of the hockey locker room only really smells good to a player when he knows he contributed to it.

Aside from simply being around my teammates, it was the impromptu conversations and pranks from guys that I also missed—like taping "99" to the back of Coach Donato's tracksuit one day before practice, the day after he said "Numbah 99 is the only guy who can skate around the ice and do whatever the fahk he wants." I heard the story later that day but when it happened I was across the street in the field house getting treatment for my back.

And just because we were at Harvard didn't mean conversations between teammates pertained to solving the budget deficit or concerns over GDP growth. No, conversations that might take place between teammates in the locker room post-practice would go something more like this: "I'm not fuckin' with you, Nicky. He wipes back to front. No wonder The Smash wouldn't dome him." Then there were the creative solutions teammates had for each other, like the time one sophomore who was struggling through a dry spell found out he'd be sidelined for a few weeks with a broken right arm: "Try going inverted southpaw," our senior goalie advised. Or there was the day I walked in the locker room and saw a group of four guys standing around another guy's locker, chins propped on their sticks, as the speaker revealed to his expectant listeners what he learned earlier that day: "Just lick your forearm and sniff it right away. Smells identical, eh?" Again, I understand that out of context, it's hard to believe I found this stuff funny, but this is the type of thing I missed—the camaraderie between teammates. I no longer felt part of it. It's no wonder a hockey team is used to illustrate the definition of the word "camaraderie" in the dictionary. Look it up.

If I wanted to have any hope of ever playing again, I had to go back under the knife. So I did.

After my second operation, I was unable to take on the simplest tasks by myself like dressing and going to the bathroom and was wheelchair-bound for several weeks. Even worse, I didn't qualify for a motorized one. The pain was no longer something I experienced; it was a part of me.

To my doctors, it was an unspoken truth that my days playing hockey were over. They were more concerned that I would be able to bend over and pick up my kids one day than I would be to survive getting knocked around by a bunch of Ivy Leaguers. Unlike normal people with normal metabolisms, the months of inactivity didn't lead to massive weight gain but rather I withered down to 150 pounds and was as frail as I'd ever been. The only remnant of my hockey player self was my hair, and even that was getting thin.

It was devastating to contemplate a life without hockey. I could survive without it but I couldn't live without it. The game was my sustenance and without it, I starved. The mental suffering was almost worse than the physical pain, and I coped with it by further alienating those around me. I lost any interest in my classes and shut myself off from everybody.

Everything happens for a reason, I'd think. *Someday this will all make sense.* The only problem was that someday seemed to grow more remote with each day that passed, and at twenty-years-old, it was tough to accept.

I hit a new low when my iTunes playlist was filled with the most depressing country songs ever recorded: "I'd Be Better Off (In a Pine Box)" by Doug Stone, followed by "Gunpowder and Lead" by Miranda Lambert, followed by "Hard Rock Bottom of Your Heart" by Randy Travis. Next up, the Cure.

But it turned out that diving into Robert Smith's depressing discography wasn't necessary, as the second operation seemed to have worked. So it was back to the gym where, under my own supervision, I built my body back up. Each of the hundreds of shoulder exercises meant being able to fend off a defender for an extra second; each of the thousands of plyometric jumps meant having that extra burst of speed to win a race to a loose puck; and each bicep curl meant I was one step closer to filling out my slim fit T-shirts. By the time school was out for the summer, I felt strong and in shape. Going into my senior year, I was confident I'd finish my collegiate career on a positive note.

I don't know who Murphy is, but I think we could add a Keenan Amendment to his law.

"Break a leg," Mom told me the day before our first preseason game. I wish I had. Instead the awkward fall into the boards on my first shift of the game left me unable to put weight on it as I glided to the bench. Unfortunately, I didn't break any bones; compared to the hell of the back-to-back ligament surgery—not to mention the unwelcome addition of two screws and one plate—breaks would've been a breeze, because bones heal in six weeks, whereas fully torn lateral ligaments take six months.

Had I known that season on Apple Core where I helped Rick DiPietro blossom into the No. 1 overall NHL pick that he already was would result in me contracting his injury plague syndrome, I would have considered playing junior hockey somewhere else.

As my Harvard teammates darted around on the ice, holding their sticks and making plays, I sat in the stands, once again, holding a pen and fabricating faceoff stats. I couldn't deal with it anymore. Against the doctor's orders, I laced up my skates for practice after undergoing my second ankle surgery. Wearing the orange jersey with the red cross patch meaning I couldn't be hit, I was as useful as the big orange pylons Donato tossed on the ice at the end of practice indicating he was about to bag us.

At our annual Christmas Party, Secret Santa gifts were exchanged. One guy, whose girlfriend had a slight gap in her front two teeth, received a box of Chiclets. Our star defenseman who grew up in Quebec but was struggling through Intro to French received *French for Dummies*. And while he wasn't technically part of the party, Coach Donato received a muzzle from the players. All gifts received a chorus of booze-filled laughs. Then I opened mine: The orange practice jersey I'd been wearing—"KEENAN" stitched to the back.

Again, I sat on the sidelines and watched the game—and my college career—skate by. I tried to block everything out and focus on my classes, but that was all but impossible, as I often needed to dive into the painkillers prescribed by my surgeons. Weekly lectures at the planetarium, however, for *Science A-47: Cosmic Connections* class was an otherworldly experience after a couple of Percocets.

I was in a constant daze and contemplated taking the semester off to fully recover, but after discussing it with my parents and advisor, I decided it would be best to push through.

Well, to say I "pushed through" might be slightly misleading. I spent my final year at college mostly cooped up in my dorm room, wearing my piss-stained green windpants, feeling sorry for myself. I could only parade around as the mayor of Meltdown City for so many hours so when I wasn't doing that, I'd binge on episodes of *Gossip Girl* which gave me some insight into what it would have been like had I actually been cool while growing up in New York City.

On a dark February night as I was preparing to throw myself another self-pity party, I flipped on the TV and stumbled upon a New York Rangers pregame show. It was the night Adam Graves was going to have his jersey retired at MSG. As the crowd, many of whom proudly wore their No. 9 Graves jerseys chanted his name, Graves himself was far less vocal, almost embarrassed to be the center of attention, deferring credit for his accomplishments to his teammates and family. Time had taken his hockey hair. He stood with swollen eyes, clutching his wife and three kids. But amidst the celebration, there was an uneasiness to Graves. It was like he was watching the funeral of Gravey, unable to recapture the highlight clips that played over and over on the Jumbotron. Standing at center ice with the Garden lights dimmed, Graves watched his legacy immortalized as his jersey slowly rose to the rafters. But as grateful as Graves was to have the Rangers honor him in this way, I knew he was looking up at his jersey in the rafters, wishing he still had it on his back.

I didn't bother watching the game. I had watched enough hockey over the past few years. I turned off the TV and stared at my closet. In the far right corner hung the orange practice jersey I'd received for Secret Santa.

* * *

I eked my way to the finish line of college, receiving my diploma in June 2009. While the recession was devastating the economy and job market, my mind was elsewhere. I knew I couldn't call it quits. I didn't need a bunch of injuries to make me realize I still loved and missed the game. Playing just flat out made me feel good.

Driving out of Cambridge with my diploma stashed somewhere underneath my hockey bag in my car, I passed Harvard Yard and noticed old Dexter Gate, one of those symbols of Harvard that tourists like to photograph. I hadn't ever noticed it in my four years. Sitting at the red light, I looked at the sign above the gate and to my surprise realized the inscription wasn't in Latin or Greek, but English. "ENTER TO GROW IN WISDOM." In my four years, I couldn't recall walking through that gate.

Back home, I also realized that yes, I missed being around my teammates and the feeling of being part of a team, but there was more to it. There's something inherently supernatural about hockey, and I'm not about to try and spew up some revolutionary thoughts here.[21] Think about it: Humans have feet and toes made for walking on solid ground. In my equipment, I was a few inches taller and more than a few pounds heavier. In skates, I could reach speeds not even Olympic runners could achieve. Every time I suited up, my gear became an extension of my body. Off the ice, I was just another scrawny kid with a bag of putrid equipment I hauled around, but that always changed when I put it on, taking on a new identity. You wonder why hockey players use the same battered jock strap or treat their skates like a newborn baby? Some may claim superstition or comfort. The fact is, the equipment becomes a part of the player and thus treated as such.

I also knew that if I turned out to be one of those old jacknobs who wears his hand-knit letterman sweater and rambles to anyone within earshot about how his college injuries prevented him from making it to the pros and eventually becoming a Hall of Famer, I would retroactively want to kick my face in. And as you know by now, I'm kind of a pussy and suck at fighting so I wouldn't be able to accomplish that.

That summer, slowly, incrementally, I worked my way into shape once again, and it was a long, boring grind of which I'll spare you the details and cue the Rocky-like montage of Bill skating from one side of the rink to the other, intercut with snippets of him at the gym lifting weights, doing step aerobics, sprinting around Central Park listening to Jock Jams Vol. 3, jazzercising with the gals, tripping on hurdles at the track, dismantling agility ladders, guzzling

---

21 Yeah, I am.

gloppy protein shakes, and researching his next move, all the while his friends and family were wondering: *When is this guy going to figure it out and move on?*

A rational person probably would have walked away. After all, it is a game, and after sending me to the operating room four times, I think it was trying to hint at the fact that it didn't want me playing anymore. But rational thinking wasn't my strength.

If I wanted to keep playing the sport, I needed to find realistic alternatives, and after hours of Googling, it became clear I had two options: The first was to start looking for a desk job in New York where I'd probably have no clue what I was doing and join a once-a-week beer league where guys (a) wore helmets with built-in ear pieces and mouthguards attached to their cages, (b) owned hockey bags with wheels, and (c) associated "the Coast" with the beach near their summer house. The other option was to find a minor league team in Europe located in an area that preferably didn't have Internet access so they wouldn't be able to look up my stats from the past four years.

Most countries in Europe hosted at least one professional league and some of the bigger hockey countries (e.g., Russia, Finland, Sweden, and Germany) had two or three, all of which offered foreigners an opportunity to play. I saw it as a chance to reinvent myself as a hockey player and maybe even as a person. Going *way* out of my comfort zone would allow me to start on a fresh sheet of ice, offer a unique way to see a new part of the world, and introduce me to dozens, if not hundreds of non-English speaking girls who wouldn't realize that I had zero, I mean negative, game.

Furthermore, the larger ice surface in Europe—rinks are fifteen feet wider—force players to focus on speed rather than hitting, which, now that I had my legs back, would favor my style of play. North American hockey, the type I had grown up playing, was more linear—right wingers stayed on the right, centers in the middle and so on—but there was more room in the European game, less congestion, additional opportunities to be creative. I'd even heard of scenarios where the goaltender was used as an outlet, much like goalkeepers are used in soccer, which is about as freewheeling as it gets. Traditionally, a defenseman might retreat behind the team's net while his linemates change. However, in Europe apparently some teams simply passed the puck back to the goalie allowing the entire five-man unit to change.

Alright, maybe I made up that last part, but who cares? It could be true.

Hockey was my forum to control the uncontrollable, to tame chaos and demonstrate superiority. In Europe, there would be more skating, more weaving, more darting, and more cutting, leading to more unpredictability. And I welcomed unpredictability, both on and off the ice, because the predictable wasn't working.

Professional hockey in Europe, however, wasn't immune to the global financial recession. Teams had tight budgets and were stingy with their money, especially when it came to their import players from North America. All the leagues in Europe have a limit to the number of North American players each team can have on its roster, in part due to the finances, and in part so teams can develop home-grown players.

After numerous emails and phone calls to teams all across the continent, landing a tryout with a team seemed impossible. My outbox-to-inbox ratio in my email was 20:1, much like the conversion rate on texts I would send to girls on Saturday nights. The one email I received from a team was usually a form letter in a foreign language thanking me for my inquiry and wishing me luck . . . a.k.a. telling me to get lost, and to think about becoming a barista.

I tried to contact sports agents, but, as I had suspected, they weren't jumping at the opportunity to take on a client who had undergone four operations in two and a half years. I sent out email after email, flooding the spam folders of every general manager, coach, assistant coach, and equipment manager affiliated with a European hockey team.

By mid-July, I still had no leads and was questioning whether this was a fool's game. Was I kidding myself? Who would give me a shot? Is this all worth it? At times, I wondered what the hell was wrong with me. *It's just a game*, I would tell myself, *move on*. But I couldn't.

While my friends prepared for their jobs on Wall Street, the pressure mounted to make something of myself. I spent nights staring at my ceiling trying to figure out how to get myself beyond these feelings I had for the game. I still had my Graves poster hanging beside my bed and pucks displayed in front of my bookcases.

I envisioned my life as just another average guy with above-average hair. Then I got a phone call.

"Bonesy. What's crackin', brotha?"

"Kubes, how the hell are you? Long time no talk." It was Jakub Kubrak, my old friend from junior hockey who ensured my face didn't get rearranged each game.

"Good, my man. Just finished playing a season of pro over in Poland."

"That's awesome. Back to the motherland, huh? How was it?"

"Time of my life. Met my wife over there, and I'm gonna be a father in seven months which is why I'm calling. I want you to be my kid's godfather."

"Wow. Congrats, Kubes. I'd be honored. Sounds like an offer I can't refuse."

"Good shit, Corleone. It's been too long. How's your back? What're you doing these days? You working?"

"Honestly, I still got the hockey itch so trying to keep the dream alive. Not ready to sit at a desk all day. Plus, my grades didn't exactly have anyone knocking down my door."

"Come on, fuckin' Harvard grad. You probably got one of those diplomas with Latin shit all over it. No way I woulda got through those fuckin' SATs without your help."

"Yeah, yeah, well I got the diploma but it was more like *sine laude,* not *cum laude.*"

"Keenan, I don't understand half the shit you say, but I love you. Seriously, though, what's your plan?"

"I've been skating and trying to get a place over in Europe to play next season. Not much luck finding anyone who'll give me a tryout."

"You in shape?"

"Yeah. Been skating at Long Beach and—"

"Willing to play in whatever country?"

"For sure. I don't care. Just looking for a shot."

"I got you. Be ready August 1."

"What? I've tried to get in touch—"

"Keenan, I got you, buddy. August 1. Be ready to go."

PART TWO

SECOND PERIOD

CHAPTER FIVE

White Cap Lifeline

IT'S GO TIME. I'm headed to Belgium, where I'll be paid (I think) to play hockey.

On the drive to Newark Airport, Mom opts to sit in the back seat with me while Dad drives and Lil sits shotgun. "Did you pack your boots? You're going to want boots if it starts snowing," she says.

"Yes, I packed them." No, I didn't. I never bothered buying boots— didn't even cross my mind.

"How about towels. Do you have enough towels?"

"Yes, Mom. I have three." I have no towels in my luggage and think, *packing one or two might have been a good idea. Boots sound good too.* Mom's got a BA in History, an MBA in Finance, and a PhD in Bill.

They park and walk me to the ticket counter. I check my hockey bag, five hockey sticks, and suitcase. My backpack stays with me as does my mindset, hopeful with a healthy dose of delusion. "I guess this is it," I say, hoping to avoid any real emotion.

"Okay, Bill. Have fun. We love you," Mom says, as she and Lil come in for a group hug, holding me tight like I'm about to deploy for some military mission. I see a tear trickle down Lil's cheek. I turn to Dad, who tells me to take care of myself. The last time I had to say goodbye to my family is when I left for Harvard. My goal is to spend more time with my teammates than with doctors—funny how expectations become more realistic with age.

The girl seated next to me on the plane converses with one of the flight attendants in what I assume must be Flemish, but I don't have a clue. She's pretty good—a nine at Harvard, a soft six in real world standards, but I'll bump her up to a seven 'cause she's foreign and I'm the one telling the story. After three hours to compose myself, I make my move.

"Belgian?" I probably could have come up with a complete sentence, but usually the more words I say, the worse off I am.

"I am. And yourself?"

"American but actually going to be in Belgium this year. Headed to Turnhout. I'm playing—"

"Are you the new American on the team?" She adjusts her body towards me. "I'm from outside of Turnhout, but it's all over the papers—the new American who's going to save the team!"

"Yeah, Turnhout. Wow, I didn't realize there was much hype. Not sure about saving the team, but I'm excited to do whatever I can to help. So it's a big deal over there? Lots of fans at the games?"

"Of course! Everyone goes. The stadium is always sold out—at least 15,000 people every home game, cheering and chanting."

"Holy shit. 15,000? That's unreal. I had no idea." I saddle up on my mental high horse and begin galloping.

"My little brother dreams one day of playing for the senior team. Right now he's ten years old but he loves football, or sorry, I guess you call it soccer. He has the autographs of all the players on the team—if you wouldn't mind, do you think you could sign this?" She pulls out a pen and sheet of paper from her bag. "It would mean the world to him—the first of his friends to get an autograph from the new star American footballer."

"I'd love to." I scribble down my best Mickey Mouse signature. "Hope I can meet him at one of the games. So, other than soccer, or football, I guess, are there any more sports in the city?"

"There's a hockey team."

"Oh yeah? Ever been to their games?"

"I haven't, but I think they have good supporters. Not as popular as the football, but people enjoy watching it."

When we touch down in Brussels at 7:00 a.m. local time, I get a sudden head rush. I'm alone, in a new time zone, out of my comfort zone, and I have to pee.

Moments after exiting the plane, I see a sea of people waiting to clear customs, and the disorganization is overwhelming. Some jabber in an unidentifiable language, while others stare into space, shell-shocked. Me, I'm a man on a mission. I weave my way through the crowd until I'm not too far in the back of the line that I'll be here all day, but not too far up front that I'll feel guilty about cutting. When I finally reach the customs officer, he takes my passport, quizzes me on my name, and lets me on my way. I continue down the terminal towards the baggage claim. After forty-five minutes of anxious waiting, I'm relieved to see an airport attendant walking towards me with my hockey sticks.

On my way out, I stop at the currency exchange booth where I spot the attendant slapping at his keyboard while dividing his attention equally among three computer monitors. I slide two fifty dollar bills through the small glass opening separating us, then the FX trader gets to work, no doubt engaging in a variety of cross-currency swaption straddles, naked hedges, and arbitrage plays. After sixteen glances at each of the monitors, he agrees to provide me with the USD/EUR exchange rate that is displayed in illuminated red lights behind his head.

After completing my sales and trading internship, I walk outside to the bus stop, greeted by a spitting rain and a nippy breeze. I hear Mom ask, *Did you bring enough warm clothes?* The bus is supposed to arrive every hour on the hour, but time drags by with nary a bus to be seen although plenty of tiny cars whiz by. Two interminable hours later, the bus arrives. I throw my bags into a bin underneath and grab a seat in the back of the bus.

Thirty minutes, or thirty hours later, I arrive at the Antwerp train station, where I call the general manager of my new team, the White

Caps. His name is Guy and he tells me he's going to send someone to pick me up and they'll be there in half an hour. I sit at a table outside for thirty minutes, which turns into sixty minutes, which turns into ninety. In Belgium, the concept of time seems skewed.

Suddenly, I'm starved, so I wander into the station where I hope to find some place that serves American-ish food. Thank goodness there's a Mickey D's, where I order four plain hamburgers and a large fries. In a fruitless attempt at gaining weight, I've developed an eating disorder—anti-anorexia.

I've had to take a leak since halfway through the flight, but due to my lack of confidence in the cleanliness of airplane toilets, I've been holding it in. After lunch, the dam is about to break, so I ask an older man sipping a coffee by himself, "Can you watch my bags while I head into the McDonald's to go to the bathroom?" I speak slowly, enunciating each word clearly and holding out my index finger from my crotch.

He nods and says in perfect English, "I have to leave in five minutes."

"I'll be back in two," I say, then run upstairs.

There's a woman sitting outside the restroom, perched on a stool that's far too small for her ass. "Pay me, you must. One Euro."

"But I just have to take a pee." She makes a face, so I make a peeing motion.

She holds out her hand. "One Euro, you must pay."

I look over her shoulder into the bathroom as the door swings open. It's like somebody detonated a grenade full of shit in there—unflushed toilets, crap written all over the walls, balled up paper towels on the ground, not to mention the smell. There's a door on the far side of the bathroom, presumably the entrance to a quarantine area for anyone leaving this bathroom before returning to civilian life. Sea Bass kicked in one of the toilet doors and there's an earthquake occurring behind the other stall door, so I eye the lone urinal.

The fact that people don't give a damn about cleaning up after themselves in public bathrooms irritates me. The fact there's a pay-to-piss rule is more irritating. The fact the bathroom attendant talks like Yoda is great.

I pay the toll, cross myself with my right hand, then take a final gasp of air and enter, hoping my immune system will protect me from whatever I'm about to be exposed to. I pee, and after a second-degree white belt karate kick to activate the hand dryer, I exhale, flash a passive-aggressive glance at Yoda, then leave, and look for the gentleman who's guarding my bags.

He's gone.

As are the bags.

I get dizzy. My passport and money were in my pocket but everything else was in the luggage: My clothes, my sticks, my skates, *everything*. I calculate how much it will cost to replace everything, and if I'll be able to do so here in Belgium, or if I'll have to order everything online from the States, and the shipping costs will be astronomical—

Before I jump into oncoming traffic, I notice the gent had kindly hidden my stuff under a table. I wipe the sweat and rain from my forehead and decide that Belgians are pretty damn cool.

When I sit down the jet lag catches up to me and I get trapped in a spiral of neuroses. *Is someone actually going to pick me up? What have I gotten myself into? I can't understand what the hell anyone's saying.* I hear my heart thump as if my chest is an amplifier and figure that the entire station can hear it too.

A voice brings me back: "Bill? Bill?" I look up and see a hulking man who directs me towards his car. I pick up my luggage and heave it into the under-sized European automobile.

"I'm Marcel," he grunts. "Ice stadium first."

"Sounds great. So how are you affiliated with the team?" Before departing, I'd spent a good two hours on the team's website trying to gather as much information as possible but considering that my Flemish is nonexistent, I didn't get that far. I had, however, come across one page that seemed to show the team personnel, but Marcel's face doesn't look familiar.

"English not so good." He turns on the radio—it's an unfamiliar rock song in Flemish, or Urdu, or something. "We do this."

On the dashboard I see a piece of paper with my name written on it—spelled correctly. That's a positive.

Marcel dodges through highway traffic at break-neck speeds and after forty-five minutes including a harrowing two-minute detour on the wrong side of the highway, he gets off at the Turnhout exit and races through the town, zipping by pedestrians and bikers without much concern for their safety, or ours. Not only does he not brake to make the turns, but the guy accelerates into them. His reckless style reminds me of a New York City cabbie screaming down Park Avenue, trying to make as many of the lights as possible. Finally, Marcel mercifully screeches into the parking lot of the rink, Kempisch Ijsstadion.

Okay, I wasn't expecting Madison Square Garden—there's no sky box seating, just a stack of empty boxes waiting to be taken to the trash out back; and no upper bowl seating area, just seven or eight rows that encircle the rink. It seats a thousand spectators. Maybe. No jumbotron hanging above center ice, which is probably for the best considering the cracks in the ceiling look like a drop of pigeon shit might cause a collapse. Right on cue, a small bird flies across the length of the ice only to disappear somewhere in the rafters.

Welcome to European minor league hockey.

On the plus side, there's a clean sheet of freshly cut ice, so I'm good. I've been to a lot of rinks, walked my equipment into a ton of locker rooms, but this is distinctively different. I'd always recognized at least a few faces in the locker room or a few rink employees; now I don't even know if I'd recognize my team's logo.

You smell the locker room before you see it. That's almost always the case. Making my way through the door, I pass the stick rack. I haven't seen this many wood sticks since my mini-mite days. Pro hockey players using wood sticks? It's like a professional photographer using a Polaroid camera. Some old school NHLers like Ryan Smyth use wood sticks, claiming they give them more feel for the puck, but that's by choice, not necessity.

No large flat screen TV hangs on the wall like the one at Harvard. The only electronic devices in the Turnhout locker room are a large boom box with a stack of CDs on it and a heat gun on the floor. In the far corner is a training table in desperate need of a Lysol wipe down.

I spot an empty stall and hang up my equipment although as I survey the surrounding lockers, there doesn't seem to be any set guidelines on which pieces of equipment go where. No carpet with a team logo in the middle, just some black rubber mats. The large trash cans on both sides of the cramped locker room are overflowing with tape balls. The sides of the barrels provide evidence that another player was here not long ago as a glob of spit slowly inches down to the ground.

In the lobby, I spot Marcel at the cafeteria, chugging a beer and chatting up a server from the rink's restaurant. The area is dimly lit, and as I look back onto the ice surface, I see the main source of light inside the arena is sunlight that comes through a large window above the rink's far side. As I wonder how the bright light will affect the ice—after all, sun has been known to melt ice—I see a small rainbow appear on the opposite side of the rink, as the light is somehow diffused on its path indoors.

In the car, Marcel once again dodges and darts through the narrow streets, and any chance of me trying to familiarize myself with my surroundings goes out the window. After winning another time trial, we pull up to a structure that looks like either a former military barracks or a condemned building. Long weeds shoot out from the cracks in the pavement outside the entrance. One of the window curtains upstairs is partially collapsed. It looks like where happiness comes to hang itself.

Home.

"I go now." Marcel hands me a house key. "Bye-bye."

Before he speeds off, I take out my luggage and haul it up to the second floor. No one is around. In college, I had eleven roommates, not including the three mice who made their home in our common room couch. I'm not sure how many guys will be living with me here, but I hope the ratio of humans to animals will be higher.

I walk cautiously around the apartment doing my normal Inspector Gadget routine, testing light switches and examining the furniture. On the floor inside the hall closet is a rotary phone and VHS player. After walking around a pair of fire hazards, I spot the bathroom behind a half-open door and lift the toilet seat—murky brown water in need of flushing, but I can't find the handle. Dark, scraggly hairs litter the bowl and the tiled floor is suspiciously sticky.

When the time comes, I'll be nesting or heading to the woods.

I turn on the shower—not very hot and even at full pressure it's more of a steady leak, but it works. There are three bedrooms all of which have single mattresses that look like they were last used for conjugal visits. A folded set of non-matching sheets are stacked on an armchair. Exhausted, I don't bother unpacking and instead collapse on the common room couch into a deep sleep.

Ten minutes or ten hours later, someone shakes me. "Bill? Bill Keenan?"

I jump off the couch and am greeted by Guido, our German coach. A stout man with a square head and thick bowed legs, Guido looks in his forties and like a guy who doesn't enjoy smiling. His dark hair is cropped tight and he has no sideburns.

After handshakes and how-you-doin's, Guido shows me to my room. As I open my suitcase and reach for my dopp kit, Guido pokes his head through the door. "Take a few minutes to make you beautiful, then we go to rink. Practice."

The last thing I want to do is make my first impression on the ice in this physical and mental state. But I hear Mom's voice in my head: *Don't be a bitch.*

I suck it up.

On the ride there, Guido gives me a rundown of the team: "I want fast, tough lineup dis season. We will do good in dis league if we can do dis. I have two Canadians coming tomorrow—good toughness. Dey will live at da apartment wid you. We have four guys from da Slovakia—great skills but little odd in da head. Den we have da rest guys from Belgium, good mix of young and veteran players."

"Where'd the Canadians play before?" I ask.

Guido turns his head to me, his hands at nine and three on the steering wheel, and smiles. "Major junior boys."

Major junior hockey is comprised of three separate Canadian leagues, the "Q," the "O," and the "Dub."[22] Players between the ages

---

22 Quebec Major Junior Hockey League, Ontario Hockey League, and Western Hockey League.

of 15–21 are eligible, but by playing major junior hockey, one loses eligibility to play US college hockey. There's a ton of debate about the pros and cons between college and major junior, but I won't bore you with my opinion. The fact remains major junior hockey is loaded with big, tough, Canadian NHL prospects. In other words, everything I wished I had been.

In the locker room, everyone prepares for practice—sticks are taped, skates are stoned, and pieces of equipment are sniffed before being strapped on. I immediately recognize a distinct hockey scent, that of a blow dryer blasting high heat from deep inside someone's glove, emitting a putrid stench. I love it.

Some players come over and introduce themselves, but I fail to remember a single one of their names. Guido had assured me that all the players speak English, but I quickly realize just because they have the capability to do so does not mean they will.

I sit in my stall, which happens to be adjacent to the Slovak Corner. Directly to my right sits a thirty-something Slovakian forward who's played on the White Caps for the past six years. Above his stall is his nameplate: Marek Ziarney, No. 9. I stare at the inscription, wondering if there is any chance he would change his number so I could take it for the season. But when Marek removes his shirt, I realize my chances of getting my lucky number are nil, as "9" is tattooed on his back. I look down at the small "9" trinket I've had dangling on my neck since I was seven years old. I start thinking about another number, any number will do.

While the faces of my new teammates are unfamiliar, the sounds of the locker room are familiar and comforting—clear tape ripping off a shin pad, a collective laugh from a small group of guys listening to some story that's most likely embellished or stolen from a friend.

Considering my lack of sleep, I practice well, running on adrenaline and the intense need to make a good initial impression on Guido and my teammates. I haven't felt a part of a team for what feels like years, and I *have* to be accepted. On the ice, I'm at ease for the first time since arriving in Turnhout. I recognize the energy immediately. It's the same feeling I've experienced at the beginning of nearly all my hockey seasons. United by our love of a simple game—that's at least what I'm thinking—and the desire to win, we begin the year's story. The game exists on so many levels—the theoretical game, the actual game, the games we play with ourselves inside of our heads, the games coaches play with players, the games players play with refs.

Once off the ice, I hurry up and shower so Guido can drive me back to the apartment. In front of the barracks, Guido shoos me out of the car. "I return to da Germany. Be back Monday. Be rest dis weekend."

Exhausted as I am, I can't fall asleep. I've never experienced home-sickness, primarily because my parents never sent me to overnight camp and, thank god, because camp sounded *awful*. Mom even used camp as a threat: "Bill, if you break another window with that puck, I'm sending you to that sleepaway camp in Maine!" I doubted she'd follow through, but I shot the puck low from then on. With no clue how to access the Wi-Fi and no functioning cell phone, I do the only thing I can think of doing—have a meltdown and cry myself to sleep.

I wake from my coma at three o'clock in the afternoon, starved. There's a box of cereal and some expired milk in the fridge; three bowls of Cocoa Puffs later, I hear muffled voices echo through the stair-well—the words are English, the accents, Canadian. I swing open the door and meet my two new roommates, Chris and Rene. I help them carry their bags into the apartment, and then we sit down on the nasty couch in the living room to get acquainted.

Chris, a forward from Vancouver, is the type of guy who has all the answers. I've played alongside dozens of guys like him. His blue-tinted aviator sunglasses hang off the front of his black shirt, a V-neck just deep enough to reveal he shaves his chest. His stonewashed jeans are hemmed just above his white snakeskin shoes. Everything's accounted for. He's got one of those faces that make you want to knuckle him for no good reason, and his hair is gelled into a faux-hawk—like my hair freshman year minus the frosted tips. Chris dresses like a douchebag and has hair like a dickhead.

"Guido said you guys played major junior?" I say.

"Yeah," Chris says. "Played in Prince George, decent team but we had a brutal coach—he gassed a few of the boys then traded me to

Notre Dame in Saskatchewan, eh? Worked out alright though—put up twenty G's and thirty-six apples. Fuckin' bunch of beauties[23] out there." This is the guy who says "beauty" a lot but he himself isn't one. He may be a blowhard—and probably a liar—but his obvious love of the game mitigates at least some of his obnoxiousness. I'll refrain from belaboring the point about Chris's douchedom and henceforth allow his dialogue do the talking.

Rene, a hulking defenseman with a strong Canadian accent, is the anti-Chris, an easygoing guy, the type you want on your side, who has a smile so big it swallows up his almond-shaped eyes when he laughs. He has high cheekbones on his tanned face, thick, dark hair, and a top right tooth missing. The sleeves of his gray Henley shirt are rolled up to his elbows, and his khaki cargo shorts have scattered paint stains. "Yeah, I played in the Dub three seasons, three different teams. Had a couple shoulder operations last two seasons so didn't play much last year which blew."

"I'm in the same boat. Had some issues with injuries too last couple seasons," I say.

"Let's leave that shit in the past, eh. We'll tear it up this season, buddy!" Rene is what my six-year-old self thought all Canadians were like: friendly, laid back, and obsessed with the sport, the type of guy I would have been good friends with had we grown up together.

After Chris inflates his tires some more and sets up his Xbox, the three of us walk into town. We wander around the narrow streets of Turnhout, keeping our eyes peeled for any restaurants and bars that look appealing. The small houses in the city center tiptoe the line between charming and depressing depending on one's state of mind. There's a medieval feel to Turnhout—like one of those places I was supposed to read about in my sixth grade European history class. I wouldn't be surprised if a knight appeared riding a horse and carrying a lance preferably aimed at Chris's nuts.

---

23 Beauty (as well as the derivative "beaut") is the most overused hockey expression ever. Hard to define—no one really knows what it means, but it's good to be one; the same way no one really know what a 'douche bag' is but it's not good to be one.

"Boys, over there, eh?" Chris points at a large black building, the type that only looks good in the darkness of a drunken weekend night. "I can see us getting rowdy in there a few times this year, eh?" And then he's off. "I was in a place like that once with a couple beauts this summer and I met this broad, eh, and she was all over me the entire night. Ended up dragging me into the men's room at this place, and I let her sample the goods. But she was real sloppy drunk. Kept crushing Bud heavies. Late round pick, boys, not gonna lie. Real sturdy stems, eh. Fuck, good times back in the Sask." Chris looks at Rene who smiles. As Chris looks away, Rene turns to me and shakes his head.

"Looks empty now . . . except for some creep standing solo in back," Chris says looking at the dark tinted windows of the place.

"Think that's your reflection, bud," Rene says.

"Fuck off, chief."

The town's most popular means of transportation seems to be the bicycle, which proves hazardous to pedestrians. The riders are reckless, racing inches from us, one after another, fueled by that sense of entitlement shared by 100 percent of hardcore cyclists across the world.

"Maybe they ring a bell," Rene says after nearly getting sideswiped by a cruiser. "Or at least a hand signal."

On the positive side, the frequency and speed with which bikers travel allows us some favorable visuals of a few of the female locals who have no qualms biking in skirts. Staring longingly at a particularly cute brunette, I think, *Maybe they'll be into the shy American. Maybe I'll find a girl who has negative game and our forces will multiply to create positive game. Maybe it's stupid math references like that which account for me having negative game.*

Chris elbows me in the ribs, then shoves me into a supermarket, where we stock up on provisions.

"The boys call me Magnum, so . . ." Chris trails off as he pushes the cart idly through the pasta aisle, periodically pausing to check nutrition facts.

"Hey, asshole." Rene emerges from another aisle holding two bags of generic-labeled cereal. He removes the Fruit Loops box from the cart and whacks Chris on the head with it. "Quit picking the brand name shit—costs twice as much and tastes the same."

Armed with six overflowing grocery bags, the three of us exit the supermarket and instinctively begin tailing the first set of girls in distressed jean shorts we see. When a new set, wearing shorter shorts with more holes and tighter tops enters our line of sight, we begin following them at a reasonable distance for another few minutes until we see a sign for the Dutch border and it dawns on us we are completely lost. We remove our heads from our asses and retrace our path through the labyrinthine streets, most of which are lined with cozy bars and cafes which provide outdoor seating for old couples sipping from wine glasses and smoking leisurely.

"This way, guys," I say pointing down a street.

"You sure?" Rene says.

"Positive. I remember that thing up there pointing to the street our apartment is on."

"You mean that graffiti dick?" Chris lifts his aviators from his eyes to his forehead.

"Yeah, I remember the tip facing the street we need to walk on."

"I don't know. Following our dicks got us lost in the first place," says Rene.

"You sure that's the right dick? I've seen a whole slew of them," Chris says.

"I know it's right. I remember thinking how weird the ball to dick ratio is."

"Shit, you're right. It's almost like three nuts," Rene says.

"Or like regular balls with testicular cancer," I say.

"You two done?" says Chris.

"I think Billy's right."

"Fine." Chris lowers his shades back over his eyes. "But is it the street the dick tip faces or where the jizz is going 'cause that veers off to that street," he says pointing down another alley.

"Dick tip," I say, ending our circle jerk. And miraculously we find our way home.

At the apartment, Chris takes it upon himself to cook up a meal, and, to my surprise, it's good: grilled chicken over linguini with tomato sauce, and a medley of peppers, onions, and garlic. But the vegetables worry me. Chris spills them on the floor before adding to the dish. I'm not about to make a stir out of it, as he's doing all the work, but I hesitate when taking my first bite. Since I don't keel over and die within three seconds, I scarf down the rest of the meal.

"Hey buds, you know these trash bags are different colors for a reason. Blue one's for recycling. You don't just throw shit in it when the black one's full." Rene removes some chicken from the transparent blue bag.

"Relax, chief," says Chris. "Guess I'm a shitty recycler. Sue me."

"You're pretty good at it with those hand-me-down Mother Goose tales you've been telling today," says Rene, swiping his hand over Chris's gelled hair.

"Sorry I get laid."

"Not sure how impressed Billy would be if he knew that one story involved a handicapped chick." Rene tilts his head in my direction, looking for me to get involved.

"Physical or mental?" I ask.

"She was missing a toe, not a fuckin' chromosome."

"She still got one of those parking passes though, eh?" says Rene, nudging Chris in the stomach.

"A kill's a kill." Chris picks up an Xbox controller. "How 'bout I slay you two pussies in vids."

After a few games of Halo on Xbox which Rene dominates, Chris tosses his controller on the ground.

"Chief, you fill this thing out yet?" Chris pulls a piece of paper out of his pocket. Rene shakes his head.

"How 'bout you, buds?" Chris says turning to me.

"Took a look, but haven't written anything yet." Chris flings the sheet on the coffee table.

"I played hockey so I wouldn't have to fill out goddamn home-work," Chris says walking to the kitchen.

"It's just three questions, buds." Rene picks up the sheet and reads the form Guido had left for us in an envelope. "What are your strengths as a player? What are your weaknesses? And what are your goals this season?"

"I'm here to play, not write a book about it," Chris says dumping his dishes in the sink.

"We'll get you a box of crayons. You can draw him a picture," says Rene. Chris puts his hands in a "V" shape and gives Rene the international "suck it" sign.

"I got no problem with strength testing bullshit. At least that applies to the game." Chris flexes his right bicep and kisses it while winking at us.

"But even some of that stuff we did in juniors like that grip test . . . who gives a shit how strong my left grip is?" Rene says.

"You're just rattled I had the highest score on the team, eh, buds?" Chris says.

"You get enough forearm work in every night, Popeye," says Rene. Chris contorts his face, rotates his body, and unleashes a burst of farts like a semiautomatic machine gun before wafting the air in our direction. "Let those marinate." It smells like hot sewage from a third world country.

"Alright, ladies." Chris reaches in his pants checking for seepage. "Time for a Skype sesh with my girl. Said she's gonna put on a show for me. Maybe I'll take screenshots for you queers. And when you're done playing grab ass, how 'bout you work on your Halo so I can try next time." He tosses a controller on my lap.

"Tell your mom I say hi, buds," Rene says. Chris, his back turned to us as he walks into his room, extends his right arm behind him, lifts his middle finger, and closes the door.

"Big stats guy, huh?" I say flicking my head in the direction of Chris's door after it closes.

"Yeah, he could tone it down, but he's harmless," Rene says.

"Who calls him Magnum?"

"Shit, he's been pushing that nickname since Juniors. Haven't heard a single person call him that. Ever."

"Told me he had thirty-two kills last season."

Rene smiles. "Maybe in Halo. Thing is, if you knew his parents, where he came from, you'd see why he's like that. Before juniors, I played with him one season in peewees. His mom was nuts. Made him run home in full gear behind her pickup after every loss. I remember after one blowout, it was like twenty below, piss would freeze midair if you took a leak outside, and you could barely see this little kid pumping his arms in a cloud of diesel smoke, sprinting to keep up with the truck. Hockey parents, eh?" he says shaking his head.

I had a teammate on the Connecticut Yankees whose dad made him do the same thing. He plays in the NHL now. I wonder if my parents had been like that, would I be in the NHL now too? Would it have broken me and made me quit the game? Would I have ended up like Chris?

"My mom used to tell me I looked invisible if I played shitty," I say. "Or ask me if I'd rather play baseball or soccer—but just mind game stuff, nothing physical. How 'bout yours?"

"They didn't really give a shit. Don't think my mom saw me play more than a couple games. Mind if I use your computer?"

I hand him my laptop.

"Look at this fancy shit." Rene takes my MacBook, running his palm over the front and back before opening it. "I gotta get a contract here—need a paycheck bad." He stares with squinted eyes at the computer screen, typing carefully with both index fingers. "Credit card's maxed. Good thing I bolted the country, eh?" He forces a smile.

"I hear ya," I say even though I have no idea what it's like to be living off a maxed out credit card. Mom slipped fifty bucks in my pocket before I got on the plane to Belgium. Dad slipped me another fifty.

Rene closes the computer, then tosses his feet on the couch and lies down.

"I don't give a shit what I have to do to. I just don't want to go back home," he says looking at the ceiling, tossing his Velcro wallet up and catching it. "You're a college guy, eh?" He turns his head towards me. I nod. "Aren't you going to do something with your degree?"

"Frame it probably."

The left side of Rene's mouth curls up in a half smile.

"How'd you lose the tooth? Stick?" He shakes his head. "Puck?" He shakes his head again.

"Wasn't from hockey."

"Guido's pretty jacked you guys played major junior hockey. How was the coach on your last team?

"Decent guy, but not sure he could pick me out of a lineup. And he wasn't all that confident putting me in one either."

"Where you from?" I ask.

"Manitoba, up north on the border of Saskatchewan."

"My first travel coach was a Saskatchewan guy. From Regina. You grow up on a farm?" I remember all those drives through Canada when I was a kid, staring longingly at the farms where the land produced miles of crops and tons of NHL players.

Rene swings his feet back on the floor. His head drops between his shoulders as he stares at the ground, exhaling slowly.

"OCN," he says, his eyes fixed to the ground between his feet. He rests his head in his hands, and for the first time, I notice his large, swollen knuckles and the mounds of thick scar-tissue built up on his eyebrows.

"OCN?"

"Opaskwayak Cree Nation." He raises his head. "The farm boys have it good. They're across the river in The Pas."

I nod my head slowly, readjusting my body as the room goes silent. "Your parents still there?"

"Not sure," he says quietly, his eyes still fixed on the floor. "I got out when I was fifteen to play juniors. There's a lot of pride there, but life . . . It's casinos, booze, and fighting." Rene runs his fingers through his thick, jet-black hair. "You're from New York City, eh? Like Manhattan?" I nod my head.

He looks up at me, his eyes briefly making contact with mine before focusing somewhere on the wall across from him. "When I was seven or eight, we had a tournament in Saskatoon. We played this team called the Boston Icemen in the finals, all these rich kids with one-piece sticks, new skates, names on their sweaters, all that. They were nice guys though, and good players. I think they pumped us like six or seven to one. After the game, we ate dinner with them at some steakhouse and traded pins. We gave them these little Maple Leaf pins and they gave us these real nice American flag ones, like this big." He holds his thumb and index finger a couple inches apart. "When we got back home, I used to wear that fuckin' thing on all my jackets. I remember thinking how sick it would've been if I was one of them, growing up in the States." A smile envelopes his face as his eyes gets swallowed in it. "I still got the damn thing. My coaches thought something was wrong with me. But there was this one teacher who kind of understood. You probably think I'm fuckin' nuts too, eh?"

CHAPTER SIX

Hamstrung Home

GAME DAY. FINALLY.

I set my alarm for 8:30 a.m., but anxiety wakes me at 5:32 a.m. I wake up again at 7:16 a.m., but that's 'cause I have to pee.

Yeah, it's an exhibition game, but the team's anticipation is palpable, because we're finally playing against another team instead of beating up on ourselves. That, and it'll be nice to wear something other than our practice jerseys which were last washed during the Belgian Revolution.

There's an old cliché in sports (well, there're a ton of old ones and most hockey players myself included talk solely in clichés) that goes, "You're only as good as your last game." It might be true, might not be; either way, I can barely remember my last game.

"What time's the draft, bud?" Chris says as I enter the common area, cinching up my tie. Rene and Chris stand by the front door, both wearing jeans and T-shirts, with duffel bags slung over their shoulders. "You can save the suit and tie routine for when you make it to the Show." I change out of my suit and toss on my jeans before the three of us begin the ten-minute stroll to the rink.

Our opponent is Herne EV, a perennial powerhouse from the German Oberliga. The Oberliga is the third division in German professional hockey, but, as is the case in most European hockey leagues, the classifications here can be deceiving. Sometimes, due to new ownership or sponsors, a team in a technically lower division may be much better than a team in a higher division due to a franchise's financial resources. Herne, for example, has an owner who has signed a number of dual Canadian/German players from the American and East Coast Hockey Leagues in hopes of dominating the Oberliga. This season, we'll also be playing teams from the Belgian Elite League and the Dutch Eredivisie. Due to the small size of both Belgium and Holland, each country has one professional league and teams play for both an inter-country championship as well as intra-country championships. Truth be told, the structure is so complex, you have to wonder how a bunch of hockey people came up with this.

Warmups are twenty minutes away and there is no place I would rather be than sitting in this stall putting on my hockey gear. The rest of the team doesn't seem as excited. Aside from the jacked up Slovak Corner, where Marek and his posse take turns tucking their dick and balls between their legs to see who has the best mangina, the pregame mood in the locker room is tense. Although I don't join in, there's something comforting watching the Slovaks as it takes me back to familiar locker room scenes in juniors and college.

I've seen guys drink before games, but not if they're in the lineup. Above Marek's stall stands a small, unmarked bottle filled with clear liquid. Periodically, each of the Slovaks returns his genitals to their God-given position then swigs a gulp, before cringing, burping, and blowing the gas in the direction of the nearest teammate. I don't ask what they're guzzling, but intuition tells me it's best I stick to drinking from my own water bottle.

Suddenly Guido storms into the room. Dressed in a dark suit, his short hair glistens with gel, and his face remains void of sideburns, though he now sports a short, dark moustache.

Rene, sitting to my left, taps my elbow, then leans in and whispers, "Getting an early jump on his playoff beard, eh."

Guido stands on a chair and roars, "Yellow line stahhhts da game! Yellow line stahhhts!" *Yellow line*, I think, *that's my line*. I look over at Chris, my left wing on the yellow line, and we nod at each other—although there is a mirror behind me, so he might be nodding at himself. I glance at my right winger, whose name I can't pronounce, and he flashes me a quick smile before tilting his Red Bull upwards then tossing it in the garbage. It's a good feeling looking at guys in the room, feeling a shared purpose, knowing they're relying on you. It's been a long time since I've felt this way.

Our first shift isn't what I'd imagined when I'd played it out in my head before the game. Off the opening faceoff, Unpronounceable Name takes a high sticking penalty and we're immediately short-handed. Chris and I stay on the ice to start the penalty kill. Although I know the most important part of playing on the penalty kill is being patient and staying in position, I'm unable to curb my enthusiasm and chase the puck as it's shot into our zone. Hurling across the ice, I can hear The Lizard's voice in my head: *What the fuck are you doing out there?!*

After darting across the ice and gaining control of the loose puck, I pick up my head and see Chris streaking across our blue line, so I saucer a pass over no sticks and hustle to join him on the rush. The safest play on the penalty kill would be to fire the puck into the opponent's zone (recall Coach Donato's affinity for "good dumps"). However, as Chris skates through the neutral zone, one of the opposing defensemen catches an edge and falls. Seeing this, I push harder to catch up and find myself on a two-on-one situation—an odd man rush—a dream scenario when you're shorthanded. When we enter the zone, Chris slows up, forcing the defensemen to make a decision as to which one of us he wants to cover. Clearly recognizing that I'm not much of a threat to score, the d-man chooses to block Chris's shot lane. The moment I see this happen, I haul ass to the far post of the net with my stick down. Chris sends a hard pass in my direction, which deflects off the defenseman's stick, sails through his legs, bounces off my ankle, clangs off the post, and trickles over the goal line—just like we planned.

I raise my hands and my stick high in the air nearly taking out the referee. Chris and our two defensemen skate towards me, huge smiles plastered on their mugs. "Fuckin' greasy, buddy," Chris says, rubbing the palm of his glove in my face as we embrace. I could literally kiss my teammates after a goal. Even Chris. But I don't, because it would probably be misconstrued. Plus, I might catch one of them mid-spit.

Ask any hockey player to describe a big goal he scored and he'll tell you more or less the same thing. Well, guys might use different words depending on brainpower, native language, and their tooth count, but the short pause and smile that consumes their faces will be the same.

Skating to center ice, I can't help but notice the bewildered looks on the faces of the opposing players whose stares translate roughly into, *What the hell is wrong with this guy? He just scored an absolute garbage goal in a preseason exhibition game.*

If they only knew how long it's been.

The fun continues as the puck follows White Caps players around the rink, and when the final buzzer sounds, we celebrate a 7–1 victory. Guido walks through the locker room, fingering his moustache and offering each player a congratulatory kick on the shin pads. There's happy and then there's hockey-coach-after-a-win happy; in the hour or so after a victory, you can get away with doing pretty much anything to a coach. I consider clocking Guido in the jaw just to test the boundaries, but settle for smacking him on the ass with my stick, and he gives me a big grin in return. If we'd lost, however, and I tried that maneuver, the stick would most likely have wound up splintering off my head.

As Guido exits the locker room to meet with a local reporter and reel off a bunch of hockey clichés, Marek walks around the locker room, slapping each guy on the leg, wearing his jockstrap and a piece of black hockey tape fastened below his nose.

So far, European hockey is pretty damn great.

After devouring some sausages at the rink's cafeteria, I wander outside for some fresh air when a little kid, no more than ten years old, wearing a White Caps hat flicks his cigarette butt into the street then hands me a pen and motions for me to sign the brim of his hat. I haven't signed many autographs—occasionally the entire team at Harvard would have to sign a jersey or stick for a Harvard grad wearing corduroy pants and Velcro sneakers—but who am I to refuse? I scribble down my name like I did back in my stint as Malkin's passing bitch a few summers ago. The kid then nods at me as he shows it off to his friend standing nearby. I give the kid a wink as he points up at me and I hear the words "Chris" and "Canada" amidst some other Flemish I don't understand. I interrupt the boy and explain to him that I'm not "Chris the Canadian" but rather "Bill the American." The other little kid slowly retracts his game program and pen from my reach. Then they both scurry away.

After avoiding the rest of the rabid, autograph-seeking fans, Chris, Rene, and I decide to walk back to the apartment and check out the local bars along the way. As we walk down the narrow alley that connects the rink's entrance to the main street in town, I hear some faint giggling sounds behind us. I turn around and there are two girls, around eighteen years old, pointing at us.

"Looks like we got a couple gamers, fellas," says Chris. We slow our pace so the pair can catch up.

"Hey, girls, watch our game?" Thank god they're young and foreign, because Chris's delivery is dumb.

"Yes," they say in unison amidst more giggling, whispering, and hair tossing.

But I shouldn't cast stones, because my move—a less-than-subtle head-to-toe appraisal of both girls' bodies—isn't much better. Dressed in jeans that looked painted on and tiny white tops that reveal more skin than they cover, the pair have stellar builds. We introduce ourselves, and, as is customary in The Land of Negative Game, I don't register either of the girls' names because I'm too busy congratulating myself for not fucking up my own name. I feel like Charlie Brown listening to adults when girls talk to me.

Chris drops several tons of bullshit, but it must be convincing, because the girls agree to head back to our place. At the apartment, everybody settles on the couches in the TV room except me. I take a seat in our rocking chair because (a) I'll probably be less shaky if there's some distance between me and the girls, and (b) the chair is the cleanest of all the seating options.

After Chris finally shuts his mouth and goes to the bathroom to touch up his hair, one of the girls says, "We plan trip to New York. Probably go to clubs all night and see famous celebrity actors. We have little black dresses all picked and selected."

"Do you know famous celebrities?" the other girl asks.

"Have you ever seen somebody get shot?"

"Or mugged?"

"Or killed?"

I want to say, "I've mugged, shot, and killed a number of famous celebrities," but I keep my mouth shut. I can hear the voices of all the teammates I've ever had yelling the same thing they would if I were skating behind my net with the puck: "*Wheel! Wheel!*"

It soon becomes clear that neither of the girls has any intention of going back home tonight. However, my high from the game is wearing off and I'm too exhausted to come up with any material that won't make me look like a moron, so I go to my room to change clothes, collect my thoughts, and switch bed linens with Chris, whose sheets look less stained than the ones I got. As I empty my pockets onto my dresser, I come across the crumpled up napkin (pressed up against the Trojan Her Pleasure condom that has been waiting, patiently yet hopelessly, in there since sophomore year) on which Kubes had scribbled down a few important rules to abide by when playing hockey overseas. Included on his list of dos and don'ts are: Do toast the fans after every game, do act like a professional, do stay well hydrated, and then, underlined and in caps, DON'T MESS AROUND WITH DAUGHTERS OF COACHES/MANAGERS! I put on some comfortable clothes and return to the battlefield.

Before I can sit down, Rene stands up, takes my elbow, and pulls me into the kitchen. "Listen," he says, his eyes wide with panic. "I know you wanted dibs on the blonde but we might have an issue."

"What? She fucked in the head?"

"I wish. She's our general manager's kid, eh?"

"Guy's daughter?"

"Yeah. Guy's daughter."

When I step through my bedroom door, I almost turn around—they were wearing the hell out of those jeans—but three doesn't go into two evenly, and sometimes the odd man is out.

*   *   *

Over the next week, Guido blitzes us with a final stretch of preseason conditioning, much of which involves running around the city of Turnhout. During one run, out of nowhere, my hamstring tightens up. I ignore it, choosing instead to focus on what the Slovaks wear during our runs.

Noticing that I'm staring at my teammates, Rene catches up to me.

"Think it's a style thing or a comfort thing?" I ask.

"No clue, but there must be a Lululemon store here with a big men's section, eh?"

"Don't know if I can pull that look off."

"You can't."

"Probably right, but those two over there sure as shit can." Two young Belgian girls cross the cobblestone streets a block ahead of us.

Rene takes the scene in as the pair disappears behind a building. "Yeah, but gotta be careful, dude. Those spandex companies do magic on girls' bodies. You take it out of that contraption and who's to say what you're gonna get?"

"True. Whoever came up with those yoga pants deserves a Nobel Prize in Trickery." Our jog around the streets of Turnhout continues, and from behind me, I hear Chris squawk, "No traffic when you go the extra mile, boys."

The buildings are all four or five stories high, and large, old, white-haired women poke their heads out of windows to chat with passersby on the street. The sidewalks are lined with quaint cafés where seated couples wearing befuddled expressions enjoy unfiltered cigarettes and pastries as we jog by.

"Looks like they take the soccer serious here, eh?" says Rene as the impressive Stadspark Soccer Stadium comes into view.

"I heard they—"

Laughter erupts behinds us. I turn around, now backpedaling, and there's Chris, lying face-down on the concrete, his shorts wrapped around his ankles. He points at two of the Slovaks who are high-fiving. "That fucker pantsed me, eh? I swear, I'm gonna . . ."

Chris jumps to his feet and hikes up his shorts as a group of twenty-something girls bikes by, three abreast. "Hey, ladies," says Chris. "I live on that street next to the preschool there . . . Mastergas . . . Mistergra-ss, Maga . . . ahhhh. I'm on the Caps. Come to a game, eh? I'm Chris the Canadian!"

The next day, we travel fifty kilometers north to Eindhoven, Netherlands, for our final preseason tune up. Although the ride is a short one, from Turnhout to Eindhoven, I'm jacked up that our bus is big enough that the first-year guys don't have to double up. I settle into a seat towards the middle of the bus, far enough away from the storytelling group in the back and just behind the uncharacteristically quiet Slovaks, who spend the duration of the drive silently staring out their windows like prisoners being transferred from the Turnhout state penitentiary to the Eindhoven correctional facility.

In the back of the bus, I hear Chris turn on his faucet of bullcrap.

"So I wheel her that night, take her back to my place, punch her donut, and the broad won't leave. I'm thinking, this isn't a season subscription, babe. Go grab some pavement and let me get some sleep."

What a loser, I think as I turn on my computer, insert my ear buds, and fire up some Backstreet Boys. But after three-and-a-quarter loops of "As Long As You Love Me," my computer dies because I never remember to charge it. I remove the headphones and dive into my book, *Diary of a Hedge Fund Manager*.

Before leaving for Belgium, I took one last lap around my room, saying bye to my stuffed animals and making sure I hadn't forgotten anything. My suitcases were jammed to the point where it was a two-man job to close them. My last minute scan led me to this book, and it then dawned on me why my parents had given it to me that Christmas: The author, Keith McCullough, is a former Yale hockey player who found his way into the hedge fund business after college. I still had some room in my backpack so I brought it along.

McCullough's account of the ups and downs of his junior hockey career reminds me of my own (except McCullough actually *did* grow up in Ontario, not New York City). Before he delves into his wildly successful career on Wall Street, he reflects on the emotional turmoil he experienced when his college hockey career came to a close. My goal of playing in the NHL is receding faster than my hairline, and while some find making a boatload of money enough to distract them from a fleeting dream, my five-year-old self keeps pestering me to whack away.

I feel a tap on my thigh. "Good book?" asks the guy in the seat across from me, as he leans down to examine the cover. "Hedge fund manager," he says slowly, eyeing the title then raising his eyes towards mine in search of clarification.

"It's like those Wall Street guys who invest money, a shitload of it, into some risky stuff. This book actually has to do with all that financial crisis stuff." My teammate nods his head as I glance at the sheet of our team roster trying to match his face with a name.

"There," he says pointing with his index finger out my window. "Look."

In the distance, beyond one of the many steepled villages, I see five silver windmills rotating slowly. "Windmills?" I say.

"No, dummy. The tulips." He leans over me tapping his finger on the window now as the sea of red and yellow tulips comes into focus.

"They're nice," I say trying to figure out something, anything to keep the conversation going. "You like flowers?"

"They're okay. But the tulips . . . it's like your book."

I look at the cover of the book and reply, "I guess. But I think the tulips are a brighter shade of yellow."

"No, stupid." He smiles and shakes his head as he removes his headphones and places them onto the empty seat to his right. "*Tulpenmanie.*" I stare at him blankly. "Tulip mania in English, I think. In 1600s here, there were these new tulips with many different colors—red, white, green, yellow. They got so popular, people going crazy to get them and soon just one of these tulips costs more than a house in center of Amsterdam. Crazy bullshit. It was like this," he says with open palms like he's holding a beach ball. "Then bigger and bigger until pop!"

"A bubble," I say nodding my head.

"Yes. And this all starts for one reason, buddy. One person buys this tulip just because he knows there's someone dumber he can sell it to for higher price. Best part though," he says, grinning as he removes his hat and brushes his hair back. "These tulips everyone went crazy for, thought were so fucking special . . . only reason they had all different colors was of some virus." He pauses. "But Billy, I have to ask." He takes a sip of his water. "We figured out this bubble shit in 1600s. Doesn't anyone in America learn from what happened to us?"

An explosion of hooting and hollering from the back of the bus saves me. Surrounded by five guys, one of the young Belgian players sits in a window seat, face flushed, speaking with animated hand gestures in the manner of someone defending himself.

"What's going on?"

"The guys still make fun of him for what happened last weekend in Amsterdam—he went to Red Light District and after he paid, he got kicked out before anything happened. First guy in history."

"What'd he do?"

"Asked for the one thing that's off limits."

My mind races with a montage of sex swings, pink vibrators, anal beads, inflatable dolls, and cable channel 35, as I see the player getting peppered with more verbal abuse, trying desperately to plead his case. "So what was it? What weird shit did he want?"

"Eye contact."

At Harvard, the back of the bus is where freshmen were officially welcomed to college hockey. Some guys played three seasons after graduating high school, entering college at twenty-one, in hopes of landing a spot on a Division 1 college hockey team. Inauguration finally happened when the upperclassmen ushered you to the "hot seat." The questions came in rapid-fire style. "Who doesn't deserve to be in the lineup next game? Who's the worst senior on the team? Which guy on the team would you bang?" The more rattled you get, the greater the onslaught. A few minutes of humiliation are worth the reason you're there: Welcome to the team. You made it.

The tulips fade into the distance as we enter Eindhoven city limits. Some guys stand up to remove bottles of water and energy bars from their bags stashed in the storage area above the seats.

"Harvard, what's this garbage, eh?" Chris slaps my book on his way down the aisle as players file out of the bus, the majority crop dusting farts.

"It's about a guy who played hockey, Canadian guy actually—"

"For fuck sakes, you wanna read about hockey or play it? Let's go. We got a game to win."

I utter a phrase I never thought I'd say: "I agree with you, Chris."

The four-team showcase in Eindhoven is comprised of teams from the Netherlands, Germany, France, and Belgium. The tournament is a round robin format and we draw Eindhoven Kemphanen, the tournament host, in the first matchup. They're a perennial top team in the Dutch Eredivisie, since their team consists primarily of former major junior dual-citizen players who don't count against the import player limit, as they possess EU passports.[24]

After unpacking my equipment and changing into my team sweats, Guido calls me into the hallway as the rest of my teammates head back outside to warm up with a game of two-touch, a common warmup game for hockey players at all levels and a terrific way to tear up your knee and end your season.

Guido puts his hand on my shoulder, gives me a meaningful look and says, "Bill, how you feel you play last game?"

"Felt like my line had some good chemistry. We were gripping the sticks a little tight at first, maybe, but we were able to find each other pretty well off the rush and get some good scoring opportunities. Once we got our legs under us, it seemed like we got some good cycling down in the corners. I think we need to get a little tighter in our d-zone play, but I'm sure that will come as we get more familiar with one another on the ice."

---

24 If none of that made sense to you, don't worry. It didn't make much sense to me either.

"Yes, yes . . . you three had some good offensive chances. I like how you moved da puck around but you need to be more responsible in our own zone. We can't beat da best teams in our league if we play dis shit type defense." *Shit defense?* I think. *We won by a touchdown.* "I have talk wid management and I want to keep you. When we get back to Turnhout, you talk wid Guy and sign papers. Okay?"

"Awesome!"

"Right, awesome. Now go warm up wid rest of guys and get ready for game."

I give Guido a firm handshake and smile. I'd signed a thirty-day tryout contract earlier in August and figured I'd have to wait the full month before I knew whether I'd be offered a year-long contract. Fortunately, Guido has seen enough.

The atmosphere in the locker room is noticeably different tonight than it was before our previous game—I suspect the realization that the regular season is almost here has led to this serious mood. Or maybe we're not spending the night in Amsterdam after all, like our manager Guy had promised the day before. As we line up single file behind our starting goalie, preparing to make our way to the ice, my teammates' voices echo through the halls, and although I still don't know one word of Slovakian or Flemish, I do know most everything being said translates roughly into "Let's kick the piss out of these shitbags."

Adrenaline pumps me up when I hear "Bill Keenan" from the public address announcer. As I skate in for the opening faceoff, I make one small clockwise circle—call it a habit, call it a superstition, call it stupid—checking the position of all my teammates. I then pause, in case there are any photographers from the local newspaper hoping to get a good shot of the American import, before spitting twice and gliding in for the opening draw.

After a few shifts of frantically chasing the puck all over the ice, my nerves settle and I find my rhythm. It's a lot like overcoming that first bit of stage fright while taking a leak at a public urinal—you stand there, stick in hand, alongside the rest of the boys and once the nerves are contained, you can feel the flow while all sorts of shit is happening behind you.

My line generates some good scoring chances but is unable to capitalize. With the game still scoreless, Eindhoven takes a minor penalty for too many players on the ice, and my line starts the power play. Although we haven't worked much on our special teams, I'm feeling good about the possibility of scoring a goal, maybe even with my stick.

I win the face off in the offensive zone and guide the puck back to our left defenseman, who skates to the top of the point, drawing a penalty killer to him. I rush to the vacated area at the top of the left faceoff circle and yell for the puck. With a quick flick of the wrists, my teammate sends a saucer pass in my direction, and I slide my bottom hand down on my stick, bury my head, and brace myself for a one-timer.

Unfortunately, I fail to take the split second to identify where the other defenders are positioned. Eindhoven's second penalty killing forward anticipates the play and, in an aggressive move, races through, picking off the pass and sending himself on a shorthanded breakaway.

I drop my head and take off, chopping through the ice furiously until I feel a snap in my right leg. It's like a sniper shot me in the right hamstring. As I fall down face-first, an eruption from the crowd drowns out my groans. The Eindhoven player scored a shorthanded goal.

"Fuck!" I shriek.

I can't move it. I can't move my leg.

Somebody puts a hand on my back. "Which leg?" I half turn over; it's Erik, our team trainer. He gently pushes my shoulder. "Don't move around."

"Right leg!"

"Okay. Grab my arm and put your weight on your left leg. Let's get you off the ice." Erik, with the help of a few other teammates, scrapes me up and helps me off the ice and to the locker room. I try to put weight on my right leg to see if I can go back into the game, but the pain is unbearable.

I carefully peel off my equipment, wincing every time I have to readjust my body. Once I get my hockey pants and socks off, Erik has me turn around to assess the damage. Seconds later, he's on the phone with the team physician in Turnhout. I don't know what he's saying but I don't like the way he's saying it. I twist my head around in an attempt to check out the damage but the knife in my leg twists more and more with each turn of my torso.

After getting off the phone, Erik hurries out of the locker room and returns with Marcel, the Belgian Mario Andretti.

"Bill, Marcel is going to drive you back to Turnhout to meet with Dr. Luyckx. It looks like you have a pretty severe hamstring pull but we need the doctor to take a look and diagnose it."

Through my injuries suffered while playing hockey, I think I've learned all I need to know about lumbar spinal stenosis, medial ligament sprains, syndesmotic malleolus fractures, and sternoclavicular joint tears. More importantly, I have a good sense of the severity of my injuries, and this one doesn't feel good.

I guess all those minor hamstring twinges I had felt during our preseason training weren't so minor.

I limp outside with Marcel who carries my bag, following him to his car. I still can't figure out how he's affiliated with the team—all I know is his English is only slightly better than my Flemish and he drives like a nut. Thankfully, these two facts ensure we will have a quiet and quick, albeit dangerous, trip to the doctor.

After a thirty-minute drive involving three near fatal car wrecks, we come to a stop in front of the home of Dr. Luyckx, the Caps medicine man. During our preseason physical, with his teeth dark red due to the three bottles of Merlot he'd shared with Guy during practice, he asked me, "Can you touch your toes?" I slowly bent down, before he interrupted me. "That's okay. You don't have to do it. Just answer 'yes.'"

"Yes."

"Terrific. And any prior notable injuries?"

"Well, in college—"

"Super. You pass."

Marcel rings the doorbell and we're met by the doctor's wife, who gives Marcel the traditional Belgian greeting of six or seven alternating cheek kisses. Mrs. Luyckx shows us into the living room/examination room, where I take a seat in the most comfortable-looking chair and try to stretch out my right leg as far as I can. Marcel and Mrs. Luyckx make small talk, but I don't know what they're saying, because (a) they're not speaking English, and (b) they're being drowned out by the dulcet tones of a Billy Joel CD. Finally, midway through "Piano Man," Dr. Luyckx makes his much anticipated entrance. I unbutton my pants and Dr. Luyckx pokes and prods at my hamstring, testing its strength and flexibility, both of which are nearly non-existent.

"Looks very swollen," he says. "Does this hurt?" I look at him then scan the room's walls for some sort of framed diploma. There is one document with all sorts of calligraphy and a couple signatures that hangs on one wall. I hope it's a medical degree but it may just be some wine connoisseur certificate.

"*Shit!*" I say as he pokes at the most swollen area.

"And this?"

"*Jesus Christ!*"

"How about when I press here?"

"*Fuck me!*"

He smiles then pulls out a small, unmarked prescription bottle from his pocket. It looks like something the Slovaks would keep in their stalls at the rink. "Here you go. Take one for pain if you can't sleep. There are ten. Don't take them all at once." He chuckles then asks, "So, how'd the game go?"

Is this guy serious? I just snapped my hamstring in half and he's asking me how some exhibition game went? What's the diagnosis? When can I play again? Judging by the look on Dr. Luyckx's drunken face, I'm guessing none of the answers are good. He hands me a pair of crutches, after which Marcel and I make our way back outside to the car.

When we pull up to my apartment, Marcel offers to help me up the flight of stairs but this isn't my first time using crutches, so I assure him I can do it myself. Upstairs, I pop one of the pills the doctor gave me and wash it down with a swig of Nyquil, aiming for oblivion.

Five minutes or five hours later, somebody shakes my shoulder. "Buddy, how you feeling, eh?"

It's Rene. "Been better," I say. "How'd the game finish?" I carefully swing my feet off the couch.

"Lost."

"You hear anything about a contract?" I ask as he hands me my crutches before pulling a folded-up envelope from his pants pocket.

"Signed after the game," he says as I rise to my feet and situate the crutches under my arms.

"Congrats, man," I say tapping him on the leg with my right crutch.

"Thanks, bud. Dream's alive at least another year," he says. "Eh, Guido's downstairs—said he wants to talk with you. Need a hand?"

"I'm good, thanks." I hop down the steps and out the front door. Sharp needles of rain pelt my head and body. As I make my way towards Guido's car, he opens the passenger side door. I negotiate my way into the seat, then throw my crutches on the sidewalk and slam the door shut.

"Hello, Bill. How you feeling?" he asks his head turned toward me, his eyes looking out the window.

"The swelling's gone up a bit. I think it's just a muscle pull though. Those heal fully within a few weeks, which is good."

"I have talk wid Dr. Luyckx and he says your back leg has serious injury, minimum eight weeks recovery time."

"I've had injuries like this before. I think I can get back within a month if I get the proper rehab started right away."

"We cannot take risk of having an injured import player on roster to begin da season. We start league games next week and I need everyone on da roster to be healthy. I have speak wid Guy and we must release you from your tryout contract. He will drive by your apartment tomorrow morning wid your ticket home." After a few seconds of silence—and I do appreciate the silence since I'm not in the mood for any *We'll keep in touch* or *We enjoyed having you here* crap—Guido extends his hand and we engage in a handshake that has the sincerity of two female Olympic gymnasts hugging it out. I open the door and grab my crutches, which are now soaking in a puddle as the light drizzle has turned into a hard, biting shower.

That's it. I'm gone.

Upstairs, drenched from the rain, I take a seat on the couch dreading the ensuing Skype session. I check the time on my computer—10:27

p.m. here, 4:27 p.m. back home—which means Mom and Lil are probably working on some seventh grade American History homework in
the TV room. One ring, two rings, three rings . . .

"Hello."

"Mom, hey it's me." I don't turn on the video.

"Bill! How are you? How was the game?"

"I got hurt, but please just relax. I'm fine. I'll be fine. But I'm done
here." I can barely get the words out. A tear splashes on my keyboard.

"What happened? Open up your video so I can see you!" I hear the
escalating level of anxiety in her voice. "I can't. Doesn't work. Mom,
listen. I tore my hamstring in the game. It'll be fine. But they're letting
me go. I'll be home in a couple days."

"Are you okay? I want—"

"Mom, please. I'll be fine. I'll let you know when I get my flight. I
love you."

"Okay. Your room will be waiting just as you left it."

"Hi, Pinhead!" I hear Lil yell in the background.

"Tell Dome I say hi."

"I will. Call me when you know your flight though." A few moments
of silence pass. "Not the best birthday you've had, but I promise they'll
be better ones. I love you."

"I love you too, Mom."

I didn't say goodbye to Rene, or Magnum, or any of the Slovaks, or
Guy, or the mad doctor, or Marcel.

But neither did I say goodbye to hockey.

CHAPTER SEVEN

Deutschland Dangles

You never get used to rehab. It's endless, and lonely, and boring, and frustrating, and painful. Cue yet another *Rocky* montage with me shadow boxing as I jog around Central Park garnering more than a few strange looks considering I'm as intimidating as Richard Simmons's fanny pack.

On the plus side, my short stint in Turnhout attracts the attention of an agent named Mario Amonte, who represents numerous minor league hockey players across North America and Europe. He signs me, but why shouldn't he? He doesn't have much to lose; all he has to do is contact teams to see if they'll give me a shot. If he succeeds, he collects 5 percent of my salary. *Sounds like a pretty good deal*, I think. *Maybe I should become an agent.*

Within a week, he lands me an opportunity in Germany. The team is struggling but willing to take a chance on a North American. No big contract, just a thousand bucks a month plus housing and use of a car. No signing bonus, just a ticket for my flight. The team, Neuwied die Bären, is set to play in the relegation round of its division.

The catch: They need me right after New Year's. The *Rocky* montage speeds up, my hamstring is more or less workable, and it's off to Germany.

I touch ground in Frankfurt am Main Airport, where I'm to meet a man named Markus. After clearing customs, I follow the signs towards the luggage claim and a pulled-together-looking guy with wavy, dark hair and a blue jacket catches my eye.

"Bill Keenan?" the man says.

I nod, but before I can get a word in, Markus says, "Alright, forty-five minutes we have to Neuwied. Hope you had good flight." Apparently, all minor league European hockey teams are forty-five minutes from the nearest airport.

In the car—which Markus drives well, thank god—he says, "Your agent Mario say you went to Harvard. What you study there?"

"Hockey and girls for the most part, but technically I was a government major."

"So maybe next president?" he responds. That's how it works. If you're a government major at Harvard, people think you want to be a politician. If you're an economics major, people assume you're going to end up with some job whose title contains words like "monetary"— just more proof that non-Harvard people are about as clueless as most Harvard grads.

"Nah. You gotta shake way too many peoples' hands." Markus laughs before realizing I'm not kidding.

Winding our way north along the Rhine, passing castle after castle, Markus tells me about the team. After a disappointing first half of the season, they fired the coach just before Christmas, replacing him with a former Neuwied legend that played for die Bären during much of the nineties. Joining a struggling team halfway through the season might not seem like a great situation, however it'll give me a chance to help the team move forward. That, or I can help sink the ship even quicker.

When we arrive in Neuwied, Markus informs me we are going to stop by my house then drive to the rink to drop off my equipment. The streets in Neuwied are much wider than the cramped, cobblestone roads of Turnhout I note happily, as any detail differentiating the two cities gives me hope this experience will be a more positive one.

Markus makes one final turn onto *Elisabethstrasse* and parks the car across the street from a big white two-story house. Parked directly outside of the house are two of the smallest vehicles I have ever seen, one red and one blue. "That is your car. You share it with one of the guys you live with," Markus says as I take my luggage out of the trunk of his car.

"Which one?"

"The small one."

"The small one?"

"This one." He taps the blue midget on the roof and it jiggles. I had Hot Wheels cars as a kid that were bigger. It's an electric car—a Smart car, to be precise—so who am I to bitch about having an opportunity to save the planet? The car is plastered with company logos and phone numbers—on both doors, the hood of the car, and even the roof.

"Sponsors," Markus says, seeing me inspect the ads. "They keep the team alive." In the small fenced-in yard adjacent to the house stands an old hockey net, the posts speckled with black marks and the net partially torn.

We walk in the house and Markus leads me upstairs to my room. Although small, it has all the essentials: a bed, two chairs (one of which actually has all four legs still intact), a table, and a cupboard. Most importantly, everything seems clean, another notch in the plus column. My bathroom is across the hallway and farther down the hall are two more bedrooms. One looks lived in, its walls covered with hockey posters and the floor covered in clothes and empty beer cans. The closet door is open and I count at least ten pairs of shoes. The other room is more spartan, with two non-matching dumbbells lying in the middle of the room, an ashtray that's been put to good use, and a single sheet on the bed's mattress.

I follow Markus downstairs through what appears to be half dining room, half clothes drying room into a TV room. A guy about my age is sprawled across the couch. And he looks pissed. I'm hoping that's just his face.

"Hi, I'm Bill," I say, bending to offer my hand. "Nice to meet you."

"Dennis. It's nice," he says, briefly making eye contact with me before returning his attention to the soccer game playing on the enormous flat screen television.

"Dennis is not so good at English. He's from Cologne, about forty minutes from here," Markus says.

"Yes, no good English," Dennis says as Markus and I take a seat on the couch. They chat in German for a bit, then share a chuckle before Dennis heads upstairs.

"He's a real asshole," Markus says, winking at me, as I hear Dennis's footsteps fade.

The front door slams shut and in walks a stocky guy wearing a crumpled suit.

"Hey, buddy. You are Bill, yah?" I nod. "Good, good, welcome, welcome. I'm Dennis."

"Wow. Two roommates and they're both named Dennis. What are the odds?" I say.

"True, but not for long. The other Dennis is out of here tomorrow so you only need to know this one," Markus replies.

"Other Dennis is leaving?" Nice Dennis says.

"Other Dennis is being kicked out."

Nice Dennis grins. "Good news for us, Bill."

After Markus leaves, Nice Dennis asks, "Are you hungry? Of course you are! I'll make us some dinner, yah." He dives into the fridge. "You like chicken and this green stuff?" He holds up a bag of broccoli. "Of course you do. Okay, I fix dinner." Thirty minutes later, he presents me with a plate of chicken teriyaki and broccoli covered in melted cheese. After we finish, Dennis insists on doing the dishes.

Screw Turnhout.

He plops down on the sofa as I linger in the kitchen after my fake attempt to help clean the plates. "Could you grab me my snus from the refrigerator?" he asks.

"Snus?"

"Yeah, you find it by my beers."

I open the fridge, and, nestled among a mountain of bottled beers, sit two containers of the Swedish chewing tobacco known as snus. I grab the one labeled Göteborg Rape and bring it to Dennis. He offers me a pouch, but I pass.

Dipping is ingrained in hockey culture. I had one college teammate who summed it up best when I noticed him dipping one day.

"I didn't think you did that shit," I said to him.

"Just tryin' to quit my habit of not dipping, Billy."

I have no problem with guys trying to get a buzz or take the edge off. Plus, it looks cool to walk around with a huge bump in your mouth and the yellowing of your teeth and long-term consequences are an added bonus. What I do have a problem with is guys leaving around Poland Spring bottles half filled with dip spit all over the place—especially in the cup holder next to the driver's seat in my car.

Dennis, unprompted, tells me about the team. "We fucked everything first half of this season. Real shit start then we keep losing and losing and losing. They change coach here for rest of season. New guy, Alex, is good I think. Used to play in Neuwied some time ago."

"What position do you play?"

"Defense, but I get suspended right before Christmas and can't play for the rest of season. Stupid, fuck call by referee, but we have a look here. I show you."

Dennis pulls out his computer and logs onto a German hockey blog. As he scrolls down to the section on our team, I notice a thread with my last name in the title. I also notice a few familiar American names, guys who have made it to the NHL, next to mine in the thread.

"What's that say there, where my name is?" I ask.

"It's talk from fans about article in the paper here which say you played with some guys who are now in NHL." I lean in, inspecting the list wondering 1) how someone found those names of my former teammates who are now NHLers, and 2) if anyone realizes the last time I played with a couple of those guys was fifteen years ago. Apparently, it doesn't matter because according to the transitive property, I have quasi-NHL pedigree. Glad the bar isn't set high.

At the bottom of the webpage, Dennis clicks on a link with a video clip from the local news station showing game footage of him knocking down a referee after a scrum in front of the net. Nice Dennis might not be so nice after all. Because of the angle at which the video is shot, I have a difficult time determining whether he intended to hit the referee as hard as he did. Regardless, it's clearly an incident worthy of suspension, although Dennis still seems to be amused by the whole thing

"Stupid, fucking *dummkopf*," Dennis says tapping the image of the referee.

While most players resort to verbal abuse rather than physical, there's no denying being a referee must be miserable. It's not like six-year-old Guy Keenan was watching the Rangers play at MSG, dreaming one day of being Bill McCreary. Sure, he had an elite moustache, but it wasn't until I wrote this part of the book that I learned his real name. To Rangers fans, he was always known as "hey, asshole."

"What's with that patch that's on every guy's pants?" I point to one of the Neuwied players in the video.

"This is a sponsor—it's insurance company who pay when we have fuck up our teeths and stuff like that." I try to read the German words despite knowing no German.

"We cover your ass," says Dennis. "That's what it says."

"Good group of guys on the team? How's the city and broads here?"

"Broads?"

"Girls."

"Good guys on the team. Neuwied is fun, and great supporters at our games—chanting and everything all game even when we suck butt in first half. And we have some good girls, I make sure you meet. You play?" Dennis holds up an Xbox controller. I pick up the other controller and Dennis slides in *NHL 10*. After a best-out-of-seven series of "Rocks, Paper, Scissors" to decide who gets home-ice (up-screen) advantage, we do another best-out-of-seven series to decide offside settings, and a third series to decide icing settings.

"Sick TV," I say as Dennis scores off the opening face.

"Got it last week at work. Once I get my suspension, I got part-time job with one of our sponsors at electronic store, *Media Markt*. Twenty percent off with employee discount." He pauses the game to reload the snus under his top lip. He un-pauses the game and scores again.

"Who's the top team we play this season?"

"There are a few . . . Essen have good club, Herford too. You must watch out with Herford, buddy. Never know what happens there. Some crazy guys."

"Got some goons?"

"Yes, well . . . not on the ice so much. The supporters, I mean. Absolutely shit hammered every game trying to fight. Last season when we played at Herford, they had one fan, over two meters high, who chased one of our players after we leave ice at end of the game. I tell you this monster ran after our guy through the rink, into the lobby, and out to the parking lot. I could see the sparks from his skates flying up until the crazy fucker caught him."

"What happened to the Neuwied player?" I ask now losing three to zero.

"When he was released from the hospital a few days later, he got kicked off team. Too big pussy." The first period buzzer sounds. "You really suck." Dennis points his controller at the screen. "You must practice in free time, okay?"

He stands up, stretches his arms above his head, rotates his torso from side-to-side a couple times, and walks behind the couch. I hear some rustling as I stay seated with the Xbox controller in my hands trying to figure out the "skill stick."

"Buddy," Dennis says from behind the couch as I fiddle with the joystick. "Know what time it is?"

"Not sure." I toss the controller on the couch and turn towards him. There stands Dennis, pants at his ankles with his dick wrapped around his right wrist. "Bedtime!"

Next morning, doorbell ringing wakes me up. I look out my bedroom window and see two girls wearing backpacks and dressed in matching plaid skirts with knee high socks. After putting on pants and performing right arm bicep concentration curls to failure with the lighter of the two dumbbells in the vacant room, I go downstairs and open the front door. Both girls are young and attractive in that

I'm-not-sure-how-old-you-are-but-you're-cute-and-I'm-lonely-so-I'm-not-going-to-ask-and-I-hope-you-don't-have-braces kind of way.

"*Guten tag,*" I mumble.

"Hello," responds one of the girls. "You are new American on Neuwied?"

"Yeah. I'm Bill."

"I am Sabrina, and this is Anna," she says, putting her arm around the other girl.

"We baked you something," Anna says, handing me a tray covered in foil. "I hope you enjoy."

"Thanks. That's really nice of you." I take the tray covered in tinfoil off her hands.

"We must get to school now. Tell Stroeks we say hi."

"Stroeks?"

"Dennis Stroeks. The one who hit the referee."

"Right. I'll tell him you stopped by. Thanks again." I swing the door closed as the two girl scouts scurry away (one on a scooter), then remove the foil from the pan and see a dozen cupcakes carefully decorated with blue and white frosting. They are delicious—I eat four.

After listening to two riveting hours of CNN analysts discuss current European debt market trends in German, I hear one of the Dennises walking down the stairs.

"Hey buddy! Good morning. How was the sleep?" asks Nice Dennis.

"Good. A couple girls came by and dropped off some cupcakes."

"Yes. Sabrina and Anna—Neuwied superfans. They like to make party with us."

"They looked young, like high school age. Where the hell'd you meet 'em?"

"Online." He removes boxers from the drying rack and folds them on the dining room table. "In the fan forum message board."

"You hook up with either of them?"

"Not yet, but they like all my pictures on Facebook so I think they want sex some time."

"Nice. You want one of these?" I hold up the tray of cupcakes. "They're good."

"I got my breakfast right here." He raises a cup of coffee and pats the tin of snus in his pocket with his other hand "Let me take some shits now. Then I get changed and show you around town."

It's a five-minute walk from our house to the center of town, an area consisting of four or five main streets full of bustling shops and restaurants. It has a distinctly European feel and is far larger than Turnhout, with wider walking streets and bigger buildings. As we pass by one of the many liquor stores, the cashier knocks on the glass window and Dennis points and winks at him. Dennis then informs me that Markus will be meeting up with us at McDonald's.

The three of us grab our food and sit at a window-side table. Across the street I spot a large poster in a shop window.

"That's our team, right?" I say to Dennis, pointing across the street.

"Yeah. Sponsors," he responds while chomping on his Big Mac.

"Very important to team," says Markus shoveling some fries into his mouth.

"Stroeksi, Stroeksi!" I turn around and there's a guy who looks about my age, a cute girl by his side. Dennis introduces me to Willi Hamann, a center on Neuwied. Willi is cheerful but his girlfriend doesn't seem as excited to see us. She clearly wants to avoid any further conversation, so we shake hands and part ways.

"Seems like a good guy," I say. "How old is he?"

"Willi is a super kid," Markus says. "So young. Twenty-four years old. He have played in Neuwied three point five seasons now. Super offensive skills, but he just got his girlfriend pregnant. So stupid move on his part."

"Yeah, having a baby probably'll make it more difficult to play hockey," I say as if I know anything about it.

"Baby is not the problem. His problem is that he is stuck now with that girl, and she's a real . . ." He pauses a second and asks Dennis something in German then continues, "Bitch. Yes, a real bitch. No one likes her."

Dennis nods. "She's awful. Cute, but I still wouldn't put it in her."

"They getting married?" I ask.

"Like breaking into jail," Markus says shaking his head and balling up his hamburger wrapper. "Enough about this shit. Time for us to get to the rink."

Pictures of three *South Park* characters are painted on the banner that displays the hockey rink's name, Neuwied Eishalle. Across the street is a well-manicured soccer field.

I follow Dennis and Markus through the back entrance. Immediately to the right is the locker room, a large painting of the team's logo on the door. There's a short hallway in front of me and a set of plastic shower curtains. As I get closer, I can feel the air getting colder. Pushing the curtain to the side with my hand, I walk through and stop just on the edge. Team benches are to my right and left. Large blue banners hang from the arena's ceiling, most of which appear to commemorate teams from the '80s. There is no ice-level seating. The stands are steep and high above the ice surface. In the far corner is a small press box.

Nice Dennis pokes his head through the curtains and says, "Come on. Meeting time."

Inside the locker room, Nice Dennis points me towards an empty stall which Mean Dennis had recently occupied. Players gradually fill the room, and most make brief eye contact with me as I sit in my stall and unpack my gear. Twinges of cologne and hair gel accent the familiar smell of the locker room as guys pass by me. From what Dennis and Markus explained earlier in the day, we are having a team meeting to discuss expectations for the second half of the season.

It's unsettling walking your equipment into a locker room mid-season, almost as if guys look at you like *oh, nice of you to finally show up*. There's a weird dynamic that the New Guy faces, like if he were to try to chime into the locker room banter before proving himself on the ice to his teammates, his comments will mostly be ignored. However, once proving his worth on the ice, those same comments are all of a sudden witty as hell.

I haven't proved shit yet here and when I make my way into the room, I get a few looks from guys that make me feel like my hockey bag has an extendo-handle and is on wheels.

Now at the beginning of every hockey season, when a team assembles for its first meeting, anything is possible. Shit, winning the Stanley Cup seems possible even if the team you play on isn't in the NHL. But joining a struggling German minor league team halfway through the season, expectations are more realistic. It's something I've started to get used to.

Once everyone has taken a seat in front of his respective stall, Markus walks in, followed by two men. Markus opens with a few comments in German before handing it over to the older of the two guys. Willi, who sits in the stall directly to my right, taps me on the knee, leans over, and whispers, "This is Alex, new coach of team."

Soft-spoken, Alex looks to be in his early forties with a friendly disposition and a slight build. He removes a folded piece of paper from his pocket and starts talking.

While the words are lost on me, the tone is not. He speaks with authority and severity—although German in general sounds severe—and I get the sense that this is going to last a while. You can always tell when a hockey team is struggling to win games—the greater the number of losses, the greater the number of meetings held, whether they be power play meetings, veterans meetings, semi-useful meetings, captains meetings, completely useless meetings, or full team meetings. In the best case scenario, the meetings get everyone revved up for three-and-a-half minutes, then seven seconds after they're finished, everything reverts back to how it was beforehand. Basically what happens is the coach feeds the players some garbage about how this dismal losing streak is an opportunity to shine, and everyone buys in. By the end of the meeting, there's a bunch of kumbaya crap flying around and we're doing trust falls. It doesn't last.

The other problem is hockey players have a hard time sitting through meetings and pretending they're interested. Even though the rest of the guys speak German (I assume), I bet many of them are spacing out just like I'm about to. Since I only understand one word out of a hundred, I brainstorm ways to entertain myself.

My first strategy is to study how my teammates respond to Alex's speech and act accordingly. I smile when the mood in the locker room turns light and frown when everybody looks serious. That guy that exists on every team—the one who always keeps a stern look plastered on his mug complete with furrowed brow, leaning in with his entire body, nodding his head up and down when the coach is making a point—the guy who I always have seen as a total douche—today that's me for eight minutes.

Next, I try to guess *what* Alex is saying, strictly based on the other players' responses. Sometimes, a look on the face of a listener can be as telling as what comes out of the mouth of the speaker. Next, I try to guess which position each of my teammates plays and speculate as to what type of player they are based solely on their look. For instance, directly across from me sits a small, wiry guy with light blond hair who I envision being a real pest on the ice, agitating opponents, while at the same time having enough skill to produce some offense.

The guy two stalls down from me is one of those audible breathers who emits a faint whistle every time he inhales through his nose. To cope with the irritating sound that now eats at me, I distract myself by trying to sync up our breathing. This lasts for two minutes and thirty-eight breaths.

Finally, I try to guess the personalities. I didn't realize it until I got to junior hockey, but hockey teams are the perfect size—somewhere between twenty and twenty-five guys, bigger than a basketball squad but smaller than a football team. With that number, you generally get a mix of personalities that complement each other perfectly. Inevitably you've got the meathead who doesn't own a shirt with sleeves; the showboat who celebrates every goal (even in practice); the guy who always plays dirty; the guy(s) who always acts dirty; the self-proclaimed ladies' man; the quiet guy who always comes up with a good line at the right moment; the other quiet guy who never comes up with a good line ever; the loud guy who pumps the team up before games; the quiet, humble guy who scores the big goals; the guy who messes up all the drills in practice; and then there's the guy who overthinks the whole thing and needs to write a book about it.

As Alex drones on, I remember how seasons were kicked off at Harvard. The team would gather in our locker room and receive three speeches, the first coming from the local sheriff after he handed us some papers which basically said we needed a notarized letter to talk to a girl holding a drink. "All youse guys got a great opportunity here, so don't go out boozin' every weekend and let some girl ruin what you got going. We don't need any youse ending up in cuffs 'cause of some Hahvahd girl claiming she was blacked out and taken advantage of. Alcohol screws with your decision-making and vision, boys."

"Thank God it does," whispered the teammate sitting next to me.

Next up was a departmental dean, who informed us we were students first, athletes second, after which he told us that we were athletes second and students first. Then he finished with how it was an honor to represent the school, blah blah blah integrity, blah, culture, whatever.

And lastly, after the other two guys had left, Coach Donato took center stage. After a full lap around the room—careful not to step on the sacred *VERITAS* logo in center of the crimson carpet—Donato would glance up to ensure no hidden cameras had been installed in the corners of the room during the off season, then roar, "Irregardless of what you have heard. . ." Then I'd tune out because we'd all heard this before from every coach we ever had: winning hockey games was our priority. That's exactly how I felt too.[25]

As Alex's speech continues, many of the players grow restless, myself included. We keep eyeing the large digital clock that hangs over the locker room door. At 18:32—over an hour after he started his speech—Alex mentions my name. I smile and acknowledge him by raising my index finger. Some guys smile back. Some glare. Most don't care. An indeterminate amount of time later, the meeting is finally over.

As I stand and stretch my back, Alex wanders over. "Welcome to Neuwied, Bill. I have some time to speak with you, if you want. I can explain everything in English." His personable demeanor stands in stark contrast to the loud, intimidating manner of nearly all the hockey coaches I've ever had. My interaction with coaches growing up

---

25   In my four years at Harvard, three guys on the team were booted from school for a year for cheating or failing classes.

was limited to "good work" after I scored a goal and "What the fuck are you doing out there?" when I didn't.

I'm thrown by Alex's proposal so I say, "Dennis offered to clarify everything for me once we get back home." That's a lie. I'm sure Dennis would happily explain what went down but I decide to remain in the dark. There's something refreshing about not knowing, like a kid free to live in a world of his illusions. That, and the thought of listening to an English version of the never-ending monologue, is mind-numbing. Hockey's not complicated. When the team wins, everyone is happy. When it loses, everyone is miserable. It's a simple concept that holds true all over the world—this simplicity defines the game, a simplicity the real world doesn't afford.

With one week remaining before the season resumes, I decide to devise a daily routine that involves more than playing video games and watching dubbed versions of *Queer Eye for the Straight Guy*. But I'm on my own, because I don't know my teammates well enough to invite them to hang out, and Stroeks is busy peddling printers at the electronic store. So I explore the city alone.

The walk into town is short and involves one turn, which is fortunate since my sense of direction is pitiful. I walk down one of the streets I vaguely remember Markus and Dennis showing me and come across a Thai restaurant called Thai Restaurant. I walk in, and a little girl about six or seven greets me and shows me to a table in the back. There's only one other couple in the restaurant, a teenage girl and a boy she looks to be tutoring. The menu is in German but there are photos of select entrees on the back, so when the server comes by to take my order, I point to the safest looking one and hope for the best. Two minutes later, my miniature waitress returns with a spicy beef stew and veggies. After some cautious exploration with my fork, I take a nibble, and to my relief, it's delicious and hearty, whatever it is.

By the end of that week, I'm a regular at Thai Restaurant, ordering "the usual" from one of the most competent waitresses I've ever dealt with, six-year-old Lin. I'm not sure whether it's the tasty food or the fact that Lin reminds me of my little sister that keeps me coming back.

Finally, practice.

In the beginning

Suiting up before bed

Lasker Rink

Mrs. Rhodie and me—St. Bernard's
Santa Lucia assembly

Gravey had been hounding me for a pic so I gave in.

1996 New Jersey Rockets—Dilly, top row, second from left

Connecticut Yankees—two-time
Stanley Cup champ pictured

New York Bobcats—wrong league to
be carrying puck with head down

Me and Matt Gilroy—junior hockey awards function

New York Apple Core—working on my crossovers mid-game

Harvard's class of 2009 on the ice (Photo courtesy of David Silverman)

Harvard's class of 2009 off the ice (Photo courtesy of Steve Rolecek)

Belgium—this sums up my time in Turnhout

EHC Neuwied fans (Photo courtesy of Reimund Schuster)

In Germany pretending to look at my winger, knowing a camera guy is poised with his Nikon (Photo courtesy of Reimund Schuster)

Iceland (Photo courtesy of Andrew Flynn)

Dean Moore (Photo courtesy of
Vimmerbytidning.se)

Röös post-game (Photo courtesy of
Stefan Igelström)

My hamstring and back are in good shape, and I'm optimistic. I see myself starting on the third line, then, after a week of solid play, moving up to the second line, then a week later, anchoring the first, averaging a couple points a game. I see myself leading the charge to the top of the division, a turnaround that'll catch the eye of some European NHL scout and he'll offer me a minor league contract. I see grinding it out in the Coast, then making the jump to the American League when a forward goes down with an injury. Then I see myself being called up to the Show. I see myself being a hero.

Or, I see myself making it through the next couple of months without a major injury.

Finally, game day.

For some players when they wake, everything is done with an eye on the game: the meals they eat, the clothes they wear, the body parts they shave. Sitting at the dining room table munching on my cereal, I consider if it's worth developing any game day habits that have the potential to take over my life. After dumping my dishes in the sink, I hear someone clamber down the stairs. Darting to the living room, I see a girl rush out the front door leaving behind only the strong stench of Abercrombie & Fitch perfume. Moments later, Stroeks slowly descends the stairs in his boxers, rubbing his right eye and inserting a snus into his mouth with his other hand.

"Who was that?" I push the curtain to the side trying to catch a glimpse of her through the window as she bikes away.

"Girl from shoe store. She always come by day of games. Good at blowjobbing." He taps me on the back while passing by me and brews himself a cup of coffee. "I can't play, but do what I can to help the team. We haven't lost a home game since she started coming over."

"That's commitment."

"Took me so fucking long time to get her. You see how many shoes I got?"

"I was wondering what the deal was."

"Almost go bankrupt buying damn Converses there, but was the only way to get to know her."

"I know the routine."

Stroeks smiles, sips his coffee, then swings a chair around and sits in it A.C. Slater-style. "Oh yah?"

"There was this one cute girl at Harvard, and—"

"Cute girls at Harvard?"

"I said one."

"Blonde?"

"Brunette—sleek, sexy brunette. She played on the soccer team. I probably spent more time studying her Facebook page than I spent studying for any class. So me and my roommates finagled our way into her sociology section. We drove a car to class since we knew she had soccer practice right after. A month into the class, we finally got the balls to ask if she wanted a ride to the soccer field. So we all piled into the car and made the fifteen minute drive to the sports facility, where the rink and fields were. Probably the only drive to the rink in college when the car didn't smell like ass. We bought air fresheners just for her."

"That's not so crazy. That's same like me spending time in shoe store."

"Just listen. The rink was right next to the soccer field. So we'd drop her off—the four of us waving goodbye to her, then drive behind the rink to make sure she'd disappeared into the soccer building. Then it was a thirty-minute drive back to our dorm to kill the remaining three hours before our own practice. Did that all semester."

"You were like her taxi driver." Stroeks grins as he gets up and walks to the bathroom. "But, buddy," he yells from behind the bathroom door after a series of grunts and a loud splash. "At least taxi drivers get paid." He was right except for one thing: I wasn't even the one driving.

Dennis flushes the toilet and swings the door open. "So you get with her?"

"Playing the long game. I think she's in law school now so I'll probably be driving our kids to soccer practice too."

* * *

I haven't played a real game since the hamstring fiasco but I'm not nervous and I can't figure out why. So in typical Bill fashion, I become nervous that I'm not nervous. Can you imagine? I have to live with this person every day.

"Feel good?" Markus asks me on the short drive to the rink.

"Excited for my first shift."

"Super. I have made bet with one of our fans. I say you have two points tonight and he say you have zero." Markus adjusts the rearview mirror making eye contact with me in the back seat.

"Okay." I hope he got good odds.

"So you must score tonight," Markus continues. Dennis, sitting shotgun, turns towards me smiling and rubbing the tips of his thumb and first two fingers. "Pays to win," he whispers.

"If you get some points," Markus says, "the fans will like you right away. That I promise. Even if you get no points, you play hard and you will get them on your side."

I look out the window and a car speeds by with a large Neuwied hockey flag waving outside of the window. And now, I'm nervous. I don't want to let the fans down. I want to help Markus win his bet. But mostly, I don't want to fuck up.

"All about fans here. If we win, we sell tickets, make more money, get more sponsors. Everyone needs to play for the logo on the front, not the name on the back. If we do that and cut out all the selfish play from the first half of the season, then we have success. We have good tradition here; we make sure our supporters never leave a home game disappointed," Markus says as we pull into the rink parking lot.

"Or sober," says Dennis, turning to me again as I unlatch my seatbelt. "Have some fun."

Although each player has different preferences when it comes to pregame routines, I like to arrive at the rink a solid two hours before games to do important shit like look at my sticks on the rack, flex them for ten minutes, flex other guys' sticks, tape my wrists, untape them 'cause it hurts and I'm losing circulation in my hands, tape my sticks, beak a guy on how he tapes his sticks, question my taping method and decide to tape it like the guy I just beaked, clean my visor, then flex my sticks again. Once I'm done wasting an hour, I place my skates on the rack to be sharpened, then switch on my iPod. I feel a tap on my shoulder: It's Oleg Tokarev, a Russian centerman who reminds me of what many of the 1980 Soviet Union Olympic hockey players must have been like—not overly tall or burly but an intimidating figure and he knows it. His nostrils seem permanently flared and he's also strong like bull. At our first practice, he nicknamed me "American Airlines," and even after a few weeks, I can't figure out whether that's a compliment or an insult or he just doesn't know my name. To show some vertebrae, I call him Mother Russia since I'm not creative enough to come up with any other references to his home country.

"You get me puck on power play, American Airlines," Oleg instructs, sounding more like a coach than a player.

"You got it, Mother Russia. I'll be back door so don't be afraid to pass it down to me either." He nods his head while waxing his stick blade and I put my earbuds back in as I go over the game plan which Alex left in each guy's stall. Like all game plans, it's scanned by each player for comic relief then wadded up and fired into the trash.

Taping my shin pads, I hear Willi call my name. He holds up a large roll of plastic tape plastered with a VISAM logo all over it. (VISAM is Germany's version of Home Depot.) "Gotta use this tape," he says handing it to me. "Sponsors."

As the team gathers in the hallway leading to the rink, I hear fans chanting in German. When the lights in the arena are dimmed in preparation for our entrance, I realize I don't have any clue what the pregame protocol is. As a matter of fact, I don't know that the power didn't just go out. I peer out through the hallway and notice a sea of orange sparklers light up in the rafters as the chanting grows louder.

The best pregame introduction I ever saw was at a Trenton Titans ECHL game when I was eleven. The Devils had just acquired a French-Canadian winger with the royal sounding name, Pierre-Marc Grand-Bouchard St. Germain-DeLaCroix. Hyphen Man was supposed to be a sniper, but nobody could confirm that, as he had yet to make his debut for the team, and the Internet wasn't a big deal yet. After being introduced on the loudspeaker, Hyphen Man, gripping a wood stick whose straight blade was wrapped in duct tape, skated with his ankles bent in at a 45-degree angle. When he went to stop, he dragged the toe of his right skate blade behind him.[26] The crowd was silent, fearing that their sniper was a stiff. Turns out the French-Canadian was a great actor—he scored two goals that night and set up another on a nifty backhand saucer pass.

I'm number 85, and I have nineteen opportunities to check out the protocol. There isn't much in the way of hotdogging, so I decide to save the theatrics for someone who can pull them off. Moments before I'm introduced to the crowd, I feel a whack on my ass. It's our equipment manager whose wry smile tells me he's debating on whether to tell me that I still have my skate guards on. Thankfully, he saves me.

As the player in front of me takes three quick steps on the rubber mat before launching himself onto the ice, I hear the chanting reverberate from the rink's ceiling. Maybe it's the much anticipated debut of the American forward that has the fans in a frenzy. Or maybe hockey games don't have much competition on Tuesday nights in Neuwied.

I skate onto the ice surface as the guy maneuvering the spotlight struggles to find me. The crowd maintains its cheering before erupting into a chorus of boos. Usually this reaction is saved for the arrival of the referees or the opposing team.

"What was with the booing after I skated out?" I ask Willi when we get to the bench and the arena lights illuminate the surface. He squirts some water down his back then in his mouth.

"They don't like American imports. Bad experiences with them in past." Willi hands me the water bottle and I squirt some in my face.

"Hope I can change their minds," I say cleaning off my visor as it starts to fog up.

"Just fucking with you. They boo because announcer say no booze will be sold after end of second period. Had some problems last year."

Our opponent, ESC Darmstadt, has all black uniforms with bright yellow numbers, and it's clear a group of their fans has made the trip to Neuwied, as the far right side of the stands looks like a large bumblebee. I'm starting the game on the second line, playing right wing. My centerman, Daniel Walther, or Tönner as everyone calls him, is a

---

26 This is the equivalent of a baseball reliever limping in from the bullpen, putting his mitt on his head and hurling warm up pitches into row Q.

Neuwied veteran and at age thirty-five is probably the team's most fit player. On the left wing is Willi who is tall and lanky but deceptively strong, with great ice vision.

After my first few shifts, I'm distracted by the unrelenting chanting of the standing crowd. Oversized Neuwied flags are unfurled and wave back and forth and the shirtless conductor whose chest is painted blue and white leads the raucous symphony with flailing arms. Standing beside him is a large man wearing a Neuwied jersey and banging on the drum that hangs around his neck. Whether it's the supply of booze or a strong passion for Neuwied hockey (most likely a combination), I can't help but wonder, are we players that entertaining or would this group be chanting regardless of what activity is taking place? As I hop over the boards for my next shift, my mind remains on the bench, and as the puck rims around the corner and onto the stick of my blade . . . *BOOM*, my head hits the ice and my stick boomerangs into the corner as a Darmstadt defender levels me. I stagger up, grab my stick, and head to the bench for a line change. I hear Tönner and Willi yelling on the bench in German. Are they pissed at me? Are they angry with themselves? Are they blowing off steam? Should I just start yelling at myself?

Two hours later, we celebrate a satisfying 4–2 victory. Markus wins his bet as I finish with two points assisting on a goal by Tönner and another by Mother Russia.

In his postgame speech, Alex is brief and, I can tell from his smile, pleased. A few minutes later, he pulls me aside. "I told the team, good work tonight. We played good but need to work on a lot of areas of the game if we want to compete with the good teams in the league." I appreciate Alex's self-translation but it's tough not understanding what he says when he addresses the team. I consider investing in *Rosetta Stone, German—Level 1.*

As I undress, Tönner comes over and smacks my shoulder pads before taking a swig of his Fanta Exotic. Willi pops open a Hefferveisen and offers me one, which I decline, as I don't like to drink (a) immediately after a game, or (b) when I'm naked from the waist down surrounded by twenty-two guys. Always the first to arrive and last to leave, Willi sits in his stall, still in his gear. It might have something to do with avoiding his girlfriend. Before I can ask him about her, a local reporter approaches and gives me an opportunity to talk about how great I am for five minutes.

Dennis waltzes into the locker room with a beer, toasting a few of the players, and sits next to me.

"Looked good out there. What you think?"

"Happy we won, but I got to admit, I've never been on a team where more guys are drinking beer after a win than are drinking recovery shakes."

Dennis takes a gulp from his bottle then wipes his mouth with his sleeve. "Remember what Markus said before the game?" I nod unsure of exactly what he's talking about. "Guys need to play for the logo on the front, not the name on the back." He lifts his beer, showing me the *Krombacher* label. "Recognize this?" He points at the game jersey hanging in my stall. The same *Krombacher* logo is displayed across the front. "Just like Markus says. We have success when we play for the logo on the front."

All the players gather in the rink cafeteria postgame with their families. In the bathroom after pouring out the third glass of absinthe Stroeks handed me, I notice a familiar logo on the splash guard of the urinal. It's the same logo that appears on the right sleeve of our jerseys, for a local water park.

After finishing his fourth "last beer," Dennis decides it's time to head home. Sitting down in the car, I feel something in my back pocket. I reach in and remove a wad of euros. Attached is a note: "Super game. Your cut from the bet! Markus."

"I told you. Pays to win here." Dennis reaches into his own pocket as I hold one of the twenty euro bills taut and raise it to the illuminated overhead light.

"Got another something for you. Anna and Sabrina, the cupcake girls, ask me to give you this." I open the sealed envelope and unfold a letter which reads: "Dear American Bill, We are so happy you play in Neuwied now! Me and Sabrina hope you enjoyed the treats. We would love to come to your house one day. We could watch some TV or have sex if you want! ;) Sorry, my englisch is not so good, but I hope you understand. We could have relationship, like sex :) Please return letter to address on front!"

"Take a look at this." I hand the letter to Dennis. He props it above the steering wheel and begins slowly reading out loud. The car comes to a stop at a red light. Dennis digs out the snus that's tucked under his top lip, tosses it out the window then replaces it with a fresh one.

"So which box you going to check?" he asks pointing at the bottom of the letter where two small boxes are, with "*Ja*" written above one and "*Nein*" above the other.

"What's their story? You met them on the online message board, right?"

"This is true. And Anna . . . she's Alex, the coach's daughter." A figure appears outside of the car, knocking on Dennis's window. Dennis and the stranger engage in conversation for a minute as the man occasionally glances at me and smiles. We miss two green lights, but with no cars behind us, it's not an issue. Finally, the man taps the car on the roof, before bending down to look at me. "Good luck," he says then disappears down the street.

"Neuwied fan?" I ask.

"Yes." Dennis put the car back in drive. "He's your number one fan. Wants to blowjob you. Said everyone was talking about you after the game."

"Really?"

We pull up to the house. "No. He saw the advertisement on the car and wants to buy a printer from me. But you did do good today."

It's been a while since I've called home with good news about me and hockey. Mom has grown accustomed to the whining and is a good sport about it.

"Hello?" Mom says.

"Mom, it's me . . . listen, everything will be fine . . . it happened again."

"Bill! Don't tell me that? What happened? Are you okay?"

"It's my shoulder . . . My flight leaves tomorrow—"

I can feel Mom's hand shaking.

"Kidding! We won tonight. I had two assists, and I'm in one piece."

"You're awful. Don't you do that to me!"

"I got you going though, huh?"

"You know what—the Internet is broken again, and I—"

"I'm four thousand miles away. No way I could've screwed it up this time." I can hear her necklace jingling as she shakes her head, convinced I'm the culprit.

"You can redeem yourself by helping me decipher your sister's text messages—what's it mean when she writes "IDK?"

"I don't know."

"You're useless! Hold on, Dad wants to talk to you. He just got home."

"I saw the AOL article about you joining the team. Congrats!" What he means is that he signed into the AOL account I made for him eleven years ago, typed my name in the URL bar, got an error message that sent him to the search bar, then retyped my name and encountered a small blurb in German from the league website with the press release about me joining the team for the remainder of the season.

"Thanks, Dad."

The next afternoon, I head to Thai Restaurant. The dining room is empty—no customers, no Lin, no Lin's mother—but the kitchen is loud, a cacophony of pots, pans, and screaming. I take a table and see Lin poke her head out of the kitchen, then scurry out of sight, only to return moments later, wearing a huge smile. She places a copy of the *Blick Aktuell* on my table, opened up to an article about last night's game, which features a picture of you know who.

Even though I can't understand it, I know it must be something positive judging by the picture and the fact we won the game. I just don't understand why Dickie von Dunn chose a picture that looks like it was taken with a Game Boy Color. Lin hovers over me, awaiting my reaction. I smile, flash a thumbs-up, then put my hand out, palm up, and receive a low five, in which she puts every ounce of her strength, going airborne on her downward thrust. The publication's circulation may not be more than a few miles around our rink, but at least the

Blick aktuell - Neuwied Nr. 06/2010

Bill Keenan verwandelt nervenstark

Neuwieder Bären feiern zwei weitere Erfolge in der Pokalrunde - Daniel Walther und Andreas Halfmann verlängern

Treffsicher und nervenstark: Als es am Wochenende in den EHC-Spielen eng wurde, schlug der Amerikaner Bill Keenan zu. Foto: DEL

Neuwied. In der Eishockey-Regionalliga-Pokalrunde bleiben die Bären mit vier Siegen aus vier Spielen auf Kurs. Der erste Platz dürfte zwischen dem EHC Neuwied und dem verlustpunktfreien EHC Troisdorf ausgespielt werden. Einem spektakulären 9:5 (3:0, 4:4, 2:1)-Erfolg gegen den Herforder EV ließen die Deichstädter in Darmstadt ein 4:3 (2:2, 0:1, 1:0) nach Penaltyschießen folgen. Beim Tabellenletzten Darmstadt kamen die Bären mit einem blauen Auge davon. Nach einem schnellen Rückstand brachten Stephan Petry und Daniel Walther die Gäste in Führung. Kurz vor der ersten Pause überraschten die Hessen mit dem 2:2-Ausgleich und gingen nach 30 Minuten 3:2 in Führung. Den Deichstädtern gelang es nicht, ihr Potenzial abzurufen. Die Zeit eilte Neuwied davon. Erst drei Minuten vor dem Ende erlöste Willy Hamann den Favoriten mit dem Ausgleich. Im Penaltyschießen bissen sich sämtliche Schützen an den gegnerischen Torhütern die Zähne aus: Mit Ausnahme von Bill Keenan, dessen verwandelter Penalty den Zusatzpunkt für den EHC bedeutete. Gegen Herford verzettelten sich die Neuwieder nach einer 5:1-Führung in viele Scharmützel mit zahlreichen Strafzeiten. Die Gäste kamen so auf 5:4 heran, sodass sich EHC-Trainer Markus Fischer zu einer Auszeit gezwungen sah, um das EHC-Schiff wieder an Kurs zu bringen. Diese Maßnahme hatte in der 36. Minute Erfolg, als Andreas Halfmann einen Schlagschuss von der blauen Linie ansetzte und Willi Hamann den Abpraller zum 6:4 einnetzte. Nur 60 Sekunden später bereitete Tim Grundl durch ein überlegtes Zuspiel sehenswert vor und Marco Herbel traf zum 7:4. Mit diesem Spielstand ging es dann auch Richtung Kabine zur zweiten Pause. Doch bevor die Mannschaften das Eis verließen, gerieten zunächst Lucas Klein und Stephan Petry aneinander. Christian Czaika wollte in dieser Situation zunächst schlichten, erhielt aber von Klein eine Kopfnuss. Es kam zu einer kurzen Schlägerei, mit dem Ergebnis: zwei Minuten Strafe für Petry, fünf plus Spieldauer für Czaika und eine Matchstrafe für die Gäste. Die Gemüter hatten sich in der Pause dann auch wieder etwas beruhigt, doch Neuwied musste nun zu Beginn des letzten Abschnitts eine 3:5-Unterzahl

überstehen, was auch gelang. Kaum wieder komplett zeigte Neuwieds Neuzugang Bill Keenan seine technischen Fertigkeiten. Zunächst spielte er einen Verteidiger aus und ließ dann Goalie Frenzel keine Chance. Den Schlusspunkt in dieser torreichen Begegnung setzte dann allerdings erneut Keenan mit seinem zweiten Treffer an diesem Abend in der 47. Minute zum 9:5-Endstand. Ein hart umkämpftes, aber auch unterhaltsames Eishockeyspiel war beendet. Trainer Fischer: „Die Mannschaft hat nach der Schwächephase im zweiten Drittel Charakter gezeigt und sich ins Spiel zurückgekämpft." Tore: Hamann (drei), Keenan (zwei), Walther, Petry, Herbel, Czaika.

Am Rande der Bande

Die ersten Verträge für die kommende Saison sind festgezurrt. Dabei wurde von Seiten des Vereins eine Vertragsoption bei Daniel Walther gezogen, mit der er auch im nächsten Jahr weiterhin das Trikot der Bären tragen wird. Ebenfalls verlängert wurde der Vertrag von Andreas Halfmann, bei dem die Option einer Vertragsauflösung nicht eingelöst wurde. In den nächsten Tagen und Wochen wird es in den Reihen des EHC Neuwied weitere Gespräche mit den Spielern geben, die auch für die neue Saison gehalten werden sollen.

Ausblick

Am Karnevalswochenende müssen die Bären nur einmal ran. Auf Antrag vom ESV Bergisch Gladbach wird die geplante Begegnung am Samstag in Bergisch Gladbach auf den 27. März verschoben. Damit bestreiten die Bären ihr letztes Saisonspiel, wie so oft in den letzten Jahren, erneut bei den Realstars. Die Bären bestreiten am Freitag um 21 Uhr das Rückspiel in Herford.   · DEL ·

TuS Rodenbach

Damen I belegen 2. Platz beim Mons-Tabor Cup 201

TuS Rodenbach II Damen scheitern in der Vorru

Neuwied. Trotz Schneechaos machte sich der TuS Rodenbach mit zwei Mannschaften auf zum Mons-Tabor-Cup 2010, der von den Damen des 1. FFC Montabaur ausgerichtet wurde.

Der Schnee war auch der Grund, wieso der komplette Spielplan fast minütlich über den Haufen geworfen werden musste, wollte man doch einen regen Spielfluss für alle Mannschaften garantieren. Das erste Spiel für die TuS Rodenbach I Damen verlief sehr erfolgreich. Gegner in der 1x15 Minuten Spielzeit waren die Damen des VfR Niederfell. Nach 15 Minuten hieß es 8:0 für die Rodenbacherinnen. Erfolgreiche Torschützinnen waren Daniela Müller (3), Nicole Karls (2), Sandra Czornitzek, Kerstin Funk und Melanie Herpich. Im zweiten Gruppenspiel traf man dann auf den Gastgeber 1. FFC Montabaur II. In einer spannenden Partie hieß der Gewinner mit 3:1 TuS Rodenbach. Die Treffer erzielten dabei Daniela Müller (2) und Sandra Czornitzek. Im dritten Gruppenspiel wiederholte man das Ergebnis des Turnierstarts mit einem 8:0 Erfolg über die Damen des TV Kruft II. Die Tore in diesem Spiel erzielten Nicole Karls (3), Melanie Herpich (3), Kerstin Funk und Laura Hansen. Das darauf folgende Gruppenspiel gegen die SG 99 Andernach wurde nach Ablauf der 15 Spielminuten mit 1:1 beendet. Den einzigen Treffer dieser Partie erzielte Nicole Karls. Im letzten Gruppenspiel traf man dann auf die Damen der Fortuna Freudenberg. In einer sehr schwachen Partie hieß es nach 15. Minuten wieder 1:1. Den Treffer in dieser Partie erzielte Laura Hansen. Das erste Gruppenspiel der TuS Rodenbach II Damen war ein kleines Nervenspiel. Ging man doch innerhalb der 15. Spielminuten mehrfach in Rückstand, ehe es nach Ablauf der Spielzeit dann 3:3 hieß. Alle drei Treffer erzielte Sarah

Roth. Im zweiten Spiel traf die Damen des TV Kruft I es nach 15. Minuten 3:1 fü bacher Seite erzielte Yvon artz. Im dritten Gruppen: man auf den Titelvertei Kirn-Sulzbach. Hier muss sich unglücklich nach 15. mit 2:3 geschlagen geb Siegtreffer für die Damen Kirn-Sulzbach fiel kurz vor Spielzeit. Die Treffer erzie Rodenbach Sarah Roth un fer Heyden. Im letzten Grup sel gelang dann endlich de Sieg im Turnierverlauf für Rodenbach II Damen. N Spielminuten trennte man einem 4:1 Sieg. Die Treffer dabei Sarah Roth (2), Yvon artz und Denise Herpich. Im Halbfinale trafen die Dar TuS Rodenbach I auf die des SV Kirn-Sulzbach. N Spielminuten hieß es 5:1 für men aus Kirn-Sulzbach. Torschützinnen waren Dani ler (2), Melanie Herpich, Lau sen und Sandra Czornitzek. Im Finale traf man dann zu ten mal an diesem Tag auf men der Fortuna Freudenl der gesamten Spielzeit wo ein Treffer fallen und der v Damen der Fortuna Freu vorbehalten. Eine Unacht nutzen diese eiskalt zum 1 stand. Auf der Gegenseite die Damen aus Rodenbac Chancen, jedoch wollte einf weiterer Treffer gelingen. **Es spielten für TuS Roden** Angela Stoffels, Laura Han lanie Herpich, Sandra Czc Daniela Müller, Kerstin Funk Karls. **Es spielten für TuS** **bach II:** Sandra Härtel, Fr Schneider, Denise Herpich, Hauptmann, Melanie Blischk nifer Heyden, Sarah Roth.

(Reprinted with the permission of Marco Lindner)

hockey section comes before the big local figure skating feature. I rip out the page and pocket the article.

On my way out of the restaurant, I notice brochures for a massage parlor. As I pick one up, Lin's mom appears out of the kitchen.

"Good game! I read in paper," she says in her unique Thai-German accent. Seeing the brochure in my hand, she adds, "My sister. Best massage in all of Germany. Very relax."

"Thanks. I do have a little back pain, so I think I will go see her," I say, enunciating each word as clearly as possible.

"Yes. You must. Best massage in Germany!" I bid goodbye, but before I'm a block away, Lin's mom runs down the street, hands flailing. "You forgot money! You forgot money!"

"That's the tip!"

She halts in front of me and with a motherly huff, shoves the money in my pocket. "Oh no, don't leave money. If you want to tip, wait when my sister give you massage. It has special ending."

"What do you mean?"

"Gentleman's facial. You deserve it!"

* * *

Over the next month and a half, we rack up a respectable 8–5 record, which puts us in the top three of the league standings. Despite passing on the gentleman's facial, I'm feeling nice and limber with my weekly "best massage in Germany," where Lin's aunt uses my back as a trampoline for a couple hours at a time.

I know things are going well all-around when I'm included in the weekly video game night at our veteran defenseman Tim Grundl's home; his girlfriend, Svenja, and their newborn daughter spend those nights at Svenja's mother's house to avoid being the target of stray video game controllers flung through the air.

Playing in front of the rabid Neuwied fan base is an added bonus. Even after losing 5–1 at home against our biggest rival, Herforder EV on fan appreciation night, the team is greeted with a long line of autograph seeking supporters that wraps around the rink. Not only is it an honor to sit in our gear for three hours after the game, not showered and not fed, but it is also a contractual obligation. I can't help but wonder from time to time if there's anything else to do in this city. And then there's the booze thing: In what must be some sort of German hockey tradition, fans present players with postgame bottles of alcohol.

None of this would be possible without the support of our sponsors, which Markus and the rest of our management work diligently to maintain. Securing good sponsors prior to the season is vital, since they provide a large portion of players' salaries. Professional hockey in Europe is a volatile business especially at the lower levels—it's common for a few teams to fold midseason due to the loss of a sponsor's financial support.

Our jersey is essentially a billboard, covered with the logos of Neuwied's local radio and television stations (98.0 and okneuwied. de), Medicon (the team's exercise facility), as well as many of the city's restaurants and bars. (Thai Restaurant doesn't have a spot on our jersey. I think I need to speak with Lin about that.) You can barely see our team's logo, a growling bear's face.

Another major sponsor of the team is Agostea, the region's biggest nightclub, located in Koblenz, a twenty-minute drive from Neuwied. Most nights after home games, a group of players head to Agostea, where we hang out at our reserved section near the dance floor. One night after a victory against Frankfurt—an evening when Willi's girlfriend loosens the leash and lets him come out for a few hours—Mother Russia, signature dirty martini in hand, ushers me to a table of women who appear ecstatic to speak to an American.

"We love USA," the blonde says. "*Sex and the City* we love. I'm the Samantha and she's the Carrie." Since Samantha was easier of the two, I focus my attention on her. But talking to girls is like trying to play hockey lefty. Before I'm exposed as not being Mr. Big or Aidan but more like one of those guys Miranda dates for one episode, I'm distracted by our goaltender, Hans Neurath.

Since he's a goalie, I'm not shocked by his dancing, which consists of various standing convulsions and violent twists and turns. It's like watching the devolution of dance. I'm not sure whether to call the paramedics or finish my beer and join him. Mother Russia, now with his arms securely around the shoulders of both girls, gives me a nod telling me to get lost so I join Hans on the dance floor. Despite my ballet training, I'm a better skater than dancer, but compared to Hans, I look like Usher.

Returning to the bar, I see Dennis and Willi entertaining a group of four girls, three of which are doable. After a few minutes, the two guys clear some space and stand about ten feet apart, facing each other. Using imaginary ropes, they begin a game of double dutch, swinging their arms in unison as their heads rock slightly back and forth.

"Here we go again," says Hans as he sits next to me and situates himself towards the action.

"What's going on?"

Hans touches his finger to his nose. "Billy, when the boys go fishing for girls here, sometimes they use too much line, and the only thing to do is use it to play the jump rope game."

One by one, each girl in the group takes a turn hopping over the imaginary ropes, as their friends cheer them on. After some coaxing, the fourth girl, visibly heavier than the rest (and I'm sure reallllly nice), emerges from the pack. Her friends clap and urge her on. She hands one girl her purse, then removes her heels and steps into the game.

Seconds later, Willi and Dennis stoop down to retrieve the imaginary ropes now lying on the floor.

* * *

In March, the last month of the season, we have our final matchup against our rival, Herforder EV. Three months ago, I didn't know Herford, Germany, existed and while I still can't locate it on a map, I now hate their team. Nothing beats playing in an intense, inhospitable environment.

To further the drama, Oleg played the previous two seasons in Herford before a falling out with the coach which, knowing Mother Russia, must have been ugly. But wait, there's more—tonight's ref is the same *dummkopf* who gave Stroeks his suspension.

I find a seat somewhere in the middle of the bus and pull out my computer. Today's bus ride video: Game 7 of the 1994 Eastern Conference Final—the New York Rangers vs. the New Jersey Devils.

Even casual hockey fans know about this game, one of the greatest playoff contests in NHL history, a double overtime thriller capped off by Stephane Matteau's wraparound goal that sent the Rangers to the Stanley Cup Final and the New York fans into a frenzy. I was eight at the time, and reenacted that play a thousand times in the living room rink.

As our bus approaches the arena, I see a group of Herford supporters, wearing their team's bright green jerseys, loitering outside, taking turns swigging a bottle of Jägermeister. A cloud of smoke hovers above them and bright orange cigarette tips flicker in the haze. A few yards away stands a man teetering like a single bowling pin about to topple as he pisses, steam rises from the snow.

Powering off my computer, I hear a loud thwack near the back of the bus. I spin around and catch a few of the guys blurting out curses in German (*missgeburt*[27] and *scheisse*[28]) as a second raw egg splatters against the window. Mother Russia, wearing a stocking cap that fits his head like the end of a condom on a dick, glares out the window, muttering to himself in Russian.

When the bus stops, a small boy emerges from the crowd of Herford fans and stomps through the snow towards our bus, stopping just a couple steps from my window. He cups his hands around his eyes and I rub the condensation off my window. As he puts his hands back at his side, we make eye contact. Clad in a big winter jacket with the Herford logo on it and wearing a New York Rangers winter hat, he looks about eight. I wonder if he feels the same way about this game as I did as an eight-year-old watching Game 7 of the '94 conference finals. I raise my left hand and give him a small wave. He remains still then removes the mitten from his right hand, and gives me the finger.

---

27 Loosely translated: Fucker.

28 Tightly translated: Shit.

As we haul our gear from under the bus into the rink, a group of riot police stand nearby, some talking, some laughing, some smoking, and all holding large shields and billy clubs.

No dramatic pregame speeches are necessary. Motivation will not be an issue tonight. I'm still on a line with Tönner and Willi, and although we had little success against Herford in our first game, we're optimistic about creating more offense tonight by being aggressive on the forecheck and firing shots on net from all angles.

Predictably, the first period start is intensely physical, as both teams try to establish themselves. The focus is on playing stingy defense, so there's little offense created at either end of the ice. Every player on Herford finishes his checks on us, making it difficult to create many scoring opportunities, but we're taking the same approach. The first period comes to an end with the score knotted at zero.

A group of Herford supporters descends from the stands, some chanting and some threatening us with fists raised. "Someone needs to get the cowbell out of that beast's hands," I say to Willi as we wait for the armed guards to clear a path to our locker room for us.

"Or put it around her neck where it belongs," he replies.

During the intermission, Hans does his gummy bear routine as Alex drops some knowledge, and before you know it, we're back on the ice. Five minutes into the second period, a Herford defender high-sticks me in the face, drawing blood. His intention was probably to lift my stick and take the puck, but that makes no difference to the refs who assess him a four minute double minor. Blood drips in my eye as I leave a trail of dark red splotches on the ice on my skate to the bench. I catch a glimpse of his number, 42.

On the bench, Mother Russia nudges me. "Zis number 42, you must go after him next time."

"Yeah," I say grimacing, as our equipment manager rubs something on the cut then sprays it with some other crap.

"I hate zis guy. Played with him last year, and he is real fuck."

Tönner, Willi, and I jump out on the ice for the final seconds of 42's penalty. The Herford penalty-killing unit, unable to clear their zone in the last two minutes, shows signs of fatigue, hunching over their sticks and no longer applying much pressure. Tönner skates the puck to the point before dishing it off to Willi on the half wall. Willi then darts behind the net before throwing a slick behind the back pass to me, forcing the goalie to sprawl to the near post. With a Herford defender desperately diving back into my shooting lane, I slide the puck across the crease to a wide open Tönner, who has sneaked down to the back door. Tönner sweeps the puck across the goal line, then drops to one knee and pumps his fist so hard he nearly dislocates his shoulder.

The celebration sends our bench into a frenzy and Tönner receives a flurry of face washes. I time my return to the bench so I pass by 42, who is in the midst of the longest skate known to a hockey player: The trek from the penalty box back to his bench after his team gives up a power play goal.

We take a one-zip lead after the second period. In the locker room, I walk to the bathroom and splash some water on my face, as Hans begins sorting the gummy bears. Before returning to the ice, Tönner addresses the team with some short but rousing words in German. The message is clear: Let's fuckin' finish this game.

My line starts the third stanza, and as I glide out to my spot on the right wing, I see 42 lining up at left defense. A drop of sweat from my forehead drips into the cut over my eye, and it stings like a bitch. The last thing I want to do is take a selfish penalty and give Herford an opportunity to tie the game, so I must be smart about how I retaliate. After we gain control of the puck off the faceoff, our defenseman dumps it into 42's corner. Pivoting backwards to retrieve the puck, 42 races to the nearside corner, clearly concerned about Tönner, who's coming at him like a pissed off bull. I build up some speed and, coming from the opposite side of the ice, skate towards the far post of the net. Just as Tönner forces 42 around the net and up the ice, I take two final, hard strides and, with my shoulder lowered and core braced for impact, I dismantle him. Now considering the last time I knocked an opponent down and inflicted some real damage was when I was eleven and playing mini sticks with my little sister who had just learned to walk, I may have a skewed perspective of what it means to "dismantle" someone. Anyway, the force of the collision leads me to fall as well. We both scramble to our skates, and I know we're not through. The referees break us up and attempt to escort us to our respective penalty boxes. Refs can keep players from physically assaulting one another, but they have no say over the verbal stuff.

"How many goals you score at Harvard? Fuckin' useless American!" There's no time to walk him through my Harvard sob story. But I'll take it as a compliment that he took the time to research me.

As the PA guy, who sits in between the two penalty boxes, announces the penalties, I hear a roar from the crowd. After four minutes to regain my composure and spit blood all over the place, I'm released from the sin bin and on my skate back to the bench, I hear my name again, this time louder and not on the arena's loudspeaker. When I sit down on the bench and squirt a few shots of water in my mouth, I realize it's the crowd chanting my last name in unison. Has my spirited play won over the support of the Herford fans? The chant catches on and within seconds, nearly all the Herford fans are screaming it. I hear my last name, but I can't make out the rest of it. I tap Mother Russia, who's sitting next to me.

"What're they saying?" I say. Oleg pauses, taking in a few more repetitions before responding.

If you recall, the crowd was chanting, "*Keenan du arschloch.*"

If you recall, that translates to, "Keenan is an asshole."

And if you recall, we won.

CHAPTER EIGHT

Cold War Truce

EVERYBODY IN THE organization is in a great mood because we've been winning. After back-to-back victories this week, we remain in the top three of the league standings. Unfortunately, the most recent win is a pyrrhic victory since we lose Willi to a shoulder injury that will end his season. I'm not sure if Willi is more devastated his season is over, or that he'll be forced to spend more time with his girlfriend.

In light of Willi's injury, it's time to make some obligatory comments about violence in hockey. Hockey is dangerous and sometimes, downright scary. Large men play the game and some of them are fucked three sheets to the wind in the head. What separates hockey from most other team sports are the lengths to which teammates will defend one another. Physical, borderline violent play presents opportunities for players to stand up for teammates and ultimately create that bond that exists between them. What makes that goal you scored in the third to give your team the lead, a goal you'll never forget, is that you almost got dummied digging for the puck in the corner. If you walk into a locker room with guys who have played at any sort of high level, you'll see knee braces, lower back wraps, shoulder harnesses, and other remnants of past injuries. My bet is that those whose bodies are taped together are the guys who love the game the most.

Everyone is surprisingly loose in the locker room before our game against Essen. Although we've yet to beat them this season, we've been playing well, and, with the exception of Willi, the team is healthy. In his pregame speech, Alex reminds us to capitalize on our power play opportunities; Essen is a strong, offensive-minded team, but they have some holes in their penalty killing units. After Alex wraps it up, Tönner and Mother Russia call us together and go over our power play strategy one last time. I've never seen Oleg this intense, and that's saying something, as he practices intensely, drinks intensely, and pees intensely.[29] "Look here," he snarls, slashing his marker across the dry erase board. "If puck is here, give it to me at top, zen I pass here, zen shot. If puck goes here, pass to him, zen up to me, zen I find you on back door for shot." This carries on for a few minutes, and my mind drifts because I know that all the plays involve Mother Russia either shooting or being one of the last two players to pass the puck before a shot is taken ensuring that as long as we use one of his ideas, he'll end up with a point if a goal is scored; self-interest in the guise of team play—we've all been there.

Yes, Oleg is the point man on our power play, and the plays he draws up usually work, but some games, he's completely disengaged and a liability on defense. Signing him is like investing in an unsecured, synthetic, high-yield fixed-income instrument: high risk, high reward, and nearly impossible to understand. I wonder if I should start calling him Junk Bond instead of Mother Russia, but I realize it'll be lost on everybody and even if someone does understand, he'll think I'm a complete douche.

Marc Blumenhofen is taking Willi's spot on our line tonight, and I'm looking forward to playing with him. He's a quiet guy in his late twenties who doesn't have a high skill level, but he plays hard every night, which more than makes up for any dearth of talent. As we begin

---

29 Don't ask.

the meticulous process of taping our game sticks, I say, "Bloomy, how you feeling today?"

"Good. Excited to play with you and Tönner."

"Me too. Our power play'll be important tonight. These guys aren't big on blocking shots so we should generate some chances."

"Oleg's got some good plays. We can move the puck to him at the top then crash the net."

"Bloomy, you notice how all the plays go through Oleg at the point so he knows he'll get a point if we score?" He makes one final wrap around the blade of his stick and rips the black tape.

"Oleg likes the puck on his stick. I wouldn't make a big deal about this to him. You ever look at his career statistics?"

"Nope," I respond even though I've tried but still don't know how to spell his last name.

"Go on the Internet and check it out some time. Two years he doesn't have any stats, didn't play hockey." Bloomy places his newly taped stick on the rack and leaves me to myself. I guess Mother Russia and I have something in common: an extended time away from hockey. I'll have to find out—maybe we can even talk about it. Maybe we can even be friends, and go out for drinks, and pick up Russian beauties, and . . . nah, that'll never happen. I later lift the Iron Curtain on this mystery and find out Oleg spent two years in Kazakhstani prison on a drug-related charge.

Essen has come to play. By the middle of the second period, we're trailing 3–0 and all our power play planning was for naught. Our guys (me included) are taking penalty after penalty, leading to two first period power play goals. Compounding the problem, Hans isn't as sharp in net as he usually is and I'm wondering if the local candy store was out of gummy bears.

After the second period, Alex storms into the locker room and for the first time since I've been on the team, he goes into a tirade that involves water bottles ricocheting off the locker room walls, sticks javelining through the air, and large gobs of spit shooting from his mouth. In my junior and college days, I trained myself to switch on the mute button to avoid listening to these irrational diatribes, but because

Alex exhibits this type of behavior so infrequently, I try tuning in even though it's all in German and my *Rosetta Stone, German—Level 1* is still wrapped in cellophane. When he stomps out of the locker room and slams the door shut, the room is silent. Staging a comeback trailing 3–0 with one period remaining against the first place team in the league is improbable, but we've got twenty minutes to get our heads out of our asses.

Essen has a defense pair, numbers 27 and 72 who are twin brothers, both stocky and probably the two ugliest players in all of hockey. Tweedle Dick and Tweedle Douche are hard-nosed players but not particularly nimble on their skates, something I hope to expose.

Three minutes into the final period, I receive a perfect stretch pass from one of our defensemen, sending me on a breakaway. As I dart through Dick and Douche and break in alone against the goalie, I feel a tug on my right foot. I lose my balance and crash head first into the Essen netminder. Stroeks has also been making me watch a lot of Italian Serie A soccer and I've been taking notes on diving. I'm not sure if it's Dick or Douche who drags me down, so to play it safe, I tell them both to fuck off.

The sudden roar of the crowd tells me that I've been awarded a penalty shot. I skate back to the bench to wipe off my visor and catch my breath and look for Stephan, our backup goalie. Spending as much time as he does on the bench watching the game, Stephan (and I suppose all backup goalies for that matter) is a spy. I've spent enough time sitting and watching hockey to realize that to someone passionate about the sport, there's incredible enjoyment from simply getting lost in the game from the sidelines.

"Any ideas on where to score on this guy?" I ask trying to keep my nerves in check.

"He comes out too far. Throw a quick fake shot, make him bite on it, then go wide forehand or backhand, and you'll beat him five-hole."

My first thought is, *Jesus, this fuckin' guy has a good command of the English language. Maybe I should start hanging out with him more.* My second thought is, *maybe I should go Gunnar Stahl on this one, triple deke, high glove 'cause I like to get fancy.* My third thought is, *that's one of the dumbest ideas I've ever had. I can't believe that entered my mind. Plus, Julie the Cat stoned Gunnar on the triple deke penalty shot in D2.*

Now some players say they don't premeditate their move, they wait for the goalie to make the first move and react. Well, I'm not good enough to do that. I need to think it all out beforehand.

I've done this move a thousand times if not on the ice then in my head, sometimes better than others. This is the type of situation I dream about, but when it becomes reality, I really just want to get it over as quickly as possible and hope that the reality ends the same way as the dream.

The referee blows his whistle, signaling me to skate to the center faceoff circle for some obligatory instructions. As he relays some message to me, I nod, too deep in the zone to understand or even care what he's saying. I take a deep breath, brush the snow off the blade of my stick with my glove, then skate through the center ice dot, picking the puck up with my backhand, and break in with heightened awareness.

As I close in on the goal, I cut left, then right, then left, all the while stickhandling both wide and short in an attempt to make the goalie move laterally. The more side-to-side movement I force him to make, the greater the odds that he'll lose his position in the net, giving me the slightest advantage that could determine the difference between a goal and a save. Once inside the hash marks, I lift my left leg up, drop my right shoulder, and cock my stick. The combination of these three movements causes the goalie to freeze momentarily as he tenses up, expecting me to shoot. This hesitation on his part opens the door for me to sweep the puck all the way to my backhand. In a desperate maneuver, the goalie slides his right leg across, opening up his five-hole and I slip the puck through the large gap between his legs.

The sight of that piece of black rubber crossing that thin red line never gets old. It's a damn good feeling. *Man,* I think, *If I'd done this more often, I wouldn't be writing this book.*

My momentum carries me into the corner. To my right, I spot the ref, arm outstretched, pointing at the puck lying still inside the net. It's almost like he's taunting the goalie. Maybe refs aren't so dumb after all.

I drop to a knee and, making certain to time it perfectly, I perform a world class fist pump that begins at one end of the Essen bench and continues to the far end, careful to dodge any tomahawk swings aimed at my head. It's displays of good sportsmanship like this on which I pride myself. Coaches always tell players to play every game like it's their last, so why shouldn't we be able to celebrate every goal like it's our last? It might be.

Unfortunately, the celebration is ephemeral. We still trail by two goals, and Essen isn't the type of team that folds at the first sign of adversity. We continue to battle, and halfway through the period, our fourth line made up of teenagers is able to do something that the other three lines have yet to do in regulation—score a goal. However, time is always the enemy for the team staging a comeback, and the buzzer beats us. Essen wins, 3–2.

Alex is pleased with how we respond in the third period, but no points are awarded to teams for losses and moral victories don't exist. We probably outshot Essen by a ratio of three to one in the third period and controlled most of the play, but the scoreboard is the final measure of success. Only the top two teams at the end of the season get a chance to qualify for a spot in the league above for next season. It's a positive sign we're able to compete with Essen, but we need every point we can get, and tonight we go home with zero.

After most losses, Markus parks himself outside the locker room and without being too abrasive, seeks answers from players. We're rarely able to come up with anything other than "sorry, we tried but didn't get it done tonight." Not tonight though. Alexander, Markus's ten-year-old son, is visiting and the pair walks hand-in-hand, while Markus has a smile so wide you'd think we just somehow qualified for the German Elite League tonight with our loss.

Now I'm no parent, but the site of Markus and his son reminds me of playing youth hockey. Hockey parents are a unique breed, and by unique, I mean they're nuts. Hockey parents are really just an extension of their kids—not that they live vicariously through them (some may), but that they just want like hell to see their kids succeed. As players we may have to sacrifice our body to make a play, but hockey parents sacrifice their lives to give their kids a chance to follow their dreams. I don't want to get sentimental, but when a hockey player hangs up his skates for good, he's hanging up the skates his parents got him. Even halfway across the world, I know what the scene is at home when I play a game here: Mom, at her desk, using Google Translate to figure out what the hell the game report says, while Dad, sitting in his tighty-whities on the couch, furiously tries to figure out how to power on his new laptop computer (swiping his fingers vigorously across the blank screen that isn't a touch screen) he just bought so he can follow the live stats on this thing called the "Internet."

Wednesday evening, Essen clinches first place after defeating Darmstadt, thereby eliminating us from the playoffs. Even though our final game is meaningless in terms of league standings, the game is at home, and we've got the best fans in the league so we owe them an exciting game.

Although Willi's injury ended his season, it doesn't stop him from being the first guy in the locker room on game days, and here on the last day, as is the case every other day, he's gripping a beer lovingly, as if it were the Stanley Cup. He approaches my stall. "You played in Turnhout earlier this year, right?"

"For a minute. Why?"

"They fired their coach—Guido. He's from my city, Trier. I know him from when I played junior hockey at home."

"Doesn't surprise me. I wasn't his biggest fan. He's kind of a dick," I say, then start lacing up my skates. I don't feel like getting into the full story and working myself up before the game.

But Willi doesn't let it go. "He wasn't my favorite coach either. He's here tonight."

"What? You gotta be shitting me."

"No shitting on you. I just talk with him outside."

Guido is *here. Tonight.* I would like nothing more than to toss him into the nearest elevator shaft, or just have a good game and make him regret releasing me.

Our opponent, Grefrath, is just below us in the standings, and we've beaten them in all our meetings this season. But tonight, the bounces all go their way. We're unable to generate much offense and after two periods, the game remains scoreless, with Grefrath out-shooting us 22–4.[30] What makes the game even more frustrating is that Lin and her mom are in attendance and, in a misguided Babe Ruth-ian moment, I promised Lin that we would win tonight.

With one period remaining in the season, I implore the hockey gods to give me and the team a boost. It takes them a while to work their magic but with three minutes remaining in the game and the score still knotted at zero, Tönner dekes out a Grefrath defender before sliding the puck across the ice to me, for an easy redirection into the net. Tim Grundl adds an empty net goal with a minute remaining in the game, and just like that, we finish the season with a shutout.

After the game, everyone stays on the ice to salute the fans of Neuwied one last time. I spot Lin in the crowd and we exchange a smile and a thumbs-up. As we skate off the ice for the last time this season, I see a familiar face down the hallway outside the locker room. It's Guido, dressed in black from head to toe, talking with Markus. I'd like to present him with the game-winning puck, but luckily when I return to the locker room, there aren't any pucks around, game winners or otherwise, so I'm spared any pangs of remorse. Hockey is a business, be it in Germany, Belgium, or Nigeria. I wasn't an asset to his team after I got hurt, so he had to let me go. Not sure I'd feel the same way though had we lost.

After changing out of my gear and showering, I hear commotion in a room down the hall. Other than the locker room entrance, there's only one other small room that acts as a storage room for the team. I'd been inside once at the beginning of my stint in Neuwied to spray paint my hockey gloves blue because the ones the team ordered for me had apparently gotten lost by DHL. Approaching the room, I hear two distinct sounds, one of metal banging around and the other of music. Opening the door cautiously, I see Mother Russia, barbell on his back, sweat dripping down his forehead into a puddle on the floor, getting in a workout after our final game of the season. It's like

---

30 That's like a baseball team being outhit 22–4.

an updated Russian version of that scene in *Youngblood*: Oleg, shirtless still wearing all his lower-half hockey equipment, has one barbell and a set of dumbbells with a boom box blasting Russian techno music. Tucked behind his ear is a cigarette. We exchange smiles then I shut the door before he forces me to spot him.

The next night at an impromptu team party, everyone says their goodbyes and the mood is upbeat thanks to the open bar provided by Agostea. Markus thanks us all and the season is deemed a success because we weren't relegated to a lower league—it's all relative, I guess. As discussions turn to plans for next season, some guys are more willing to voice their intentions than others. I tell Markus I'm excited about possibly coming back to Neuwied for next season, but honestly, it's a lie. I'm thankful for the opportunity to prove myself and finally play a few months of injury-free hockey, but now with some decent statistics, I'm hoping to have a new team, at a higher level, for next season. Okay, it's true I've had to scale it back a bit, but the dream is still alive and I intend to keep moving up. Until then, the booze flows, as do the stories, and tonight, some are even in English.

But something is missing. And that something is Oleg. Mother Russia is at the hospital, awaiting the arrival of his first child. Despite our differences, I'll miss the big lug, and it's sad I won't get to say goodbye.

The next afternoon, I swing by Thai Restaurant where Lin and I exchange email addresses, as well as promises to stay in touch. Back at the house, Dennis and I perform one last deluxe clean before we leave. Thanks to me, the guy has become even more of a neatnik.

Once the place is spotless, Dennis pops in some snus and grabs his suitcase. "I'm happy to have met you, buddy. It was a lot of fun living with you."

I lump up. I'm a bitch when it comes to goodbyes. "You too, Stroeks. I had a great time. I just wish we could have played together. Maybe next year."

"Maybe next year." Dennis reaches into his suitcase. "Want these?" He holds up a pair of Converses. "I have five pairs." While they don't fit me and are heavily used, I appreciate the gesture.

We hug it out and just like that, he's gone. Minutes later, there's a knock at the door. "Forget your snus, Stroeks?" I say opening the door. There stands Mother Russia, gripping the handle of a baby stroller as if he was afraid I'd steal it.

"American Airlines! You haven't left yet!" he yells, flashing me a never-before-seen grin.

"Mother Russia!" I'm shocked he's here. I'm shocked he's a father. "What're you doing here?"

"I want you to meet Oleg Junior."

"Congrats." I give Baby Russia a rub on his tummy—Oleg's wife must be a hottie, because that kid didn't get his good looks from his daddy. "Nice of you to come by."

"Of course, buddy. Zis was my first season playing with American guy. I enjoyed zis very much. You can play higher level next season. Train hard and eat good." Oleg takes one last long drag of his cigarette then flicks it over the baby's stroller into the street. "That is the key."

"I know you have a lot going on now with the new baby, but if you ever come to New York City, you have a place to stay."

"Thank you. And you have home in Naberezhnye Chelny, my brother. I wish you much luck next season."

Seriously, who needs the NHL?

PART THREE

THIRD PERIOD

CHAPTER NINE

Iceland Economics

THE OFF-SEASON IS a scramble in the European minor leagues. Regardless of country or league, European teams (yes, all of them) think they're going to land the next Gretzky every season. First, the top players sign in the top leagues then it filters down. So the more coveted you are, the earlier you sign. By late July, it's the equivalent of the scrawny kid with glasses and suspenders who signs a contract. I get the call from Mario the first week of August.

"Billy, you got two options: Return to Neuwied with a guaranteed contract for the season or take a month long tryout offer with a team in Sweden."

As we discuss the differences between the teams and leagues, my choice is easy when talking about the Swedish team, Mario says those three words every hockey player wants to hear: "One step closer."

You don't need a taste to keep hope alive; you only need a whiff.

I'm in, and I'm psyched. And I'm even more psyched when I find out that *Forbes* rated Sweden as the third cleanest country in the world.

Lindlöven is a member of the Swedish First Division, *Hockeyettan* as the locals call it. Each team is allowed two imports, and it looks like most North Americans who played in the league recently are former college or ECHL players with a smattering of former AHL and NHL guys who are looking to shut it down and have a good time.

Adding to my excitement is news from Mario that a fledgling hockey stick and glove company based out of New York City is interested in sponsoring me, supplying me with sticks and gloves for the upcoming season. I'm thrilled. Three days after signing all the papers and getting fitted for my new equipment, the company goes bankrupt.

Although my contract only guarantees me a tryout with Lindlöven, I plan on making the team and playing the full season, so I make an effort to learn about Sweden: the language, the culture, the food, the chances of meeting a girl,[31] *everything*. This time I want to be able to understand what's being said in the locker room, on the ice, and on the bus. I want to be in on the jokes—even if they're about me.

On August 20, I find myself at Gate 17 at Newark International Airport's Terminal 8 on flight AY 6 to Iceland. After a day layover, it's off to Sweden.

It's an accepted truth that the birthplace of ice hockey is the frozen ponds of Canada. But before my flight, I learned that thousands of years before ice hockey was "born" in Canada, Vikings in Iceland invented a game called *Knattleikr*.[32] Played on a thin layer of ice, *Knattleikr* featured two teams whose players used sticks to try and put a small, hard ball into the opposition's goal. The game featured penalties, penalty boxes, body contact, spectators, intimidation, and probably verbally abusing whoever was officiating.

It's knowing stuff like this that keeps me from getting laid.

Employing my customary strategy of being last to board the flight, I forego my assigned seat and claim an empty, middle seat I notice nestled between two cute Icelandic girls. They jabber in their native

---

31 Latest odds in Vegas have this at 1,938,048–1.

32 And you thought my Gunnar Stahl / Mighty Ducks D2 reference would be the only Icelandic hockey connection I'd have.

language, which has a melodious rhythm that stands in stark contrast to the guttural German I'd heard last season. Under the pretense of looking out the window, I eyeball the girl in the window seat, whose piercing green eyes and dark hair give me a jolt in the pit of my stomach, or maybe it's the gluten-free protein shake I downed before boarding.

There's something daunting about trying to talk to a girl you're separated from by an armrest, knowing that if you make a move and she deems you unworthy, the rest of the flight will be wildly uncomfortable. In the past whenever I've been seated next to a cute girl, I spark up lively conversations but unfortunately for me the girl isn't part of them since they take place in my head.

Thirty minutes into the flight and at 30,000 feet, the black-haired girl reaches into the bag under her seat and pulls out an economics textbook. *She's a nerd*, I think. *And so am I! There's my opening.*

"You, uh, study economics, or you reading that for fun?"

"It's for my studies. Just starting my first year in university."

"I was actually an econ major," I lie. The one economics class I took was to fulfill a requirement, and I could have sold my textbook back to the Harvard Coop at the end of the semester for a full refund, as it hadn't been cracked. "Once you get the basics, price/quantity graphs, supply/demand relationships, it gets more interesting—like cyclical swings in the level of aggregate production that emerge endogenously from empirical laws like the Beveridge curve." *Where is this crap coming from?* I wonder, while jotting down a couple impromptu graphs in her notebook, graphs that'll help her fail her class.

"These ones are driving me crazy." She points out some crap in her textbook with her right hand leading my eyes down the page as I try to remember something I learned about invisible hands. I wish my hands were invisible.

"Stimulus package," I blurt out.

"Sorry?" she says.

"Nothing . . . So these, uh, graphs are important. . ."

I scan her textbook and notice a highlighted box that reads, "diminishing returns—used to refer to a point at which the benefits gained are less than the amount of energy invested." I pause for a moment wondering if economics might have been something I should have paid more attention to. Before coming to any mind-blowing revelation, the girl jolts me from my daze.

"Have you read anything about our financial disaster in Iceland?"

I nod mirroring her expression. All I know is the Nordic countries are usually clustered in to the top right corner of economic graphs. Not sure what it means but it's got to be better than the bottom left.

"After our three big banks collapsed, it was chaos—prices shot up overnight and businesses shut down." She shuts her textbook as I intermittently blurt out a series of "sure" and "right." "At the worst point, our debt was 850 percent of GDP." She pauses. "850!"

"Real or nominal?"

"Real."

Wish I knew the difference.

"I really like your eyes." She crosses her legs towards me and brushes her hair behind her ears. "They're such an unusual color."

"Thanks. Yeah, they're brown. I guess a chestnut brown." My little sister calls them "shit brown."

"Almost no one in Iceland has brown eyes." Supply and demand? I love economics.

I have no more bullshit left to sling, and I know anything else I'd say will jeopardize the hot streak I'm on so I opt for a holding pattern. "I'm exhausted." I stretch my legs and perform a couple subtle pectoral flexes. "Hoping to beat the jetlag. I'm going to catch some sleep. Elbow me if you have any questions." And then I inch my body away from her, tilt my seat back a quarter inch, close my eyes, and pretend to nap for two hours. Hockey analysts love talking about "time and space," two keys to making good plays. Well, when it comes to trying to pick up girls, it's the same deal.

When the plane begins its decent, I "wake up," then gently nudge my econ protégé. "So I've heard there're some unbelievable sites to see in Iceland—some big waterfall, the original geyser, and, other stuff. I'm only here until tomorrow morning, but if you're free tonight, we should get together."

She rips a piece of paper from her notebook and removes a pen from her bag before jotting down her name and number. "Here. You can friend me on Facebook, if you want."

Must be my shit brown eyes.

Here's the thing though: Her handwriting is illegible. Can't read the name. Can't read the number. Looks like the chalkboard after that *Good Will Hunting* scene at MIT.

"By the way, my name's Bill," I say hoping she'll tell me hers and wondering why my voice goes up three octaves when I get nervous around girls.

She does.

"Heiða Sigurðardóttir. Nice to meet you."

After deplaning, I board a bus that provides a tour of the surrounding sights. The Reykjavik skyline comes into view twenty minutes into the drive. Idle cranes hang silently next to the half-constructed buildings. And while superficial prosperity may have halted, the fantasy-like landscape in the horizon thrives as a series of active volcanoes and rugged, granite snow-capped mountains stretch as far as I can see.

An hour later after a loop around the capital city of Reykjavik, I'm standing in front of what I was led to believe is a hotel in the center of Iceland's other main city, Keflavik. Inside, other than a few papers and an open ledger that lie on a small counter along one wall, there is no sign of life. As I turn around to go back outside and check the address, a tall, skinny man who looks in his late twenties appears from behind a door directly next to the counter.

"Hello, partner! Can I help you?" the man asks. He has long blond hair and skin so pale it's nearly translucent.

"Hi. Yeah, is this a hotel?" I ask.

"It is! Are you Bill?"

Business must be slow.

As he leads me to the second floor, he tells me that his name is Tumi, and, in addition to being a resident of the hotel, he's the manager, receptionist, maid, and handyman. After he opens the door to my room, he whips out a picture from his pocket, which he shoves in my face. It's a shot of an old, creepy looking man sitting in this very room. "This is the Bobby Fischer room! He stayed here for a few weeks in the middle of 2005! Best room in the hotel. Take a look."

Great. I'll be spending the night in a bed formerly occupied by a racist nutbag chess maniac. I wonder if there's a way I can find Heiða Sigurðardóttir. Maybe I can sleep in her bed. Or on her sofa. Or on her floor.

"How long will you be staying in Iceland?" Tumi asks.

"Just until tomorrow."

"Have you plans right now?"

"Not really. Why?"

"I can lock up the hotel and take you around. I tell you about Bobby and show you around."

This kind of thing doesn't happen in New York. How can I refuse?

Tumi darts around the corner and returns thirty seconds later behind the wheel of a large pickup truck that has seen better days, probably some time in 1986. The light snow that was falling when I landed is now heavy rain. When I ask Tumi about the weather in Iceland, he gives a knowing smile. "We have a saying here: If you don't like the weather, just wait five minutes and it will change." The maxim is borne out five minutes later, when the rain disappears, only to be replaced by hail.

En route to our first stop, the United States Naval Air Station Keflavik (NASKEF), Tumi tells me that aside from his job at the hotel, he works for the country's premier tour guide company, which explains his enthusiasm to show off all that is Iceland. NASKEF, once the sight of a seemingly active military community, has the eerie aura of a small town whose inhabitants have vanished (think Stephen King, circa *Salem's Lot*). Theaters, barber shops, banks, a hospital, and even a Wendy's restaurant are abandoned. Tumi tells me that the only activity the former military base sees nowadays is an occasional visit from teenagers, who sneak in the facility to smoke and drink. We head back onto the main road, where Tumi nonchalantly points out a few mountains and volcanoes in the distance, clearly no big deal to him, but I've barely even seen stuff like this on television. And that's the tour. So according to a key member of the area's number one tour company, the only thing actually worth seeing in the city is a dead American military base.

When we arrive back at the hotel, I dig into my pocket, remove a few Icelandic bills, and hand them over, figuring it's not every day someone shuts down his place of business to give a guest a tour of the country. Tumi sweeps his long blond hair and gently pushes my hand away. "You buy me a beer tonight." I agree, and we plan to meet up in the lobby at ten o'clock which gives me time to decode the piece of paper Heiða gave me.

I squint at what she wrote, cross my fingers, and get to work. First try: 000 354 413 5166.

"*Hallo?*"

"Hello. I'm looking for Heiða." I'm yelling into the mouthpiece, like being louder will translate my English into Icelandic.

"*Heiða? Nej.* Yadda yadda yadda yadda . . ."

Wrong number. Take two: 000 354 413 5167.

"*Hallo?*"

"Hello. I'm looking for Heiða."

"*Ekki Heiða.*"

"What?"

"*Hvað?*"

"What?"

"*Hvað?*"

Wrong again, I guess. Take three: 000 354 413 5177.

"*Hallo?*"

"Hi. Is Heiða there?"

Eight calls later, I find her. She gives me the name of a bar near the hotel and we plan to meet there.

Tumi knows the bar, so he decides to tag along, which isn't a bad thing since it turns out he went to high school with Heiða's older sister (don't even get me started on her name), which, for some reason, seems to legitimize me in her eyes.

The night is full of dancing, drinking, more dancing, and me pouring vodka shots on the floor. I generally succeed in not weirding her out, so once the bar closes, Tumi organizes an after-party at the hotel and Heiða and her friend Liza join. "We do everything together. You'll like her," Heiða promises.

As we sit in the booth at the dark and cozy hotel bar with burning candles scattered on the tables, Heiða inches closer. "I like your lip gloss. The glitter's a nice touch. Smells like apricot, maybe?" I say.

"Why don't you taste for yourself?"

I do. I'm right. It's apricot.

Then I feel the pressure of another hand on my left thigh. It's Liza. She's a ten, inflation-adjusted. Her glacial green eyes sweep me to sea. "How about mine?" She leans in close. "Can you guess the flavor?"

Smells like cherry. Right again.

I think, *What a great way to kiss Iceland goodbye.*

And then, for a change, I stop thinking.

CHAPTER TEN

How Swede It Is

"You can't leave your bags unattended, sir." The security guard at Stockholm's Arlanda Airport stands, arms folded, by my suitcase and hockey bag as I stroll towards her. "You must take them with you if you want to use the restroom."

"I wasn't in the bathroom."

"Where did you go then?"

I hold my hands up, palms skyward, and shrug. Before Iceland, I haven't been surrounded by girls that look like this since Friday nights in high school when I'd leaf through *Maxim Magazine* while watching *Wild On!* hosted by Brooke Burke.

The guard, a striking blonde herself, smiles as I finally remove the horseshoe-shaped pillow I've had around my neck since leaving Iceland.

"Welcome to Sweden," she says. I want to leave my bags unattended again just so she'll talk to me.

Eventually, I'm able to slow down my propeller head-spinning and do some more general people watching. The majority of Swedes share a common style: White Converse sneakers with either jeans (pegged at the bottom) or shorts (with a folded cuff). Shirts are tight and look like someone, at some point, had been yanking at the neck region thereby exposing the upper chest area. But while their style is far from American, their interest in American culture is clear: Yankees hats, Rangers T-shirts, Knicks jerseys—I see 'em all. If I didn't know any better, I'd guess I just got off the 4 train at Yankee Stadium. You'd think it would make me feel homesick. But it doesn't—because I'm a world traveler, an international hockey mercenary, a seasoned veteran of the continent of Europe . . . or just a twenty-three-year-old American trying to get his shit together.

I take the Arlanda Express to Stockholm City and enjoy every second with plenty of good scenery sitting around me. Plus, it's the cleanest form of public transportation I've ever seen. I doubt I'll feel compelled to lather myself in Purell when I arrive in Stockholm.

I plop my feet up on the empty seats across the aisle and pull out my computer. I click open my email and find a message from Tomas, the coach of Lindlöven, who, in perfect English, expresses his excitement to have me skate with the team and tells me he'll meet me at the train station in Lindesberg.

Once at Stockholm central station, I track down a man wearing a conductor's hat.

"Can you tell me which track has the train to Lindesberg?"

"Where?"

"Lindesberg."

He looks at me like I just asked him to solve for the cube root of negative π in his head. I dig out my ticket and show it to him.

"*Jaha!* You mean *Lindesberg*," he says pronouncing the "berg" like "berry." "It's down that way on track 3." I thank him as he stares at me still wondering how my pronunciation could have been so horrific.

"But you are American, yes?" he says. I nod. "Why you want to go to *Lindesberg?*"

Within minutes, the train chugs outside of Stockholm city limits and into the hilly countryside of interior Sweden. While I've yet to see Lindesberg, I realize it makes no difference to me what the town is like. It's like the way I saw math through a hockey prism when I was a kid. As long as I'm playing the game, hockey colors how I see everything: the people I meet, the town I live in, and even myself. What scares me, though, is that sometimes I wonder if what I'm clinging to is no longer a dream but a lie I've been weaving for myself to keep me from moving on.

Three hours later, I arrive at the Lindesberg station. As promised, Tomas, the team's coach, is waiting for me. He's impeccably groomed, and the side part in his blond hair is straight as a ruler. He's wearing white Conserve sneakers with jean shorts (shocker) that look like the bottom half of an NBA uniform from 1972, both in length and design. In other words, they're boxers.

"You made it! Let me give you a hand with this." Tomas rips the bags from my hands and heaves them over his shoulder. "We drop your stuff at the arena, then I take you to where you will be staying."

Cleanliness. Punctuality. Politeness. Great Hair. I'm in the Twilight Zone.

"This is town," Tomas says as we drive down a two-way street that features six pizza/kebab restaurants which are only outnumbered by hair salons. I count four customers total in the stores and spot another three pedestrians walking briskly with lowered heads.

Once out of downtown Lindesberg (re: Off that one street), we zip by a gas station and two supermarkets before taking a right turn at a small blue sign which reads: Lindehov Ishall.

Now Tomas may call it an arena, but either something is lost in the translation or his idea of an "arena" is slightly different than mine. To me, MSG is an arena. Lindehov, is a big, red industrial-looking structure that has three horses roaming in the field across the street, one of which is in the middle of taking a dump. It's now clear to me the origins of hockey rinks being referred to as "barns." But honestly, call it an arena, call it a barn, I don't care. They want me here, and I'm excited to play.

I follow Tomas through the parking lot of the rink, making sure to avoid a small pile of horse crap. He moves quickly, unencumbered by the tightness of his shorts. "Here is our gym. Not very big, but it has everything you need." I smile as it reminds me of the gym I set up in the laundry room back home. On one side is a squat rack with three sets of dumbbells next to it. On the other side are two foam rollers, rehab rubber bands in a variety of colors, and two spinning bikes, one with a missing spoke on the right pedal.

Between the gym and locker room is a small room that has a sink and some cupboards as well as a coffeemaker. "This is Röös's office. You will meet him soon enough." I nod my head. "This fucker never works, damn it," he says kicking the washing machine that shows a flashing red light. "We need a new one soon 'cause the boys always smelling like shit even before practice."

Tomas points me towards a stall where I unpack my gear. The logo of the team's main sponsor, Energizer, is plastered all over the pants and practice jerseys. The locker room is clean and cozy and smells like hockey. I hope I don't pack my bag again any time soon.

"Mind if I check out the ice surface?" I ask Tomas.

"Sure, through the doors there." "The Boys Are Back in Town" starts playing from his cell phone. He taps his right foot to the beat as he checks the caller ID then inserts a Bluetooth device in his ear. "I must take this. Meet you outside when you're done."

Small puddles of freshly melted ice line the rubber mat of the narrow hall that leads to the ice surface. I pause and eye old team pictures that hang on either side of the walls. While the dates of the string of pictures range from the '70s to the most recent season, there's very little that distinguishes one picture from the rest aside from the quality of camera and resolution. The names, faces, hairstyles, even jerseys seem constant from one year to the next. Nearly every last name ends in "son," and the long, flowing blond hair is either parted to one side or slicked straight back. There's a timelessness to the hockey world, something that keeps those playing pure and innocent. But the clock is always ticking. We work to score goals, stopping the clock momentarily. We harness time in the plays we make, the plays we practice over and over to get right. But the moments are fleeting; the memories are what we play for. I walk slowly down the corridor studying the pictures until I hear the sound of a puck shot into the boards.

The lights above the stands are shut off. Though dark, I can make out the wooden church style pew seating. The rink is lit up by a few fluorescent bulbs above center ice, just bright enough so I can see a little kid—he's probably six or seven—skating around the rink stick-handling a puck. Standing in net is an even smaller kid, probably a younger brother, forced to play goal the way I made my little sister gear up every afternoon in the living room rink.

When the skater sees me, he waves his gloved hand and races to center ice, crossing over around the faceoff dot before attacking the net on a breakaway. I know where his head is; it's Game 7 of the Stanley Cup, thirty seconds left in the third period, game tied. He comes in, dekes left, then right, cradles the puck through his legs, and lofts it into the empty net. The miniature goalie is busy collecting ice chips in the corner. As the puck hits the mesh, the shooter trips on his own stick and collapses—the same thing that happens to me when I try that move. I bang on the glass and give him a thumbs-up. He grins, at once proud of scoring the game-winning goal and embarrassed that he did a face-plant.

I've been there—no standing in line waiting to do a drill; no sitting on the bench waiting for his next shift; just the opportunity to try, then fail, then try again, piss and moan for a bit, fail again, and walk away with a mental checklist of things to improve. I can't help but think how much I have in common with this kid—we both share an unadulterated passion for the game and although our paths are separated by a lot of time and space, we are motivated by the same dream. Maybe the journey is the dream.

"Time to go, Bill!" Tomas yells. "Time for your cabin!"

Cabin? I won't be living in an actual cabin, will I?

Yes. Yes, I will.

Ten minutes later, we pull into Lindesberg Golfklubb. Just past the parking lot sit five small red cabins, standing only a few feet apart. Tomas knocks on the door of the cabin closest to the parking lot. A slender blond boy emerges, ducking his head to avoid knocking himself out.

"*Tjena!*" Tomas roars.

"*Tjenare!*" the kid responds.

I bust out some of my Swedish: "*Tjena. Jag heter Bill. Trevilgt att tr . . . att tr . . . at trr . . .* nice to meet you."

"I'm Linus," the boy says as we shake hands. Linus is about 6'4", but his slim build makes him seem taller. His hair, long and combed straight back, is so blond it's almost white. His facial hair is thin and wispy and I don't know if that's because he's exceedingly young, or exceedingly Swedish. He and Tomas have a short dialogue and from what I can understand, they're discussing tomorrow's practice.

After Tomas leaves, I take inventory of our *very* humble home. The cabin is slightly larger than it appears from the outside. There are two sets of bunk beds aligned flush with opposite walls, a small desk separating them. There's a single chair in front of the desk that seems to take up more space than it's worth. Linus lays down on one of the bottom beds, under which his suitcase is neatly tucked. His feet dangle off the end. His shoes are organized alongside the wall, and, to my relief, he set up a fan which provides the cramped room with some circulation. He's clean, he's nice, and he's reading a book entitled *How To Pick Up Girls*. I think we'll get along just fine.

I plop down on the bottom bed in the opposite bunk. "Any idea how long we're staying in here?" I ask as my eye is drawn to the corner of the ceiling where a spider is busy weaving its web.

"Not long, I hope. I think some time after the tryout period is over, they'll either move us into an apartment or let us go. It's not too bad though. We can eat all our meals up the hill at the clubhouse. It's pretty good food."

"How about the bathroom and showering and all that?"

"Upstairs in the clubhouse too. Tomas gave me the key so we can go up whenever we want."

After I settle in, we walk up the pebbled path to the clubhouse for an early dinner. The only employee working in the dining area takes an immediate interest in my American background. Since Linus and I are the only patrons, the guy joins us for a traditional Swedish meal of meatballs and potato balls.

When we finish dinner, Linus takes me upstairs to show me the golf locker room, where, to my delight, a man is mopping the floor with precision and purpose. Inside the room are three large showers, a few toilet stalls, a group of lockers, and a sauna.

Armed with our shower caddies and towels, the two of us enjoy a fifteen-minute sauna after our showers then return down the pebbled path for bed.

"Where'd you play last season?" I say, as Linus scribbles in the margins of *How To Pick Up Girls*.

"I had to take last year off from hockey." Linus closes the book and tosses it on the floor. "I had military duty last year. Everyone here has to do it some time."

"Your hair must grow quick. It'd take forever for me to have a buzz cut then get it your length."

"We don't have to cut our hair. We just use a hair net if we need to keep it up."

The rev of a car engine grows louder, and screeching tires followed by high-pitched yells can be heard. I lean up and peek out the small window, where a red Volvo with its high beams on zips around the empty golf course parking lot, performing donuts.

"What in the hell is that asshole doing?"

"It's *ragga runda*." Linus says casually. "Some nights in the summer, guys get drunk and drive around like tough guys trying to pick up girls. Small town shit."

The next morning, Linus drives us in his car to the rink as the remnants of last night's *ragga runda* are obvious in the form of some black tire marks and a vomit splatter.

After entering the locker room, somebody yells at me, "Hey, Bill, yeah you, Shithead, how is it going?"

I turn around. It's Tomas. "Uh, hey, Coach. Going well."

"That's good, Fuckface! Let's have a good practice week then we play our first training match on Friday!"

In the locker room, players are in various stages of undress—inspecting their sticks, equipment, and genitals. The guy next to me gives me a friendly slap on the shoulder and introduces himself as Anders Söderström, a defenseman from up north in Skellefteå.

"How far north?" I ask.

"When you play there, you don't get a car in your contract. You get a snowmobile."

Anders is in his second season with Lindlöven and has a quiet demeanor that suits his gentle-looking face. More players enter, and Anders greets them with small nods of his head as he tells me names and positions of each new arrival. A heavyset guy with a round baby face waddles in. After removing his tool belt, he makes a beeline to my locker to shake my hand. He flashes a large grin and heads to the opposite end of the locker room, where he plops onto a chair and chats with a few of the other players.

"Marcus Sjöö," Anders says. "He's the captain here. Really skilled player. Defenseman."

"What's with the tool belt?" I ask.

"He works construction part-time. Most of the guys have small, extra jobs here."

"Big guy, huh?" I say as I remove my pants and put on my jock.

"Over a hundred kilos, but he used to be even heavier, I promise you that. I've heard some stories when he played with Örebro in Allsvenskan a couple years ago."

"Like what?"

He scratches his chin and crosses his right leg over his left. "In preseason training, all the team had to run ten kilometers through the forest. He would run the first kilometer until they reached the thick woods, then he'd peel off and pick berries from some of the trees and sit there and eat until the team ran back by. Then he would hop in behind everyone and jog the last kilometer. Ran only two of ten kilometers and still finished last." Anders stands up and motions for me to follow him towards the stick rack. "Look." He points to Marcus's four sticks. One of the sticks is about five inches longer than the other three.

"What's the deal?" I remove the stick and check the curve for no other reason than that's what every player does when he picks up a stick. "He use it for penalty killing?"

"No, no. He uses the long one when Tomas makes us do skating at the end of practice. We usually do sprints from board to board, always touching our sticks to the glass. He uses this long one when we skate so he doesn't have to skate as far."

"What's our mascot?" I ask Anders as we return to our stalls and continue changing into our gear.

"Mascot?"

I point to one of the players sitting across from us who's wearing a Rangers hat. "Like New York's the Rangers. What are we?"

Anders acknowledges me with a small nod as he puts in a snus. "We're leaves."

When you're the New Guy on a team, the only players who introduce themselves aren't your direct competition. Anders and Marcus are defensemen, so I can't take their jobs. Being friends with my fellow forwards might take a while. I notice two guys sitting across from me checking their skate blades, occasionally stealing glances at me, almost an appraisal trying to figure out what type of player I am, whether I'm a threat to take their spot. I know that's what's going on in their heads, because it's exactly the same thing running through mine.

"Meet Röös yet?" Anders asks as we lace our skates.

"No, but Tomas mentioned him. He works with the team, right?"

"Röös! Röös!" Anders yells. Out from the equipment room appears a bearded man, probably in his fifties, wearing full Lindlöven warmups and a winter hat that can't hide his Ross Perot ears. Draped around his neck is an enormous pair of headphones.

"Röös. This is Bill. He's from America," says Anders in Swedish.

"*Tjena*," I say as Röös inspects my face like I'm some foreign object he doesn't recognize. Which, I suppose, is exactly who I am.

"*Tj- Tja-Tja!*" booms Röös.

"Röös is the king," Anders says. "*Du är Kungen*, Röös. *Lite kaffe, tack!*" Röös clambers to his office, the coffee station, and scoops beans into the coffee maker. I hear him counting, "*Ett, två, tre, fyra . . .*"

"Hope you like strong coffee," Anders says, as the counting goes on, and on, and on. "*Röös, han är törstig!*"

"*Va-va-vad faaaan,*" Röös responds, before beginning his counting back at one.

"I just started getting into coffee this summer. Not sure if I'm ready for his blend."

"Probably not. I've seen days where he must have fifteen or twenty scoops in there." Röös returns to my stall handing us small cups of coffee that have the consistency of a milkshake. I can feel a caffeine buzz from the smell. Röös then puts his headphones on his ears, bobbing his head from side to side as he walks away.

Coffee is endemic to European hockey though they've never heard of decaf. It's offered in every hockey room, both home and away. It's enjoyed morning, noon, and night. Also for snacks.

As practice nears, Tomas stomps out from the coaches' room wearing his skates and posts a sheet with the day's drills. The ninety-minute practice is fast-paced and involves lots of competition drills—1-on-1s, 2-on-1s, all in tight spaces below the hash marks, which forces guys to make quick decisions and ensures plenty of body contact. The level of play is higher than in Neuwied—the players are faster and always in the right position.

Although the large ice surface encourages a fast tempo, no one shies away from the physical play. There's one guy who's all over the ice, and I seem to play either with or against him on every drill. When playing against, he makes a point of going after me. It's a rite of passage every player must go through when landing on a new team—the New Guy is treated like he's wearing team-issued NHL gear and requested number 99. You're a skating bullseye.

When Tomas whistles us in to take a water break before the conditioning portion of the practice, Marcus Sjöö labors to the bench to grab his other stick, and the guy who'd been taking runs at me skates over. "Hey. I'm Jocke," he says as I squirt some water in my mouth, spit it out, and hand him the bottle.

"Bill," I respond. Before I can say anything else, somebody taps me on my ass with his stick.

"Hey. I'm Danny."

They're twins—identical twins with matching stubble on their upper lips and some whiskers on their chins.

"Good playing," Danny says to me. "But buddy, don't touch mine again." He holds up his water bottle that has his number taped to it. "That's how guys get sick. Röös will fix you your own."

I like it here already.

Tomas skates us for twenty minutes while Röös stands on the bench, yelling at us and trying to peg the stragglers with pucks. Not a damn clue what he's saying, but I love his intensity.

In the locker room after practice, Marcus turns on some Swedish rock music, but my attention is focused on the twins, who sit next to one another. Noticing my scrutiny, Jocke wanders over. "Good practice today," he says. As a new guy, it's always encouraging to hear words like that from a teammate, especially a guy that plays your position.

"You too." I point at the tattoo bursting with bright colors on his shoulder. "What's going on here?"

He sits down next to me. "Those are hockey sticks, and that's a puck, and underneath that, that's my and Danny's initials. And next to that is our grandmother's name, Elin. She was like a second Mom— died almost a year ago."

"Sorry to hear that." I point at his calf. "How 'bout that one?" I ask as I study the intricate design that looks like it might have some religious ties.

"That one . . . I was shit drunk in Greece. Some guy from Norway pay me 5,000 krona to get a tattoo of whiskey bottle with his name on it, so I do it." He shrugs. "What can I say: 5,000 krona is 5,000 krona."

The next morning at practice, after downing a quadruple espresso shot courtesy of Röös, a trio of serious-looking Latvians joins the team, arriving with their gear in trash bags, and hit the ice for our forty-five minute practice. Renars Undelis, a diminutive forward, has quick feet and deceptive strength on the puck. Although he's Latvian, Renars must be part Russian as he doesn't pass the puck. I can barely differentiate the other two, Sergejs Louskins and Sergejs Tjoluskins (yeah, I was just as confused). They're both big defensemen who resemble one another, and while one seems to be more offensive minded than the other, they have similar skating strides and make good, hard passes. Both Danny and Jocke welcome the two Sergejses with some hard blindside hits that don't seem to faze the newcomers in the least. Something tells me any on-ice blindside hits pale in comparison to what they've faced off the ice.

After practice, I introduce myself to the Latvians, who, while pleasant enough, aren't overly friendly. It might be a language barrier, it might be jet lag, it might be that they're jerks, it might be that I'm the jerk. Only time will tell.

Walking into the locker room with Röös at his side, Tomas says something in Swedish, before switching to English. "Good practice today, fuckers. We have two more practices this week before our first training match against Mariestad. They always have a good team, many players remain from their Allsvenskan years. Let's continue with the intense, high tempo practice and be ready to beat the shit out of their asses!"

Clapping and cheering fill the room before Tomas takes it upon himself to dole out nicknames for the two Sergejses. Sergejs Louskins, the taller of the two, is called Chara, referring to Zdeno Chara, the 6'9" mammoth defensive star of the Boston Bruins.[33] The other Sergejs, for a reason never explained, is Sigge.[34] Tomas gives Renars a nickname as well, probably so he won't feel left out. His is Ragge. Mine remains Shithead.

Friday morning, Anders drives Linus and me to the rink for a pregame meeting before the bus departs for our game in Mariestad. In the locker room, Tomas goes over the keys to the game. For ten minutes he speaks in Swedish, and I'm lost within six seconds. However, I do accomplish one feat during this time. I'm finally able to identify a distinguishing feature between the twins: Danny *always* has a large snus tucked under his upper lip like a chipmunk with a nut. I have yet to see what his top front two teeth look like—I'm not even sure he has them. Although the majority of the players on the team use snus,

---

33 Sergejs "Chara" Louskins is so tall that the team has to send in a petition to the league to grant him the ability to use a stick that exceeds the stick length limit mandated by the league.

34 Sigge, also for reasons never explained, didn't return to the team after that practice.

Danny has one lodged in his mouth so often that he looks peculiar without one. For that matter, so does Tomas.

Once finished in Swedish, Tomas give a condensed version of his speech in English.

"Boys, it's just a training match today but it's important we focus because this is where our season begins. Four keys to the game: Be accountable, both for yourself and teammates—no stupid penalties. Next, make sure we time our plays well. Centers, watch your defenseman on the breakouts so when he hits the winger with a pass you're open as an outlet. Third, battle level must be high—I know it's August and everyone's been golfing and fucking, but now it's time to play some hockey. And last, be creative, boys. You all know how to play this game. This is the time to try some stuff out, make mistakes. Have some fuckin' fun out there!"

"Feel good, Fuckface?" Tomas asks as I heave my bag over my shoulder.

"Feeling awesome. Ready to play some hockey."

The bus ride to Mariestad is four hours. The Latvians set up camp in the last two rows of the bus. Usually reserved for the more talkative, story-telling inclined guys, the back of the bus may now be an ideal place to sit in silence. I sit in the middle, next to the native Swedes who lean over their laptops, watching Peter Forsberg[35] clips on YouTube constantly stopping and replaying certain parts, discussing and dissecting each move he makes. Sweden has a reputation for producing players whose skills make up for their lack of toughness, but Forsberg revolutionized the way Swedes play hockey by bringing a tenacity to complement his elite skill set. There was a gracefulness, ease, passion, and confidence with which he navigated the game—like watching Andrew "The Man" Chan execute a Harvard Ec 10 problem set, or watching me copy it. After huddling around a couple of the guys' computers to watch Foppa in action and wondering how in the hell he got so good at hockey, I fall asleep and am awakened by the bus coming to a jolting halt at Mariestad Ishall.

---

35 Forsberg is probably Sweden's best-known, most beloved player. He was no Adam Graves, but he was okay.

Röös, bobbing his head vigorously up and down with his headphones on, slaps each of us on the back as we exit the bus. "What's he always listening to?" I ask Anders as we remove our hockey bags from beneath the bus. Anders relays the question to Röös as I stand by waiting for a response while the Latvians, devoid of expression and without anyone having to ask them, haul our skate-sharpener, bag of jerseys, and traveling equipment trunk into the rink along with their own hockey bags. "Röös says he'll let you listen if you score today."

"I need new songs to pump me up before games," I yell, hoping somehow Röös will be able to understand even though his headphones are covering his ears and he speaks no English. Röös waves his index finger at me then says something to Anders. "Only if you score," says Anders.

After warmups, Tomas barges into the locker room, with Röös in tow. "*Gubbar*!" he begins before making eye contact with the Latvians and me. "Okay, I take this in Swedish first then in English." I give a nod as do the Latvians, after which Tomas delivers an impassioned speech, of which I understand about twenty percent. Röös isn't afraid to deliver a message of his own as he periodically yells the last words of each of Tomas's sentences; Unfortunately, the speech is so rousing that Tomas forgets to deliver the English version before he leads the team charging out of the room. Ragge leans in towards me as we strap on our helmets. "Billy, you understand what coach say?"

"Some. He said play hard and don't get outworked. Also, have fun. He mentioned that too. He also said fuck, or some fuck-related word, about forty times."

"This is normal for hockey coach," Ragge responds. "We play to maximum." Ragge turns to Chara as they engage in a brief exchange which I pretend to understand for some reason, and then they follow me out of the locker room and onto ice for the first period.

With one minute remaining in the first period, Jocke delivers a booming hit to a Mariestad defender and Danny retrieves the loose puck, avoids a head-hunting Mariestad player, and dishes me a pass in the slot, where I release a rising shot that beats the goaltender over his glove. I don't want to make an ass of myself before I know everybody's name, so my celebration is restrained.

With the 1–0 lead, we're all smiles save for the Latvians, who are their usual deadpan selves. The high spirits, however, disappear in the second period, as Mariestad's offense wakes up, burying four goals and dominating play on both ends. We continue to unravel, as Mariestad outscores us 4–1 in the third period. Ragge scores our lone goal in the third and celebrates by skating directly to our bench and sitting down.

With five minutes remaining in the game, the PA guy makes an announcement. Sitting on the bench, I see everyone in the crowd with their eyes fixed on sheets of paper in their hands.

"*ETT. SJU. SEX. SJU,*" says the announcer. A large, bearded man wearing a Mariestad jersey and scarf draped around his neck darts up from his seat and raises both hands as the rest of the crowd cheers louder than they did the entire game.

"The hell's going on?" I ask the guy sitting on the bench next to me.

"Contest. Everyone try to guess how many spectators at game. That fat guy won."

"How many are there?" I ask scanning the stands.

"One thousand seven hundred sixty-seven."

"Not bad for an exhibition game in August."

After getting blown out 8–2, I line up first for the post-game handshake (being the gracious loser and overall good sportsman that I am). Then a baffling scene unfolds once I slap finger tips with each guy on the Mariestad team. Upon completing the handshake, each player (on both teams) drops to a knee to touch the ice. According to my research (and by research I mean watching *D3: The Mighty Ducks* forty-nine times), this is a Scandinavian tradition in which players pay tribute to someone much like the Ducks did to the late Hans (RIP) prior to their rubber match against the Eden Hall Varsity Squad. Even both teams' coaches partake in the tradition but not Röös, since he's busy screaming at the wall with his headphones on.

"Danny," I say as he returns to both skates. "Someone die? I mean some Swedish hockey legend pass away? Is that who you're honoring?"

"Fuck you mean?" he says removing the snus from his mouth and tossing it over the glass as we skate off the ice.

"Dropping to a knee to touch the ice. Who's the tribute for?"

"Tribute? We just shake hands with twenty disgusting guys. We touch ice to clean our hands." Danny skates away as I hear him mutter, "Fuckin' weird Americans."

I'm starting to love this country.

On the bus ride home, the mood is expectedly somber. Not only did we lose the game but a nineteen-year-old forward sustains an ACL tear that'll end his season. As each guy on the team offers his condolences to the kid sitting with his leg elevated and covered in ice as he fights off tears, I feel his pain. I wish I had a way to tell him it would be okay, but I don't know his name, he doesn't speak any English, and I know that no words can make him feel any better.

I take a seat in the middle of the bus, and as we pull onto the highway, I tilt my seat back and do what most players do at some point after a loss: Replay in my head every play I screwed up.

"Move over, Shithead," says Tomas, snapping me out of my self-pity daydream. I slide to the window seat and he sits down next to me.

"Are you low?" he asks.

We just got shitkicked 8–2, so I'm definitely not high. "Disappointed we got throttled tonight."

"Me too. But Mariestad is a top team. Their players have played together two, three years. You looked good out there—reminds me of how I used to play."

"Yeah? What position were you?"

"Right wing. Not the strongest guy out there, but I wanted it bad, Fuckface." Tomas removes his phone from his pocket, taps the screen a few times, then scrolls down and shows me a picture of a young guy in full hockey equipment, wearing a Chicago Blackhawks practice jersey, his long blond hair slicked black and darkened by sweat. "Drafted by Chicago when I was eighteen." He stares at the picture, falling into a short reverie at the memory of it and returns his phone to his pocket.

"You played for the Hawks?"

Tomas unlatches the tray table from the seat in front of him. "Went to training camp the year they drafted me. In the final scrimmage," he grabs three tins of snus from the seat across the aisle and places them on the tray table, "I had the puck cutting through the neutral zone." He rearranges the snus tins, showing the play. "Wanted to throw a fake to defenseman so I dropped my head for one split-second and got smashed. Shoulder was fucked. Went back home, played another season in Sweden but my shoulder never was the same."

"That's brutal . . . to be so close."

"It is, but that's how it goes sometimes. I could to stay in the game coaching though. I see one thing with the way you skate—your feet come up too high after your stride. You lose speed. Keep the stride long, but your leg low and back under your body quick."

I sigh audibly, tilting my head up. "That's the first piece of instruction I think I've gotten from a coach since I was probably twelve."

"I'm here to teach too. I have two rules for my players—first, give me everything you have on the ice, practices, and games."

"Got it. What's the second?"

Tomas stands up, replaces the snus in his lip, and facing the back of the bus holding up two fingers, shouts, "*Gubbar,* what's my second rule?"

Like a kindergarten class addressing its teacher in unison, the boys on the bus respond, some in English and some in Swedish, "No shitting on the bus."

As Tomas returns to his seat next to Röös, Danny and Jocke plant themselves in the seats across from me as a few other guys lean over the backs of their seats, all grinning in anticipation. "Billy, we got something for you," Danny says. "It's a bet." Jocke pulls out a tin of snus. "Ever have this?" Danny asks as he prepares a new ball of the tobacco for himself.

"Tried Skoal back home, but it tastes like shit."

A few onlookers chuckle as Jocke molds a small nugget of the snus into a ball much smaller than the one Danny just made for himself. "Five of us have put in some money, 500 krona total. If you can keep this in your mouth for ten minutes, you win it. If not, you lose."

I stare at the snus. It stares back. How hard can it be? "Ten minutes?" I ask.

"Ten minutes."

I run my tongue over the front of my teeth as my mouth goes dry. Jocke smiles and Danny frowns as they watch me pop in the snus.

Immediately, my gums burn and my mouth floods with saliva, thanks to the mint-flavored carcinogenic dirt. I'm able to stay strong . . . for four minutes, at which point I scramble to the front and beg the driver to pull over. I then plaster the shoulder of the highway with snus, and our dinner of unidentified meat which had been sitting in the bus all game and was probably going to come up anyway at some point in the night. Röös howls uncontrollably waving his flask around and greets me when I return with a couple of hard whacks to the back and cup of his whiskey, which I decline.

"I can't believe you lasted that long," Jocke says when I return to my seat. "Here you go, 250 krona. You made it halfway so you get half the bet." I take the hard-earned winnings and stash it in my pocket, wondering if it was all worth it. I decide it was.

We arrive at Lindehov around 3:00 a.m. While our equipment manager searches for the rink key, some guys sit on their hockey bags and talk on their phones, others linger where the Zamboni dumps out the snow and pelt one another with snowballs, and the Latvians engage in some late-night partner stretching. Outside the bus, I find Röös loitering, headphones on, as he smiles at me. I call Anders over and ask him to tell Röös that he promised to let me listen to his music if I scored. Röös obliges, slowly removing his headphones and unclipping the Walkman from his pants before handing them to me. He watches closely as I drape the headphones over my head and hit play.

"*Tjena* . . . What's up. *Bra* . . . Good. *Hur är det?* . . . How's it going? . . ." It's Tomas's voice.

* * *

Monday morning at practice, Tomas calls me into his office.

"You like golf, Fuckface?"

"Love it." I take a few abbreviated golf swings with my arms.

"Good. Tomorrow, my friend from Stockholm comes to visit so I meet you in the morning at your cabin."

It's not exactly the threesome I was hoping to have in Sweden, but it sounds decent enough.

"Awesome. I'm a righty, so—I guess I'll borrow some clubs from the pro shop or, maybe yours?" I ask.

"Oh Fuckhead! You're not playing. You carry the bags for us. It will be good time!"

"Got it." I put my imaginary golf clubs back in the bag.

"And listen now. We have two new guys who show up today. Go meet them!"

Sami Martikainen is a sturdy defenseman from Finland with a head of hair that looks never to have come into contact with any sort of brush (although his face looks to have had some run-ins with high sticks and pucks).

The game has a way of carving itself into those who play it whether it's scars on one's body or affected Canadian accents.

The other newcomer is Richard Flodin, a forward from Göteborg on Sweden's west coast. Richard, like most of the guys on the team, sports the traditional male Swedish haircut with the hair on both sides of his head cropped short and the long, blond locks on the top of his head slicked straight back save for a single strand that dangles just over his right eye. He's got small features, and the only thing stronger than his jawline is his shoulders. It's like he was ripped out of an H&M underwear ad.

Monday's practice involves a lot of skating but is short to ensure everyone is well rested for the game against Ore. After practice, the team gathers in the locker room to watch video of the Mariestad game.

Video sessions at Harvard never started on time, especially after losses when we'd rearrange all the wires connected to the locker room TV. After thirty minutes and a phone call to Harvard's IT department, Donato would take out his laser pointer and replay every mistake in slow motion, drawing criss-crossing arrows, zooming in and out, commenting on our "horseshit fuckin' body position" with the occasional compliment like "best part of that shift was the change." Now to be fair, video sessions weren't *always* of actual hockey games. After Ervin's hypnotic voodoo ceased effectiveness, the coaching staff turned to *National Geographic* films. While it wasn't hockey footage, it did feature another type of game, I guess. Never mind that our power play was last in the ECAC and we hadn't once executed the Bossy or reverse-Bossy faceoff plays. There we were, the day before facing Boston University, cooped up in our locker room with the lights off and the air rich with the smell of dip spit and farts, watching footage of cheetahs chasing down a gazelle in the Serengeti, learning the importance of an aggressive forecheck. It was life and death, on and off the ice.

Tomas manages to find an equal number of positive and negative clips from our 8–2 beatdown. He uses the video session as a learning tool, pointing out what can be done better and suggesting options to ensure we don't make the same mistakes. And even better, Tomas doesn't once run clips of a pack of hyenas feasting on a freshly killed antelope.

I feel a tap on my knee as Jocke leans in with furrowed brows. "Billy boy, what you got up there?"

"Thought I'd give the snus thing another shot." I pull out the tin and hand it to Jocke. "Picked this shit up at Hemköp this morning. Tastes pretty good, and I think I can handle the buzz—at least in five minute intervals."

Jockey smirks. He lifts up the pink *Catch* tin. "This is girl snus. My sister does this—sixteen years old. Fifteen, but sixteen soon."

The last clip Tomas shows us is of Ragge following his goal. "Boys," Tomas says grinning and searching for Ragge in the pile of guys lying on the locker room floor. "Here we have Ragge showing good speed as he skates to the bench after his goal. Ragge, here in Sweden we have no problem with showing some excitement after a goal. It's a good thing. So loosen up. Later this week, we will do a little competition in practice. See who has the best celebration." He points to me. "I'm putting my money on Fuckface."

The day before our next game, Richard Flodin walks in the locker room as I sit in my stall lacing my skates.

"Know your blood type?" He runs his hand through his golden mane and smirks.

"Not sure. Why?"

"Might want to find out." He tosses a newspaper in my lap and I eye the article previewing our next game against IFK Ore. Below the headline is a large color picture of our opponent's newest North American forward: Mike Danton.

Danton, a Canadian who played in the NHL from 2001–2004, was convicted in 2004 of conspiracy to commit murder (hiring a hitman to kill his former agent, David Frost, who had allegedly sexually abused Danton on several occasions). After serving five years in prison, Danton enrolled in college for two years and now is looking to reignite his professional hockey career.

Instead of boring you with the play-by-play of our game against Ore, I'll just come out and tell you I scored a goal on an absolutely blistering slapshot that makes Fulton Reed's knuckle puck look like a mini-mite's backhander. Even more remarkable is that I scored from center ice. Had it occurred during an NHL game in the mid-'90s televised on Fox, the glowing puck would've had that stupid bright red comet tail on it as it streaked through the air. Instead, this happened in the Swedish First Division, in 2011, in warmups. Let me explain.

I'm not sure if it's genetic or cultural and I'm not sure why I care, but hockey players sometimes do things on the ice for no other reason than to piss the other team off. It makes us feel good. The twenty-minute warmup prior to each game is a terrific opportunity to express ourselves in this way since it's the only time when every player on both teams is wheeling around the ice. Add in the fact that there are seventy-eight pucks on the ice, no refs, and lots of tension building, some interesting stuff can happen. Back in the States, spectators may be familiar with the team goons chirping each other at center ice during warmups. Most of the time, once the game starts, these same players will back up their tough talk by dropping the mitts and shoving their elbows down one another's throats. Well this ain't the States.

In tonight's warmups as I go through my routine of scouting out the talent both on the opposing team and in the stands, I detect stray pucks soaring into our zone like meteors. Because the rest of my team-mates are focused on actually doing the warmup drills, I take it into my own mitts to investigate the matter further. Skating slowly along the boards to the blue line being careful not to collide with any of my team-mates who enjoy doing hot laps in our zone, I spot an Ore defender lofting full-length saucer passes into our end. With time running out on the clock, guys on both teams start filing off the ice. Not this guy, though—he's still sending high sauce down to our end like a jackass. Wheeling behind my own net and gathering speed for the first time in warmups, I pick up a puck, briefly fumble it in an unnecessary toe-drag attempt, then race to center ice, and unleash a slapshot that hums through the air neck-high clanging bar-down in the opposite net. My saucer puck-lofting opponent looks just as shocked as I am, and in a display of respect nods then skates off the ice. It's the effectiveness of passive aggressive maneuvers like this that make me enjoy this league.

Now let's get to the game action.

Richard Flodin and Linus bury a goal each, leaving us up two-zip after the first intermission. In the second period, I track down my puck-lofting friend from warmups and deliver a jab to his ribs at the end of a shift. He remains down on the ice so I know he's not coming after me. However, on my half-assed skate back to the bench, I wonder if it might make more sense to exert more effort with my legs to get off the ice than with my arms which I flail around wildly signaling to the guys on the bench that I need a change. The chippy play continues, and after taking their timeout, Ore comes out aggressive, too aggressive for Jocke, and at the end of the period he gets into a fight/hair-pulling match with an Ore defenseman.

For some reason, the sight of two hockey players trying to deposit their fists through one another's faces compels the non-fighters on the ice to engage in friendly chitchat with the opposition. Maybe it's knowing that we're not involved in currently having someone try to carve our face out that gives us relief and creates this sense of solidarity. I peer to my right, and the closest Ore player to me is Mike Danton.

His ultimate fighter head looks tiny compared to the tree-trunk neck that supports it. His face conjures up a mix of a pissed off bull and an undefeated wrestler. His nose is small and flat, most likely a combination of genes, an NHL career, and a prison sentence.

I watch his gloves, hoping like hell they stay on his hands. But I'm not as concerned as you might think. You see, I've played against Danton before. In fact, I've fought him and beat the piss out of him. Then again, that all happened when I was sixteen and playing *NHL 03* on PlayStation 2. A real life fight between us would look like an angry six-year-old Canadian thrashing an American piñata.

Danton's lips curl up, revealing a jack-o'-lantern smile. Appearing more content to observe than participate, he removes his right hand from his glove and props up his visor. While his face tells the story of punches taken, his knuckles tell one of punches thrown. He puts his glove back on then props his chin on the butt end of his stick in the pose Ken Dryden made famous. I'm not sure how to begin our conversation, so I look for common ground.

"Not a bad tilt for a couple Swedes, eh?"[36] I say.

"Don't know how to throw 'em, but they'll fuckin' swing away. You Canadian?"

"American. How'd you end up here?"

"Only place that gave me a visa. Small town, but great people. I thought we had the nicest people in Canada, but I might be wrong."

Jocke and his dance partner, nearly finished giving each other French braids, are separated by the referees and escorted to the penalty box.

"Good luck this season, bud." Danton taps me on my shin guards before skating to his bench.

"You too." I skate away and thank the hockey gods my first non-video game interaction with Danton doesn't end with my obit.

The paths Danton and I took to Sweden are so far from one another it's amazing we ended up in the same place. He grew up in a small town while I grew up in the biggest city in the world. He's estranged from his father, and I'm not. He stayed healthy, and I got injured. He's

---

36 I should probably ease off the "ehs," but it seems to give me credibility in the hockey world.

signed an NHL contract, and I've signed up for the NHL Center Ice package on satellite television.

But here we both are, looking for a fresh start on the ice, a new beginning, finding refuge in the same spot. A few months later, Danton would make national news in Sweden, but not for his play on the ice. One of his teammates began convulsing during a game, choking on his own tongue. Danton was first to react and, using techniques he learned in prison, saved his teammate's life.

I spend most of the second period in a mental haze, overthinking my interaction with Danton. While not the most skilled player on the ice, Danton is the most intense, hunting down loose pucks. He must have seen those same *National Geographic* clips Coach Donato loved. It's his unpredictability that gives him an edge. I can't tell whether he's going to steamroll a defender and barrel down on goal, or pickpocket a defenseman, slyly lifting up his stick to steal the puck. For three years, Danton lived the dream of every young hockey player, myself included, when he played in the NHL. Watching him now, I see a guy pursuing that same dream once more. I see a guy willing to play in a place he probably can't locate on a map, but playing with a passion that shows everyone watching that he believes he can make it back. Through Danton I see hope.

In the third period, after receiving a pass from Jocke in the neutral zone, I hightail it down the left wing and cut to the middle hoping to confuse the defenseman and create some options. Reading the play, Ore's far side defenseman steps up on me, forcing me to make a quick dash to one side. Skating at top speed, I'm unable to fully dodge the defender's body and my left leg collides squarely with my opponent's right knee. I lift myself up relying heavily on the support of my stick and try to skate to the bench; I make it one stride before my left knee gives. The referee whistles the play dead, and my teammates help me off the ice.

The paramedics run into the locker room and help me take off my skates and shinguards, as they begin a series of pokes and prods around my knee. *Can this be happening again?* I think, flashing back to Belgium.

As I look on, desperate to understand their conversation, one of the paramedics says, "It feels like there's some damage to the MCL. I think your ACL is fine. That's the good news. But the MCL most likely has a tear. I don't know how severe. We need an MRI to determine that. Keep it iced for the next day or two. Keep the leg high, always high."

"How long? If it's what you think it is, how long until I can play again?" The two paramedics look at each other then, after exchanging a few thoughts in their native language, the one who'd been speaking to me says, "One month. Maybe less. Maybe more." I hear an unusually loud roar from the crowd. I hobble out and crack open the door. Players and coaches on both benches are going ballistic. Röös seems especially outraged at the refs who either missed a bad call or perhaps stole his last whiskey nip. Maybe both.

My eye is then drawn to the on-ice play. One of the twins, like a human missile, tracks down an Ore player, the same Ore defenseman who took out my knee. I'm too far away to make out the face, but I can tell by the way he has the Ore player in his crosshairs that this is no ordinary attempt to finish a check but retribution for knocking me out of the game. I can finally make out the face—it's Jocke. Fueled by revenge and possibly nicotine deprivation, Jocke sails in at full speed, but the Ore defender slips to the side at the last moment. Apparently when I was helped off the ice, no one bothered to ensure the gate was properly latched, and Jocke's momentum carries him head first through the boards, clear off the ice. The referee blows his whistle as a buzz of curses and shouts fills the arena, and I hobble back to the locker room.

Not every day a guy runs through the boards for me. I lift my leg back on the bench, place an ice pack on my knee, and sit alone with my thoughts.

When the final buzzer sounds and my teammates file back into the locker room, many of them voice their concern and offer me a few pats on the back, and words of encouragement.

Most teams have a tradition after victories that involves presenting something—a hard hat, an axe, a puck—to a player who contributed in some exceptional way that game. "Boys," says our captain, Marcus. "Tonight, one guy in here showed *stora bollar*." Marcus grabs his crotch. "He took a hit and got back up, and you could tell he wanted to come back. Because of this, *Tomte* goes to Billy." Marcus walks to my stall and hands me a small wooden gnome that has a white beard and pointy hat.

"What's *Tomte*?" I ask Anders as I inspect the gnome.

"It's a very old figure in Swedish folk stories. *Tomte* protects those who believe in it from all bad things."

Tomas walks by my stall and taps me on the shin pad. "In my office when you're showered."

I finish undressing, stagger into the shower, then after channeling the mythological power of *Tomte* by rubbing his stomach and stroking his beard, I place him above my stall, hoping this isn't the last opportunity I'll have to receive the honor.

Tomas sits as his desk, turning slowly from side to side in his swivel chair. Next to him stands Henry Nordlund, one of the team managers, clicking the top of a pen. Tomas slowly raises his hand to his mouth and jams a snus into his upper lip. "Take a seat, Bill," he says. "How's the knee feel?" Something's not right—this is the first time he's called me Bill since he picked me up at the train station

"I don't think it's too serious. The paramedics said it should be fine. Nothing serious," I plead as if my repetition will aid the healing process.

Henry and Tomas turn to each other, their faces serious as they exchange words too quietly and too Swedish for me to understand.

"I'm going to be fine—good to play in a couple weeks. I know the rehab for this injury."

Tomas swivels his chair back facing me and leans forward, tapping his desk.

"That's good. Well, Henry and I have talked. We like you, as a player and a person. We want you to stay the year here in Lindesberg."

I try to remain cool and fight off a smile, but it's impossible. "Fucking awesome! This is where I want to be. My knee should be fine in a couple weeks. I can't wait to get the regular season started."

"Fucking awesome, indeed. We have the contract here for you to sign. Next week, you will move into an apartment. Linus and Richard will be living in the same complex, one building down from you. Take a look at the papers here. It has our agreement for your salary and apartment we provide. We can translate whatever you don't understand, but maybe it's good practice for your Swedish." I go over the contract with Tomas and Henry and rip the paper with the pen when I sign it.

"Going to miss living in the cabin?" Tomas asks leaning back in his chair.

"I think I'll survive."

"One more thing, Fuckface. There's something I need from you that's not written in your contract."

"What's that?"

"You must agree to be my caddy. First time I shot in '70s was when you were on my bag. What do you say?"

"Once winter starts, I'd be happy to."

*　*　*

After moving into my new apartment—and when I say new, I mean new; nobody has ever lived there, which means I'll be secure in knowing that every bit of dirt or dust is my doing—I get the MRI, which reveals a partially torn MCL—four to six weeks of rehab before I can start skating. Luckily, our preseason is long so I'll be back on the ice right around opening night.

While the rest of the team practices, I receive treatment for my knee and then ride the stationary bike in the workout room. It's painful, but it's a good pain because it's a finite pain that's being properly treated. No ambivalent trainers, no hypnotherapists, no voodoo, just sane, logical, intelligent rehabilitation.

One afternoon, as I'm spinning my wheels on the stationary bike, I see Tomas tiptoe into the locker room, peeking over his shoulder to make certain he isn't being watched. He rummages into each player's stall and digs into their pants pockets.

"Hey Coach!" I yell. "Looking for something?"

"Fuckface," he says with a start. "I didn't see you there. How's the knee?" He continues rifling through pockets.

"Better every day—couple more weeks and I'll . . . *what the fuck are you doing?*"

"Yes! Found some." Tomas pulls out a tin of snus from someone's pants. "Now I can go coach."

After forty-five minutes, as I'm just about to break a sweat on the bike, Danny enters to reload his snus before the second half of practice. "Fuck sakes! Can't Tomas just buy his own for once?"

The rehab goes as planned, and I'm ready to play with the addition of a new knee brace. Two days before I make my regular season debut at the home opener against our big rival, Arboga, a knockout reporter shows up at a practice and interviews me. After fixing my hair in the bathroom for ten minutes and doing thirty-seven push-ups (one set, no rest) in the shower, I return to my stall with a towel around my waist and wait to chat with her. Before she can ask her first question, Jocke grabs me by the elbow and whispers, "Stir pot."

I shake him off. "What the hell are you talking about?"

"Stir pot. Talk big. Make trouble. We need fans in seats. Also, get a haircut. It looks like shit."

"I don't know . . ."

"Just do it. That's what you Americans say, just do it, right?"

"Sure, Jocke. I'll stir pot."

"So, William," says the reporter as I tense every muscle in my upper body. "You make your debut against Arboga. What do you know about the rivalry, if anything?"

"As far as the Arboga team, I don't know much. But I know when the wind blows from the North, the stench from the paper mills in Arboga is enough to make you want to stay indoors. The city center must smell like a toilet most days, so I'm sure the guys on Arboga are excited to make the trip here to Lindesberg and get some fresh air."

"What do you know about their players?"

"Nothing, but if I were a betting man, I'd say none of them will ever get a whiff of Allsvenskan."[37]

"Whiff?"

"A smell."

"They won't smell the Allsvenskan league? You speak a lot about smells."

Something's clearly lost in translation. "Forget it. Don't print the stuff about Allsvenskan. Just say I think the town smells like shit."

After the reporter leaves, Jocke gives me a thumbs-up on my interview and a thumbs-down on my effort to hit on the reporter afterwards.

* * *

The sound of a shovel scraping concrete wakes me on game day. I look out the window and the town is painted white with snow. It's September. Summer's over. Apparently so is autumn.

In the locker room prior to the game, as I sip on a cup of Röös's freshly brewed jet fuel, he shoos me into the coaches' room, where Tomas sits in his chair staring at a piece of paper, a baffled look plastered on his face. "Shithead, why does your Swedish hockey federation transfer card say your name is William Keenan? You been lying to us about your name this whole time?"

"No, Coach, that's me. William Shithead Keenan."

"Fuck off, Fuckface . . ."

Jocke pops his head into the office. "Why you tell Fuckface to fuck off?"

"Because his fucking name is William," says Tomas.

"I thought it was Bill," says Jocke.

"Me too. But look at this." Tomas throws my paperwork at Jocke.

"Guys, Bill is short for William." They give me matching blank stares. "Like a nickname." Nothing. "You know, like how you guys call Marcus, Mackan, or Tomas, Tompa. And that kid Bobby Steen, Jocke's friend, his real name is Robert."

37　Second league in Sweden, the one just above us.

Jocke shakes his head. "His parents named him after Bobby Orr. His real name is Bobby. He's Bobby Lindberg Steen. I've seen the papers."

I think, *That's pretty damn cool*, then continue: "Okay, you know Bill Clinton, or Bill Gates, the computer guy, right?"

"Bill Clinton? The blowjob guy, right?" says Jocke.

"Exactly. Well, his real name is William."

"I know one Bill who is definitely *not* getting any blowjobs," says Jocke flicking his head at me as he shares a chuckle with Tomas who slaps his hand on his desk.

"Oh, Shithead. You're a funny guy with this nonsense. Whatever you say." He then says something in Swedish to Jocke, and they both crack up.

"I didn't catch that, Coach," I say.

"Was not for you to catch, William."

As the opening faceoff approaches, the scene in front of the locker room mirror is hectic. Guys scramble to find the right gel and/or wax combo to fix their hair for the introductions, because it's essential that your coif is just so and you look perfect for the debut. The vying for space in front of the mirror is fierce, as is the competition for hair spray. At one point, I swear I see bobby pins being inserted into some long blond locks. As Richard Flodin plugs in the blow dryer, I see a small spark flash at the outlet and I quickly eye the fire extinguisher as hair spray molecules begin to outnumber oxygen molecules. I sample nearly every bottle and canister of hair product before I finally settle on a style which, naturally, looks like I put minimal to no effort towards sculpting. Sami Martikainen, the Finn whose salad looks like it was last cut with gardening shears and whose face looks like it was chiseled by a blind stonemason, scrambles around most likely looking for something to buzz his hair off.

As I exit the bathroom, gasping for fresh air, I take a moment to admire my hair in the nearby mirror until I feel a slap on my ass. It's Tomas.

"Fuck me, Fuckface. You better go into the bathroom and fix your hair before the introductions. Hurry up! Only have a couple minutes to fix it so it doesn't look like so much shit."

"Actually got a haircut the other day—my first one in Sweden."

"Oh really? How was it, Shithead?" Tomas asks with a smirk like he knows something I don't.

"I don't think my head shape works well with the way the people cut hair here." I rub my hand over my greasy mop before carefully pulling my jersey on. "I will say though, the woman cutting my hair was hot. A little old, definitely past her prime, but I'd still do it."

"She's my wife, Fuckface." And for the first time, I warrant the name.

Before the game, each member of the team is introduced individually over the PA and skates out to center ice to a song of his choice. When my name is announced—Bill, not William—I skate slowly eyeing Tomas, who's singing along to "The Boys are Back in Town," as he rocks out on the air guitar. Röös follows suit banging the glass with both hands. Seconds later, my thunder is stolen by Richard Flodin, who skates out to "Ice, Ice, Baby."

On my line's second shift of the game, now with a good sweat going, a harsh, metallic taste fills my mouth. An Arboga player skates out of his zone and as I hustle after him, my eyes begin to burn. By the time I'm back on defense, I can barely keep them open; it feels like there are wasps in my pupils. The puck keeps finding its way to my point man and without the ability to see, I flail around. I can barely distinguish between my teammates and my opponents. Colors blur together. I remember those books I used to read in elementary school teaching us students the importance of seeing things from another person's perspective, and for the first time ever, I see things from a referee's vantage point.

Thankfully, the actual ref blows his whistle a few seconds later, stopping the play as the puck deflects into the stands. I rush to the bench, where I furiously squirt water on my face and wipe my eyes with a clean towel.

That is the last time I use a gel/spray/wax/mousse combination.

With the game still scoreless going into the third period, Daniel Wallen, known by all and sundry as Wally, skates through every Arboga player, before deking out the goalie and giving us the lead. Wally, an unassuming guy off the ice, has been with Lindlöven for the past five seasons, leading the team in scoring each year. He's a quiet, humble guy and makes the game looks so easy. He darts through defenders as if guided by an invisible GPS. He has what Pierre McGuire would describe as "terrific puck distribution skills," meaning he's a good passer. Sitting on the bench watching Wally, I often find myself thinking, *Jeez, why don't I make moves like that? Or that? Or that?* While professional, he possesses an indifference that I'm convinced contributes to his success. Some games, he's virtually unstoppable once he gains control of the puck, almost like Jeremy Roenick in *NHL 94*.

From the puck drop, I'm the primary target of Arboga's cheap shot artists of which there are a few; clearly, my analysis of their city's air quality didn't go unnoticed. I adhere to the philosophy of "initiate, don't retaliate," because refs always miss the first cheap shot and penalize the second. In that spirit, I perform vasectomies on two Arboga players, leaving them infertile and pissed, which results in two Arboga penalties for roughing. Thankfully, this is European hockey, which means I won't get jumped and dismantled by three guys on my following shift.

In the second period, I'm reminded once again (not like I need it) as to the miserable existence referees have, as I sit on the bench screaming at the refs along with the rest of my teammates, "That was offside, fuck! Wake up, Stripes! Make the call!" I yell with conviction, like I saw the play up close on instant replay nine times. Did I actually see the play? No, but since when does that matter? I was too busy with my head buried, trying to wipe the saliva off my pants from an errant spit I made. But, upon hearing my teammates verbally lashing out at the ref (albeit in Swedish), I'm compelled to join.

With under five minutes remaining in the game, Danny makes a good play in the defensive zone, then sends me an even better pass, as I linger at the far blue line, cherry picking behind the Arboga defenseman. Suddenly, here I am, in my favorite place in the world: The breakaway. Deke, deke, deke, *boom*, goalie is rattled, Bill celebrates awkwardly, game over.

As we sit in the locker room enjoying the postgame high, it dawns on me that although winning feels awesome, there's more to it than that. Watching the Arboga players pass by in the hall, with their heads hung, I know the awful, dejected scene that will consume their locker room in a matter of moments. As good as winning feels, the horrible feeling of losing is more intense. Part of enjoying winning has to do with knowing you've avoided that feeling of losing.

Feels good to get that off my chest.

The win against Arboga ignites a streak in which we win seven of our next ten games. The first of those victories is in the lovely city of Borlänge. (If I said anything ill about their air quality, or lack thereof, it would be a fib.)

As the bus crosses the rolling hills of the Swedish countryside on our way to Borlänge, guys begin shuffling to the back of the bus. "Come check this out, Billy," Anders says as he strolls down the aisle towards the group of players huddled around a laptop.

"I've seen all the Forsberg highlight videos nineteen times. I'm good."

"It's not Foppa. It's video of a defenseman on Borlänge." Intrigued mainly because I didn't realize people put together highlight packages of players in this league, I walk back to check out the video.

"What's this shit? Where're the highlights?" I ask gazing at some video of a poker game.

"This is it. There he is," says Anders pointing to a guy wearing a black hat, dark glasses, and not a hint of transparency on his face.

"That's the Borlänge guy?"

"Yes. Well, he started the season on Djurgården but quit because they wouldn't let him play in any more live tournaments. One of the best poker players in Sweden."

"Djurgården? The guy quit his team in the Elite League? The hell is wrong with him? That's one step from the NHL."

"Guess he doesn't care. He makes more money playing poker." Anders shrugs as the bus comes to a stop outside the Borlänge rink.

Each game always has a main sponsor, which often is one of the city's local supermarkets. At Borlänge, Hemköp is the game's sponsor, and the player who scores the game's first goal is presented with a grocery bag jammed with a smorgasbord of goodies—a bag that's presented on the ice, immediately after the goal. I tip in a shot by Marcus, so I'm the lucky winner. (It's not the Conn Smythe Trophy, but it'll do.) I accept my bag at the scorer's table. A surge of excitement rushes through me as I realize I won't have to buy dinner for the next week. In the bottom of the bag, I find a bottle of chocolate syrup. Because I'm an immature douche, I detour to the Borlänge bench, pop the top of the bottle, take a swig, and give them a chocolate-eating grin.

"Hey, you stupid fuck," I hear a Borlänge player say in perfect English as he glides by the bench, his head directing my attention to the referees on the other side of the rink.

While I was acting like a dickhead, the referees were huddling on the other side of the rink and after a lengthy discussion decide I interfered with the goaltender, thus disallowing my goal.

I feel obligated as a forward to go on a quick rant at this point on the kid-glove treatment given goalies. Goalies wear more equipment than anybody on the ice; they even have a buffer zone known as the crease, a blue colored area that designates their territory. Yet, should a player go as far as spraying a light coat of ice on a goalie, mayhem inevitably ensues. Defensemen treat their goaltenders like they're goddamn helpless wheelchair-bound grandmothers. And the worst part is, goalies play right into it. My first experience with this behavior came as an eight-year-old on the Connecticut Yankees with none other than Jonny Quick.

ME (as Jonny writhes around in his crease in apparent pain): Jonny, you okay? Coach Backman is coming. Don't worry.
JONNY (still writhing around): Yeah, dumbass. I'm fine. Move out of the way so the refs can see.
ME: Okay. But where's it hurt? He stick you in the balls?
JONNY (still writhing and adding some screams to the mix): Nah, the cocksmack barely touched me.

REFEREE (in background signaling five-minute major for spearing the goalie)

ME: The cocksmack got five minutes.

JONNY (returning to his feet): Man, I'm good at this shit. Now you guys better fuckin' score. I did my part. Now put one in the net. My girl is here and I can't lose!

As I'm licking my chocolate lips and Röös is rifling through the bag in search of whiskey, a linesman taps me on the shoulder, breaks the news, and tells me to return the groceries.

Two minutes later, a Borlänge player scores, grabs the bag, skates to our bench, and hurls the bottle of syrup at my head.

"American pussy," he calls me skating towards our bench.

"*Jävla svenska jävlar.* Wait, *Jävla . . .*" The Borlänge player comes to a complete stop. I've never been great at the verbal sparring. My best comebacks usually come six hours too late when I'm lying in bed after the game.

"Not bad Swedish, asshole. You're still a pussy though."

On the bench as I spit for no reason, Anders slides next to me. "Buddy, I hear you try to learn Swedish, but I help with the important stuff. *Sug min kuk*," he says slowly. "That's what you need to tell the guy. Try it."

"Soog meen kook," I say. "That right? So suck my cock is soog meen kook?"

"You got it. Still sounds kind of shit but you practice."

The game goes to a shootout and Ragge scores three consecutive times. He celebrates the game-winning shot with a leap onto the bench. Röös joins the pileup then proceeds to douse us all with his reserve bottle of whiskey. After the game, I tell Ragge and Chara how excited I am to see one of them show some visible signs of happiness. Then, finally comfortable enough with them to ask a meaningful question, I say, "Why are you guys always so serious?"

"Billy, we're from Latvia," Chara says. "No one smiles there."

"Yes, no smiling. This is normal."

The next evening, Anders drags Richard, Linus, and me to a Lindesberg women's volleyball game. My thinking on the way to the arena: *Who the hell wants to watch Swedish women's volleyball?* My thinking at the arena: *I wonder if they have a fan club I can join.* The game itself isn't particularly inspiring but the teams' uniforms are, tight in all the right places. Number 16 on Lindesberg stands out from the rest; she looks like she was born to wear the volleyball uni. She's the type of girl I'd kiss even if she'd just gotten over the flu and had dirty hands.

I elbow Anders. "I like that 16 girl. Maybe I should go down there after the game and ask for her autograph. Or phone number, even." I consider a potential pickup line where I weave in that my jersey number is 16 too, but decide to keep that club in the bag.

"If you want her autograph, come to my place later."

"Oh yeah? You got her lined up for tonight?"

"Lined up?"

"Are you getting in there?"

"She's my girlfriend."

After practice on the day before our Halloween matchup against Falun, I follow Ragge and Chara to their apartment, where Ragge takes it upon himself to cook lunch. I'm so appreciative of his hospitality and the delicious meal that I choose not to say anything about his outfit: A white fitted T-shirt tucked into tight, tight red track pants. The tight, tight red track pants are tucked into high, white athletic socks that have double black stripes. The outfit is complete with his Adidas sandals.

"Thanks guys. Smells great," I say as Ragge serves the grilled chicken and mashed potatoes.

"Yes, this is normal. It has good smell," Ragge says.

"You guys have to come by my place and let me make you lunch some time."

"We do that, Billy Boy," Chara says, shoveling food in his mouth. Ragge switches on the TV and surfs to a KHL game.

"How bout that guy, number 14. Unreal moves," I say.

"Latvian guy, Billy. Grew up with me and Ragge. Rangers take him in NHL draft," says Chara.

"You ever watch these guys you grew up with who get drafted, like this number 14, and make it to the KHL or NHL and wonder how the hell they got there? I mean, those guys you know from when you were a kid and think why aren't I in his position? Why is he the guy making millions playing hockey?"

"No, Billy," Ragge says.

"Ragge, you never look at guys you know who didn't really work all that hard but still made it and think what did he do to deserve it?"

"Billy, it's not always about what you do. This is life," Chara says. "Parents in Latvia teach us three things when we are childs. One," Chara says holding up his index finger, "working hard always wins. Two," he continues raising his middle finger, "luck always wins."

"How's that work? You can't have them both win," I say. "That doesn't make sense."

"That's number three," Ragge says. "No sense. This is it. You go maximum, then see what happens." Chara nods his head as I lean back in my seat.

"And this number 14." Chara points at the television screen as he chews on his chicken. "Vlady is his name. Good guy. Works very hard. We skated on pond with him every winter. You learn to skate on pond when you were boy?" Chara asks.

"Didn't really have ponds. I tried making our living room at home kind of into one—"

"Pond in living room, Billy? Make ice in home?" Chara asks.

"Tried," I say.

"This is not normal," Ragge says.

A loud shriek pierces my eardrums.

"Jesus, what the hell was that?" I say. "Sounds like someone needs some help."

Still staring at the game, Ragge says, "That is Röös. It's normal. Every day like that. He watch the cartoons in his apartment below us."

"Cartoons?"

Chara taps his head and says, "I don't think Röös has much up here." Chara then taps the left side of his chest, "Lots here, but not much up here." Ragge nods in agreement and walks to the kitchen.

"You guys like playing here?" I ask as Ragge returns to his seat on the couch with a glass in his hand.

"We have home," Chara says spreading his arms wide and looking around the apartment, "and we have hockey. It's good."

"Good for one season," says Ragge. "But I want to move up to maximum level."

"Hard to let go of the dream," I say.

Ragge holds up his glass and takes a sip, smacking his lips like a guy in a commercial. "What do you see, Billy?" Ragge says pointing to his glass.

"Your glass?"

"No." Ragge holds his glass higher and points at it with his other hand's index finger.

"I got you." I perch up in my seat. "Perspective. Your glass—half-full."

Ragge smiles and takes another swig. "Not how much, Billy. What do you see?"

"A glass—your glass of water."

Ragge extends his outstretched arm slowly towards my face, glass in hand.

"Holy fuck."

"This is my Latvian vodka, Billy. Make Russian vodka look like baby juice."

* * *

A four-hour bus ride away, Falun is the perfect place for the Halloween night game—it really is a ghost town whose dark, deserted streets provide the perfect setting for a horror film. A large church spire at the city's border is barely visible through the haze, and I'm certain that behind it lies a cemetery with vampires and ghosts.

In the locker room at Falun's arena, Lugnets Hall, I take a seat next to Anders. "You live on the same floor as the Latvians, right? You ever hear Röös screaming at the TV?"

"Every day. When I first moved in, I thought he hurt himself. I rushed downstairs to see what was going on and there he was, sitting in his chair two feet from the television, yelling at his cartoons."

"He's got passion."

"You must look next time Röös hands you coffee. His right hand, it's missing two fingers. Last winter, he was walking home piss drunk and passed out on the sidewalk. Someone found him not long after and rushed him to the hospital. They had to chop off some of his fingers."

"Must've gotten frostbite."

"Yes, frostbite. And doctors said if he had been out there only one hour longer, he might have died."

"Thank God somebody found him. He seems to be a big part of this organization."

"He's been going to Lindehov as far back as anyone can remember." Right on cue, Röös stomps up and raises his hand at me. I give him a high three although I'm not sure that's what he's looking for.

"Anyway," Anders says, "crazy odds tonight—4–37. I have this month's paycheck on the line."

Gambling is a big part of the sports culture in Europe. In Germany while watching *Bundesliga* soccer games on television, viewers will see scores on the top right corner of the screen and real-time odds flash on the top left corner. In the Finnish top hockey league, *SM-Liiga*, not only can you bet on the teams but you can also bet on each team's leading scorer who wears the "Golden Helmet." Even more shocking is that the "Golden Helmet" sponsor is *Veikkaus Oy*, the Finnish national betting agency which is owned by the Finnish government and managed by the Finnish Ministry of Education. At Lindehov, the betting culture persists—the center faceoff circle is painted not with our team's logo but rather the logo of *Svenska Spel*, a state-owned Swedish gambling company. If Lindlöven management relied on gate receipts as the sole revenue stream, we might not have enough money to maintain our laundry machine that never works.

Tonight both Lindlöven's record and Anders's bank account take a hit from the game as we fall to Falun 3–1. But for me, the night isn't a complete loss, as I perform a good deed. In the second period, after taking a slashing penalty—one of their guys elbows me above the eye, which leads to butterfly stitches, so nobody will argue he didn't deserve it—I find myself in the visiting team's penalty box. After calling the ref a few choice names in English, Swedish, German, Dutch, Hebrew, and Sanskrit, somebody calls me from the scorer's box: "Keenan, I must ask you something, please."

"Number 16. *Sexton*," I say turning the back of my jersey to him.

"I know, I know. You've already been in here twice today. It's something else," he says before pausing and putting a hand to his chin. "You played junior hockey in US? Junior league for players who want to go to university on scholarship?"

"Yeah. The Eastern Junior Hockey League. A lot of guys end up playing at East Coast colleges on scholarships."

"My son, he's sixteen years old. His dream is to play university hockey in United States. Have you any information on how he could get there?"

I see Falun putting more and more pressure on our penalty kill. "Tell you what," I say, "shave five seconds off my penalty, and I'll give you my junior coach's email address, and I'll put in a good word about your son." The guy doesn't hesitate. He passes me his pen and a small piece of paper. I jot down The Lizard's email address. "I'll message him tomorrow and give him a heads up, then you write him next week." I can already see The Lizard's response to my email: *"Who the fuck is this Swiss guy emailing me? Is the kid good or not?"*

So I return to the game five seconds sooner than expected. With Falun up 2–1 and with one minute remaining, we pull our goalie. Our defenseman dumps the puck into Falun's end, where their goalie, instead of placing the puck back on the ice and sweeping it to the corner or to one of his defensemen, decides to hold his glove up, drop the puck, and punt it with his leg pad over every player on the ice, all the way down to our zone. On the bench, we watch in awe as the puck soars over everyone's head then trickles past the goal line. If I didn't think my teammates would throttle me, I'd give the guy a standing ovation. I settle for a nod to the keeper in the handshake line.

After the four-hour bus ride home, I unpack my sweaty gear at the rink before heading back to the apartment, and hopping in the shower around 3:00 a.m. Home showers are twenty minutes, minimum, and entail a meticulous routine which ensures every inch of my body is scrubbed.[38] But before I dispense some soap on my loofah, the butterflies over my eye fall off, and blood drips across my face and down the drain, a la *Psycho*. It doesn't stop, so I decide to make the short walk to the hospital.

The emergency room is locked.

I squint at the sign which is in size three font: DOOR LOCKED AFTER 21:00. RING BELL FOR ADMITTANCE.

After a four-minute hunt, I find the doorbell, which I jab three, five, ten times. A tall man wearing blue rubber gloves opens the door and sneers at me. As he sews me up wearing the same gloves he used to open the door (I sure hope he's the doctor), he asks, "Stick or puck?"

"Elbow. How'd you know I play?"

"The smell. How you liking Lindesberg?"

"Struggling a little right now on the ice."

"I've heard. Know any Swedish?"

"*Sug min kuk*. Learned that on the bench a few days ago."

"That's an important one to tell referees. And girls." He clips the stitches and pulls off his rubber gloves. "Tomas teach you that?"

"You know him?"

He sits on the chair beside me and removes the stethoscope from his neck. "Grew up together. He was a superstar on the ice—had it all: Speed, shot, skills. NHL caliber."

"You know what type of shoulder injury he had that ended his career?"

"It was no injury that kept him from NHL."

---

38   You can read about the details of my shower routine in my next book, *Odd Man Bathes*.

"He told me he hurt his shoulder at camp one year and never recovered."

"Maybe so, but he stopped playing because of his daughter. She was born right when the NHL wanted him, but there were many complications with her." He rises and tosses his gloves in the trash. "She had problem like Röös, but more serious. Tomas didn't want to leave her behind or take her away from his family here."

"I thought it was some injury that got in the way."

"No injury. It was life."

I thank the doctor who hands me some ointment to apply every few hours to the wound. We shake hands and he walks me out.

"Thanks for stitching me up." I look in the vanity mirror. "Almost look like a real hockey player now."

He nods and opens the door. "Start playing like one."

CHAPTER ELEVEN

Odd Man Crushed

THEY TAKE YOUR pants before they send you home. It's pretty simple. You show up to the locker room and your hockey pants aren't hanging in your stall. That's how you know you've been traded or cut.

By the end of November, with our record below .500, Linus's pants are missing from his stall when we stroll into practice the day before a game against Arboga. Next stop for him is Piteå, a team in northern Sweden where a new set of hockey pants waits.

Three hours prior to the opening faceoff, Marcus Sjöö calls a meeting to discuss how we can break out of our slump. He speaks in his native tongue, and he speaks quickly, so I lead a meeting with myself.

After a promising start to the season, I've since started sucking. Players will try about anything to get out of a slump—extra shooting before practice, extra conditioning after practice, extra video sessions, extra booze—it varies. I decide to hit the local grocery store and stock up on red gummy bears. As for the coaches, in an attempt to spark some offense, Tomas has tinkered with all the lines, as frustrated coaches often do, e.g., he split up the twins, much to their dismay.

The game against Arboga also marks the debut of Lindlöven's sixteen-year-old defenseman Gustav Backström who at 6'3", 215 pounds, is a man among boys. (For that matter, he's a man among men.) Gustav plays well and doesn't back down from anyone, which is impressive considering that a handful of Arboga players are old enough to be his father. He has NHL potential and his spirited effort plays a large role in our victory. As a defenseman, Gustav's no threat to take my spot on the team, but I can relate to those he is a threat to. Every player knows there's a small window in time where one is at his peak, and now looking at Gustav, I'm starting to feel old.

The 4–2 victory is much needed and bolsters our confidence.

After the game, Andreas, one of our young defenseman who has the type of hair you can't teach, invites Richard and me to drive into Örebro with him to celebrate at Strömpis nightclub. Once in Örebro, we hit the Mickey D's, and that's when I see her.

As the girl behind the register takes my order, I fall helplessly in love with her. I want to tell her this—tell her anything so she'll remember me. But I don't have the words. She moves and speaks with confidence and poise—no pretense, no self-consciousness. My eyes search for a McDonald's job application. After handing me my happy meal, I scribble down my name and number on the receipt, check it's correct, decide against dotting my "i" with a heart, and slide it to her. Four years later, in a desperate and baroque yet heartfelt gesture, I'll still remember the way her tilted nametag was pinned to her white T-shirt, and eventually find a way to jam her in my book despite it adding nothing to the narrative.

I'm still waiting to hear from you, Caroline.

Reality resumes when we finish our meal and walk to the club. I try to dodge the wind with its ever-shifting direction from dismantling my hairdo by doing the sideways carioca, while the same wind gusts play with Richard and Andreas's hair like they're in a *GQ* photo shoot. Outside the nightclub, to avoid further decimation to my tossed salad, I approach the bouncer, tell him I'm an American tourist in Örebro for the night, I've heard great things about the club, I'm hoping he can let me and my friends inside, and blah blah blah, bullshit bullshit bullshit.

He's not impressed, but I can see it attracting the attention of a group of girls in the line and they're able to get us in.

Once they ditch us, we order drinks and circle the dance floor. When I look around, all I can think is, *man, someone should really talk to these girls.*

In what must be an attempt to stand out or look American, many of the blonde girls have dyed their hair dark brown, or red, or black. Despite the dark hair with blonde roots, their faces are stunning. The cheerleader effect is where girls look attractive as a group but not individually. Here, collectively they're attractive and individually they're gorgeous.

Andreas, who knows every girl in the place, is mobbed by admirers. He pulls off the wink without looking like he needs Clear Eyes. I take notes. Girl after girl hugs him and blushes, and even a few guys who sport unusually tight shirts and scarves wrapped around their necks receive hugs. Caught up in the scene, I barely refrain from draping my arms around him too. I don't know why, but he is completely non-threatening to girls despite his large build and seems abnormally at ease around them. His ability with females is downright Datsyukian. He possesses that rare quality where he can make just about anything look cool, even something like riding a Segway with wrist guards, knee pads, and a GoPro strapped to his helmet—he'd make that look cool as shit. As Richard and I follow him through the waves of girls, Richard nudges me in the stomach. "Look at the group of hotties over there," he says motioning with his head towards a table in the back.

"Where? I just see a couple Asian-looking girls."

"Yep," Richard responds, flicking the strand of golden hair out of his face only to have it fall right back over his right eye. "Love that shit. Let's go talk to them."

"We're surrounded by tens, and you want to go after the Joy Luck Club?"

"Great movie. You don't like the Orientals? That's racist, Billy."

"I have no choice in the matter. This is unconscious shit. I wish I was attracted to them—would've made my time at Harvard a lot more fun." Richard shakes his head in bewilderment. "It's like sports—take Derek Jeter. It's not like he chose to be an unreal baseball player. It's just one of those things he was born with—a love of the game. Not like he could explain why he wanted to play baseball over some other sport."

"Derek who?" Richard asks.

"Jeter." Richard stares at me. "Hall of Fame shortstop. Plays on the Yankees—the team whose hat you wear every day."

"Is he Oriental too?"

"No, you don't get what I'm saying."

"Yeah, I do. You're racist."

"And you're an asshat."

"Your loss. Time to get my yellow belt." He struts away, leaving me alone to nurse my beer and scan the rest of the scene. "Hi . . . *tjena* . . . hi there . . . hey . . . *hej*," I say spinning in circles as groups of girls waltz by me. I feel like one of those guys who stands outside MSG trying to hand out "End of the World" fliers.

I retreat to the bathroom for a hair check and solo pep talk. The bathroom attendant, perched on a stool, shakes his head. I shrug, drop a 50 krona bill in his jar, and he fist bumps me.

I return and notice a familiar face in the crowd: It's the girl who rings me up at the grocery store Hemköp. Erika, a former classmate of Andreas, is twenty-one with perfect features and long blonde hair which falls over her right eye, hiding it like a secret, making it hard for me to look anywhere else lest I miss a chance to see the rest of her face. I know that description sucks, but you see where I'm going with it.

I nudge Andreas, who approaches Erika and her friends. I watch as he engages them in conversation before waving me over to a table where we all sit down. He's like a miracle worker. Now *he* should write a book.

Erika and I exchange smiles as she pokes at the ice in her mixed drink with a tiny straw. Andreas kicks me twice on my shin under the table.

"You work at Hemköp, right?" I say.

"I do." She inches closer. She smells like lavender. I hope she can't smell my hockey hands or desperation. "You buy lots of groceries. I see you there almost every day." I'd been slow playing it for a couple months, trying to build some anticipation. We'd had a couple conversations while she was working: One time she told me my total was 167 krona and another time it was 282 krona.

"Yeah, well, with hockey, I need to make sure I stay fueled." Every time I was in Hemköp it was like a scene out of *Supermarket Sweep* with me flying around the aisles except instead of looking for groceries, I was looking for Erika.

"You ride?" I point to the horse keychain dangling from her purse.

"It's my passion. I have a horse in my barn; my mother has one too." I listen as she talks about her horses, pretending the entire time that I haven't seen all three horse riding albums she has on her Facebook profile.

"I can't believe you're from New York City. There must be so many funny things to do there," she says. (Yeah, the Swedes have some trouble with fun/funny, but can you blame them? It makes sense if you think about it). "What's it like? In which part do you live?"

I tell her all about it—the celebrities I never see, the clubs I can't get into, and of course, my three great roommates (although I leave out the fact that their names are Mom, Dad, and Lil). Now that is "funny" in any sense of the word.

Periodically, Erika's friends come over and they converse in Swedish, sneaking looks at me as they sport that type of smile where it seems like they know something I don't. But I don't care, as I gawk in awe at these girls who, for some reason I can't yet grasp, appear intrigued by me. I feel as giddy as Pierre McGuire surrounded by all four Staal brothers. Even more shocking, I'm near certain all of Erika's friends are named Elin.

Erika's beauty is enhanced by the melodious Swedish language. The subtle intonations and lilt lure me in like a siren song in which one can only tell the truth. Her voice is as soft as snow. Also, her skirt is short and as much as I try to focus on her words, her legs garner a good chunk of my attention. I don't want the night to end.

"I'm so embarrassed at my English." Erika brings her hands to her face. "It's so bad. I'm sorry." I imagine if the situation was reversed and I met Erika in the US, would I be embarrassed and apologize because I couldn't speak Swedish perfectly? Probably not, and I definitely wouldn't be able to articulate my feelings to her in Swedish the way she's able to in English. .

As our faces get closer, I smell a familiar minty scent. Thankfully, it's her wintergreen-flavored gum. As she reaches down to lay her hand on my leg, she pops her head up.

"What's this?" She pats my leg.

"Well . . ."

"Do you use snus?"

"Oh!" I remove the pink *Catch* tin from my pocket. "When we were standing in line, I saw a girl take this out of her purse. She was about my little sister's age, and I felt like I should intervene. I convinced her to give me the tin—promised me she'd quit for good."

"How sweet." She leans in and I feel her breath, warm against my neck. "I don't even care you're lying."

Andreas tears himself away from the quartet of Elins he's entertaining and whispers, "How's it going?"

"Great, but listen, she's not related to any of the coaches or general managers, is she?"

"No. You're good to go, buddy."

The waitress brings us the check and I hand her my credit card.

"Can I give you some cash?" Erika rummages through her purse as I sign yet another autograph on the bill.

"I'd prefer a personal check."

"I'm afraid I don't have any."

"I was kidding. I can pay for your drinks."

She removes a few bills from her purse. "That's not how it works in Sweden," she says slipping the money and her fingers into my hand. I don't want to let go.

As the remixes of the Robyn songs grow louder, she smiles and I want to know why. She taps her lips gently with her index finger and flashes her sharp, blue eyes at me. She hesitates then leans in towards me. Her hair grazes my ear and shoulder, and I feel the warmth of her mouth against the nape of my neck. Her lips tickle my ear. "I have a secret to tell you."

She tells me—our secret.

She pulls back, looking for my reaction—her eyes at once innocent and mischievous. "I didn't hear you," I say. She smiles and leans forward again, placing her hand on my thigh. Her soft, sleek hair brushes by my face, its scent intoxicating. Her lips, soft and cool, deliver the secret again.

I heard her the first time.

* * *

By the middle of December, Erika and I are inseparable, and my improvement in Swedish directly correlates with the increasing time she's at my apartment. She tolerates my speaking Swenglish on the contingency that I shave my new moustache which is understandable, since I'm a pair of transition lenses away from having Chris Hansen pop out of a closet and offer me a seat and glass of lemonade.

I ask her to teach me how to drive a stick shift. Because it takes five sessions and ten hours for me to figure it out, I'm able to have plenty of face-to-face time with her. She feels bad that as the teacher, it takes her so long to help me master the skill. I feel bad too since Dad taught me how to drive manual when I was seventeen.

One of the best things about Erika is that I don't have to play those games I do with other girls—no spending six-and-a-half hours working on a two-line text, saving it to drafts, then waiting three business days to send it, hoping like hell that the poorly constructed joke lands and she replies "hhahaahaha." Considering I can't figure out how to save messages to drafts on my Swedish flip phone, the point is moot.

And then there's the emoticon. Prior to my arrival in Sweden, I don't think I ever used or received a text with any form of emoticon, let alone in a text from a new boss. I can't see Coach Donato using one in a text message to me.

DONUTS: Willy, hope you have a nice suit and tie combo picked out for Friday cause you ain't fuckin' playing LOL ;)
ME: ,,!,,

However, in my time thus far in Sweden, I've become familiar with the full spectrum of smiley faces that are common in text messages here. Erika and I even have full conversations via text in which only emoticons are used even though half the time, I have no clue what the hell I'm sending.

ERIKA: :(
ME: :-*
ERIKA: :-X
ME: :o)
ERIKA: I-)
ME: :()
ERIKA: ????

I revamp my apartment with candles, a "Välkommen" doormat, and new window shades courtesy of the Latvians. It now feels like a home. All those hours of watching *Queer Eye for the Straight Guy* weren't for naught.

As the weeks go by, I see more of Erika's belongings in my apartment—an extra pillow in my bed, a new cooking pan in the kitchen, and a large bottle of hairspray (we share it) in the bathroom. I could be wrong, but considering that's never the case, I think I'm on the verge of something new to me: Commitment. I never really liked playing house with my sisters when I was a kid, but now, I could get used to it.

There's a Swedish word, *sambo*, which is a condensed form of a longer word (*sammanboende*) that means "living together." It's common in Sweden for a couple to have a *sambo* as opposed to an official marriage. It's a partnership that needs no fancy rings or formal ceremonies. And it seems to work—Erika's parents have had a *sambo* for over thirty years. Erika and I have only about thirty days together so far, and I don't know what our future is. But I do know that I'm excited for another thirty days with her.

After an off weekend, I track down Blom, our equipment manager, and ask to borrow the keys to the rink.

"But, it's Sunday, off day. Tomas said not to let you or the Latvian guys on the ice."

"I know, Blom, but this isn't for hockey. I want to do something for this girl I like."

Blom gives me a goofy grin, revealing a couple snus pouches tucked under his top lip. "Swedish girl got the American guy in love, huh?"

"Yeah, Blom, and I don't want to fuck this up so please give me the keys. I'll give 'em back tomorrow . . . with a bottle of whiskey."

"Make it Jack Daniel's. Love that American stuff you show me." He removes the ring of keys from his belt loop and hands me the rink key. "We have important games coming up. Need your legs so not so much funny business with her," he says slamming his right fist into his left palm.

That night, I sneak Erika into the rink and give her a skating lesson, and then we have a picnic at center ice. And despite barely knowing how to cook *Janssons Frestelse* properly, let alone say it correctly, Erika enjoys the meal.

"I want you to come to Christmas at my house this year," she says, clutching my hand tightly as we skate slowly around the rink. "My mom makes the best *julbord*—Christmas dinner with all types of food. And *jultomten* might have a present for you this year," she says.

"You think your parents would be okay with that?"

"They'll love you. And you'll love Christmas with us. We take out the horses and ride them through the trails." We glide towards the bench and take a seat, right where I'd be sitting after a shift in a game shouting at referee. Erika removes her mittens and places her hands in mine. "For someone who's never skated before, you're pretty good," I say.

"I need to confess . . . my dad was a hockey player here with Lindlöven, just like you. I used to skate all the time."

"Why didn't you tell me?"

She pauses. "Remember how long it took me to learn you to drive the manual? You knew how, but I didn't care. You think you have good game with the girls," she says smiling, "but I know those tricks."

"I promise I already know my game sucks."

"Well, I like your sucky game." She squeezes my hands tighter and kisses me. "When you were talking about me visiting you in New York after the season? Do you mean that?"

"Of course."

"It would be a dream to be with you in the world's greatest city."

"I love home, and it'd be great to have you come, but sometimes, it seems like everyone in Sweden thinks New York is some fantasy world. I've seen as many American flags flying outside people's houses as Swedish flags and half the guys on my team wear New York Yankee hats every day but don't know what baseball is. New York is just some dream land to them."

"But isn't that what this place is to you?"

"What?"

"You know Pippi Longstocking? It's a Swedish story from the start. *Pippi Långstrump*, the girl who doesn't want to grow up. Isn't that how you feel here? You come to a new country and play hockey and do what you want. Your life here is your dream. For us Swedes, it's our reality."

"I think I see your point, but it's a little different. I'm actually here, living here. Most of these guys haven't been to New York to see that it's just another city."

"I guess we all need to have dreams, though, don't we?"

The lights in the rink dim, and the Dave Matthews Band song "Crash" starts playing over the loudspeaker. I look towards the Zamboni entrance and catch a glimpse of Blom darting out the back door. Erika and I return to our skates and skate slowly, lap after lap.

Until then, I thought scoring a goal was the best feeling I'd have on ice.

The fun I'm having with Erika seems to have an inverse effect on Lindlöven's success. Our offense has fluctuated between god-awful and dogshit, while our goaltending woes are a huge concern. In four months, the team has had six netminders see playing time. From what I recall, one abandoned his promising hockey career to take an offer as a Versace model, another quit the game to focus on a career at his father's bakery, and a third got called up to the Swedish Elite League.

At our most recent game, when the PA guy prepared to announce the winner of the "Guess the Attendance" contest, I didn't have to wait for him to reveal the number. Sitting on the bench, I'd been able to tally the number myself: 174, including the entire mite team who'd been at the rink since their practice ended that afternoon. At one point, they tried to start the wave, but it was more of a gentle swell. Even the little redheaded kid who's had a broken leg for three months (or at least has had it in a cast that long) doesn't come into the locker room after games looking for autographs and stealing our white tape.

The morning after the team holiday party—during which Röös puts on a riveting vocal display that could've earned him a trip to the second round of the current *Swedish Idol*—it dawns on me how at home I feel in Lindesberg. Despite having a recent slump, things on the ice are starting to click better, and off the ice, Negative Game has vanished. I sometimes think what life would be like if I decided to start a life here, play for Lindlöven, and get serious with a girl for the first time.

With Christmas a few days away, I'm feeling in the holiday spirit. I'm excited to get some ideas from the guys on what I can get Erika. Maybe there's some traditional Swedish gift that she'll like, or maybe it's best to get her a gift certificate at a clothing store like I do with my sisters—can't get that size wrong. For the first time in a long time, things are going great for me on *and* off the ice.

Monday afternoon, I arrive early at practice, excited to ask the guys if they can help me lure out my inner ladies' man. I'm the first one at the rink, jonesed up for the day.

When I get to my stall, my pants are gone.

CHAPTER TWELVE

All Swedish, No Finish

"HAVE A SEAT, Bill," our general manager Henry says as I trudge into his office. I try to peak across the table at the papers Henry thumbs through.

"Today is the transfer deadline, and I've had to make some tough decisions. We've spoken with your agent. I don't know if he talked to you yet, but we've traded you to Kramfors."

My stomach sinks.

"It wasn't easy," Henry continues. "We like you here, but we have been given a good deal."

"I understand . . . I mean . . . I'm disappointed to end my time here . . . but I realize it's a business . . . I wish I could have been more productive." I wait for him to say something, but he doesn't. "Who'd I get traded for?" I ask as if I'd know the Kramfors player who's taking my spot.

"Technically, it was no trade. It was a transfer. We received a sum of money in exchange."

I take a deep breath as the door creaks open, revealing an unfamiliar face. Henry and the man have a brief exchange before the door closes again. "Kramfors have given us money for your train ticket there, so you can schedule that when you want. We wish you luck up there."

I shake Henry's hand. "I appreciate the opportunity here."

"Yes. And please leave all team gear in your locker."

When I exit the office, I see the man who had been speaking with Henry setting up a new washing machine and blender.

The locker room is empty. I can hear Tomas blow his whistle on the ice and Röös losing it because someone missed the net. I take a seat in my stall. The team had been struggling and changes were bound to be made. The writing had been on the wall, but I guess it was in Swedish and I couldn't read it.

As disappointing as it is to be sold, it feels good to be bought by another team regardless of how many electrical appliances I'm valued at. After packing all my gear—stuffing as many Lindlöven sweatshirts, shorts, and mugs into my bag as possible—I send the family an email and think about how I'll break the news to Erika on my way back to the apartment.

But I can't think too much because, after practice, nearly half the players on the team come to my apartment to say goodbye.

"Billy, you promise us you come to Riga some time," Chara says. "We show you famous Pussy Lounge Club."

"I promise, guys," I say knowing that probably won't happen, not because I don't want to but because life will inevitably get in the way.

"Billy," Ragge says hesitating as he looks at his feet then back at me. "I have question. You broke stick in practice the other day. May I keep?"

"Sure. But I don't think it's usable."

"Bottom part is good. My friend have son back home who can use. So this is okay if I keep?"

"Definitely, Ragge."

Shortly after the Latvians leave, Tomas arrives with Röös.

"I asked you to do two things—give me everything you have on the ice, and never shit on the bus. You did both and I want to thank—"

"The Boys are Back in Town" starts playing on his phone. He reaches in his pocket and silences it. "I want to thank you for that. I told Henry and management I wanted you here, but I don't make these decisions with the money." Tomas turns to Röös. "Now Röös has something he wants to say." Tomas taps Röös on the back.

"G-G-G-Good l-l-l-luck," says Röös.

As they leave my apartment, Tomas turns around. "And Fuckface, one more thing. I want to see you after the season for some golf. I'll need a caddy this summer."

That night Erika cooks one last dinner for the two of us. "Think there's enough room in your suitcase for me?"

"I wish." Her smile morphs into a pout, then the pout morphs into tears. It's shocking to think that somebody who isn't a blood relative likes me enough to cry at my departure. A small part of me can't help but wonder, *what's wrong with her?* "I'll call you when I get there. It's really not too far and once the season is over, we can meet up."

"This isn't so easy for me, Bill."

"Me neither." Although I suspect it'll be easier for me. I know myself, and I'm well aware that I'll be busy trying to fit in with my new team. "I'll miss you a lot," I say holding her close.

"Why'd it take you so long to talk to me?"

"It's not easy trying to start a conversation with a girl that looks like you."

"I hate that guys always say that. Just come up and be funny. It's so simple."

"Do you have any idea how hard that is? I wish I'd said something earlier though."

"I may be a small town girl, but I'm not stupid. I knew this day would come."

As she nestles her head under my arm, I feel another tear of hers drop on my chest. She may have seen this day coming, but I hadn't.

I stare at the ceiling as my eyes adjust to the darkness and think about what Erika meant when she told me about Pippi Longstocking. Maybe she's right. Sometimes I feel like it's not a reality I'm living in. The game requires an unrelenting, alienating self-absorption. Or maybe that's just how I see it. When was the last time I called home and the conversation didn't revolve around me and hockey? It's like

I'm on this delusional journey and all these people around me are extras, these places just pit stops. Is this just another memory for me to tuck away, never to return to? How long can I go with my life only concerned about myself?

The next morning, Erika drives me to the train station. We ride mostly in silence, the type that precedes long separations, exchanging forced smiles every few minutes. She grips my two fingers with her fist, squeezing harder as our time grows short. Her nails dig gently into my skin, communicating more than any words either of us could say.

At the station, people shuffle on and off the train. "This isn't goodbye," I whisper in her ear as she clutches me tight to her body. We kiss one last time, and I taste the salt of her tears.

The conductor pops his head out, instructing me to board. "I'll see you soon. I promise." Parallel streams of tears inch down her soft, flushed cheeks.

I haven't seen her since.

When I board the train, I can feel the town slipping away. I wonder what else is slipping away too.

* * *

On the train, I whip out my latest book, *Liar's Poker,* and once settled in, I lose myself in Michael Lewis's story of Lewis Ranieri raking in a fortune by focusing on mortgage bonds in the early '80s. The book reaffirms my confidence in deciding to nickname Oleg, Mother Russia and not Junk Bond.

Ranieri's instincts are similar to that of a clutch goal scorer. Broadcasters refer to it as the "scorer's touch," and like Ranieri, goal scorers' prowess comes from developing instincts of where and when to cash in.

It's rarely the players involved in the mad scramble around the net who put the puck past the goalie. Being opportunistic has a luck component, but there's so much more to it. Goal scorers understand the game and may appear to be doing nothing at times, when in fact they're carefully calculating where to be when the puck squirts free. Sometimes, it's not about chasing the puck all over the place if you want to score, but rather patiently waiting for the play to come to you.

I finish the book and as I stuff it in my bag, I notice a small white box with a blue ribbon on it. Attached to the outside is a folded note: *"Dear Bill, Don't forget me. Love, Erika."*

Removing the ribbon, I open the box. Inside is a plastic baggy filled with red gummy bears. I reach underneath the bag and find a snow globe: Inside is a little boy holding a hockey stick, standing on a pond. I hold the snow globe in the palm of my hand. It's like the boy's staring up at me, smiling. Then, almost as if someone else is controlling my hand, I gently shake it and the little player disappears amidst the large, white snowflakes. I close my palm and drift to sleep.

A brief time later, my cell phone's buzzing against my right leg wakes me. I open up the new text message which reads: "Hello Bill! Welcome to Kramfors :) Hope you have good trip here. Look forward to having you on the team. Regards / Niklas."

Ah, the emoticon.

I rifle through my backpack, in search of the paper Henry had given me with all the information about my new team. I scroll down the list of names and identify the texter as Niklas Gulliksson, the team manager of Kramfors, then read some of the history he's provided. I'm guessing Niklas used the same extensive research methods to obtain this info as I used to get me through college.[39]

Kramfors, located in Sweden's Norrland, lies just south of Örnsköldsvik in the shadow of Swedish hockey's most storied franchise, MODO. With a population of just under 30,000, Ö-vik, as the natives call it (or Onskoikdliskdcivk as Americans call it) is the birthplace of hockey stars Peter Forsberg, the Sedin twins, Markus Näslund, and Victor Hedman, among others. There really must be something in the Ö-vik water; I hope Kramfors receives its water from the same source.

Now when I was a kid, I thought there was some correlation between how far north you were and how good the hockey was.

---

39 Wikipedia.

Buffalo was better than New York City, Toronto was better than Buffalo, Calgary was better than Toronto, and so forth. According to that theory, I should be surrounded by a bunch of Sidney Crosbys in Kramfors, but clearly that theory, I know now, is stupid.

Pressing my forehead against the window, I can tell it's cold up here, like really cold, so cold that offering a numerical degree won't do the temperature justice.

There's exactly one person waiting at the train station. He's about my height, with a much thicker build, wearing a backward-facing baseball hat. The patch of facial hair on his chin makes him look like any one of my former Harvard teammates. He's dressed in shower sandals with socks and board shorts, and the only reason he hasn't frozen to death is that he's wearing a thick hoodie. He stomps the ground as I see him working on a wad of gum. We exchange head nods as I depart the train and he helps me carry my bags to a white utility van which is plastered with ads for *Micke's Måleri*, a painting company that I suspect is the team's primary sponsor and benefactor.

After slinging my bags into the back, I hop in the passenger side door. Before closing the door, I spit, watching the small bit of saliva turn into hail before hitting the ground.

Candy wrappers, old scratch lotto tickets, McDonald's French fry cartons, and a few empty energy drinks litter the floorboard of my seat. We introduce ourselves as my new teammate, Dean, scrapes the fresh layer of snow off the windshield then saddles in the driver's seat and blasts the heat.

Born in the hockey hotbed of Tampa, Florida, Dean played in the same junior league (the EJ) as me, just a few years later. He moved away from home at sixteen to pursue the game at a higher level and, after three years of juniors, he made the jump directly to pro hockey. He spent the past two seasons bouncing around the minor league hockey circuits in the US and decided he wanted to explore options in Europe, landing in Kramfors a couple months ago.

"So Harvard, huh?" he says as we drive down the two-lane road lined with massive evergreens on both sides.

"Yeah."

"What's it like there? People sitting around reading dictionaries and shit?"

"Pretty much. How you like it here?"

"You go to school with that guy who invented—"

"Nah, he dropped out the year before I came. So how is it up here?"

Dean swigs of a large plastic bottle then swipes his hand across his mouth. "Their version of Gatorade blows. Try this shit." He hands me the drink. "Way too sugary, huh?"

"This is syrup." I sniff it then examine the label. "You should mix this with water."

"That makes more sense." I hand it back to him then he takes another gulp of the cherry syrup before switching on the radio. "How 'bout their language too? Goddamn nightmare trying to figure out what they're saying."

"Not easy," I respond, especially considering the guy on the radio is speaking Finnish. "How's the living situation?"

"It's nice, I'd say, pretty nice. They put us up at the hotel—me, a forward from Stockholm, our coach, and you. We get all our meals free there. Team has some hookup with them. All got our own rooms, nothing fancy but people clean 'em once a week, give us fresh towels, even leave those mini shampoo and conditioners for us. No lotion though." Dean turns up the speed of the windshield wipers as the snow falls in blankets. "As far as the town, they got all the nature stuff—mountains, lakes, shit like that." Dean lifts his index finger off the steering wheel, pointing at a small red church that stands in front of the towering pine and birch trees that occupy much of the land that's at once rugged and serene. "They also got a lot of Africans up here, like legit off the boat—you'll see 'em walking through town in a herd, women bouncing groceries on their heads. Sometimes you see 'em crammed—five or six of 'em—in a two-seater. Called the Somalia Express. No clue what the hell they're doing up here . . . How 'bout that movie that just came out, uh, *Social Network*. That shit true? Like those rich guys trying to steal Facebook from that nerd?"

"Not sure. How 'bout the girls here?"

"Broads here are ridiculous. I fell in love like six times at the airport. The Mickey D's—like a goddamn runway show behind the counter. Plus, they're not like the girls back in Florida who think they live in some rom-com."

"Same deal with the Golden Arches where I was playing before."

"Actually was wheeling this dime last night at the club, this chick who works at the McDonald's in Sundsvall."

"How'd it end up?"

"I put my time in—probably like an hour talking about her fuckin' dog . . . she's showing me her blog on her phone and all sorts of stupid shit. So right when I try to get her to come back with me, she starts quizzing me on a bunch of crap."

"Like what?"

"Where she's from . . . her name, her dog's name. I mean, at that point what's the difference, right? I can tell you one thing, I knew the important shit like the color of her panties."

"So what happened?"

"Screwed up her name. I guessed 'Elin.' Figured I had like a 50 percent chance. Turned out she's got a sister named Elin."

"So what was her name?"

"No clue. But you should've heard how she talked—'there must be so many funny things to do in Florida'—not a clue what 'funny' means."

Erika used the word "funny" in the same way. I found it endearing.

"Dumb as shit!" Dean continues. "So once what's-her-name bailed, the cops started ushering people home. Goddamn cops were two rockets—thought about punching the guy next to me just so they'd take me in, but they love Americans so much, I probably would've had to kill someone to get their attention."

"Yeah, they love the American card. It's like everyone thinks the US is the answer to all their dreams."

"They haven't seen the shithole towns near Tampa—ain't all Disney World, tell you that much. Shit, this one guy last night congratulated me, like shook my hand and said 'congratulations' when he found out I was American." Dean swerves into the left lane to pass the only other car I've seen since we left. "Anyway, there's this one girl or woman I guess—first rounder, just unfuckinreal. Saw her last night too. Her kid plays on one of the youth teams here. If you Google Imaged 'Swedish blonde hottie,' her picture would pop up, yeah, she's a smoke. You'll know her when you see her around. She's always got a red jacket on."

He then offers to give me the grand tour of the downtown area, which entails driving down one street and back up a parallel street; it lasts two minutes. Aside from a mother pulling her child on a sled along the snow-covered sidewalk, no one is outside. There are two shopping marts; the state-owned liquor monopoly *Systembolaget*; three pizza/kebab restaurants; a tanning salon in which the black lights outnumber the employees five to zero; two clothing stores with "Everything 50% off" signs in the windows; and four hair salons.

I also see the white lights and greenery dangling from the lamp-posts lining the streets, remnants of the Swedish celebration Santa Lucia. A wave of undefined feeling breaks over me. My first grade teacher, Ms. Rhodie, led our class in an assembly where my nineteen male classmates and I dressed in the traditional Santa Lucia garb and marched around the halls singing. How would my six-year-old self feel if he knew then where he'd be seventeen years later? Dean notices me gaze at the decorations. "They had some big celebration, like pre-Christmas shit without the presents. Everyone dresses up in white gowns and pointy hats—like the KKK—kinda fucked up."

Our home, Hotell Kramm, lies at the edge of the city, across from the train tracks and main highway, the only road that leads to the south. Dean parks outside the lobby entrance in a spot designated for fire department parking only.

"I think that sign says this is just for fire trucks," I say.

"Nah, man. It's cool. I got it covered." Dean taps the front dash-board. After grabbing my luggage, I peer through the front window and see a piece of paper on the dash barely visible now as the snow-flakes accumulate quickly. On it, in large black sharpie is the following: "Dean Moore #9, Kramfors Hockey."

We take the elevator to the fourth floor (the top floor) and make our way to my room which is directly across the hall from Dean's. Johan, a forward from Stockholm, lives one room down from me, and our coach, Peter, who's currently back home in Östersund for the Christmas break, lives across from Johan.

"We got a kitchen in there." Dean points to a door halfway down the hall as we continue down the narrow hall. "And nice thing is there hasn't been anyone else checked into a room on this floor since I've been here. That's like three months."

Room 434 at the Hotell Kramm—home sweet home.

Before flicking on the light, I smell the antiseptic scent of a freshly cleaned bathroom. Sure enough, the bathroom is sparkling with three, freshly-laundered white towels hanging on a heated rack. The water in the toilet is aquamarine, and on the sink are the mini-shampoo and conditioner bottles as well as a shower cap.

Entering the room, I see a wooden desk with a chair tucked underneath. My bed, although small, has crisp, white sheets with hospital corners.

I open the curtains and take in the view: one stoplight, railroad tracks, and a burger joint that has a guy peeing behind it. The backdrop, however, is breathtaking with evergreens and snow-laden fields as far as the eye can see—like a screensaver you'd have to pay for.

"Peter's not here for a couple days," Dean says barging in my room, "but a bunch of guys are going down to the rink to get a skate in, if you wanna join. We'll probably do a few warmup drills then scrimmage."

"I'm in."

"How's the hockey here?" I ask as Dean unplugs the van from the electrical device that ensures the car will start.

"It's a shitload different than back in the States. Can't understand what the fuck the coach says half the time."

"How 'bout the competition?"

"Lotsa skilled guys up here, but players on the other teams are brutal chirpers. They speak English pretty good, but they got one line: 'Fuckin' kook.' I must hear that shit ten times a game when a guy gets in my face. Calling me a 'kook' ain't exactly news to me. They want to see some real kooks, they should see some of the guys I played with in the Coast." I nod and smile. "Played with this one nutjob, Turnstile Tony, in South Carolina. Guy couldn't cross over to the left, but he absolutely speedbagged the toughest guys in that league. Now, *he* was a kook."

"Any good places to eat?"

"The food—pizza is brutal here, just awful. Can't get a slice any-where; ask for pepperoni and they give you green peppers. Bernaise sauce on it all the time." Dean has a point. The pizza sucks and nearly every restaurant only offers pizza pies, which are as close to being cir-cular as the shape kindergarteners make when gathering around for story time. "As far as the team goes . . . whatever you do, don't put your skates on the rack to be sharpened on Saturdays, even if we've got a game that day. The equipment guy, he's a boozebag."

"Comes in hungover or what?"

"The guy's still drunk. I just change to my extra set of blades, because I don't want him to fuck up my sharpening or to sharpen his arm, or leg, or whatever."

Pulling up to the parking lot of Latbergshallen, Dean yanks the emergency brake as we come to a skidding halt in front of the large red structure. The glare of the sun on the snowdrifts blinds me temporarily as I exit the car, heaving my hockey bag on my shoulder. I follow Dean in through the back entrance.

The rink is brightly lit, with wooden stands. In the rafters hang two retired jerseys and three championship banners.

Dean occupies the first stall near the door; I take the empty one directly to his left and glance around the crowded, buzzy room, almost relieved that my presence seems to go unnoticed. As I unpack my bag, Dean gives me a rundown on each of the guys. Adrian, a defenseman who sits on the opposite side of me, looks so similar to Anders from Lindlöven that at one point when we make eye contact, I half expect him to start talking about his volleyball-playing girlfriend. To my left sits Matty Dahlberg, who reminds me of Danny, in part because of the hunk of snus parked in his upper lip. As we get to know each other while getting changed into our gear, I learn that Matty has a twin brother who plays on a team in the south of Sweden. I also take note of the automatic coffee machine that stands on the opposite side of the locker room; I know it won't compare to Röös's brew.

Leaning back in my stall after lacing my right skate, I scan the locker room. It's like déjà vu, like I've already been here. It's this familiarity with everything—the characters, the humor, the smell—this sameness that is tied up and perpetuates the pursuit of my dream. But sometimes I feel I'm stuck—like being in this environment, surrounded by my teammates playing the game we love, is the only way to feel good about myself. The personalities are preserved in time—like a play where the characters and story will live on but the actors will inevitably be replaced. I know eventually whether I want to or not my time will be up, and it won't be the general manager who takes my pants from my stall but rather the hockey gods.

Just as I expect, practice is like all the other first practices I've had with new teams. I play hard but not too hard so as to call attention to myself.

After practice, I see one of my teammates struggling to remove his shoulder pads. A heavyset guy with blond scruff, wearing a tool belt, glasses, and pencil tucked behind his ear waddles in. He speaks briefly with the player who tries unsuccessfully to lift his arm then the two disappear through a door on the farside of the locker room.

"That's the equipment guy," Dean says removing his socks and wrapping his towel around his waist. "Remember, don't give him your skates on Saturdays." Moments later, a howling sound comes from the room where the injured player and equipment guy just entered. On his way to the showers, Dean turns back to me, pointing a finger towards the other room. "Almost forgot. Don't get hurt here either."

I slowly remove the rest of my equipment being extra careful not to inadvertently injure myself, then head into the shower.

The steam-filled room smells like Old Spice body wash. It's not that the guys on the team spend half their waking (and possibly sleeping) hours in the tanning salon; it's the ultra-skinny, identical tan lines they all have that gives me pause. Before I can spend too much time staring at the sea of wet, naked guys, I hear Dean's voice, "The hell happened to your back?"

"Had some trouble in college."

"Fuckin' injuries, man. I broke my arm last season. Out two months—just brutal. Thing clicks all the time." He bends his wrist back and forth. "Tell you one thing, it better not happen again or I'm fucked. I can't afford to have a bad season or I'll be back home working at the fuckin' GNC, you know what I mean?" I nod but wonder whether I would have been a better hockey player or would my dream have died long ago had Dean's reality been mine. "Or maybe I'll just get a job flipping burgers at McDonald's here with all the blondes." He smiles. "Dude, check it out." He holds up his body wash and reads the label. "Douche gel. Gotta love this place." He works it into a lather. "Little heel curve, like a Modano." He twirls his dick clockwise. "Chicks here love it."

I take a few steps back, and as much as I try not to acknowledge it, Dean's right: I used the Modano heel curve in college.

"Whatever that meat is they serve us at the hotel, reindeer or some shit, stuff goes right through me," Dean says. "I gotta drop the Cosbys off at the pool. I'll meet you in the car in like twenty mins. Get the heat pumping. Want it like a furnace when I get in there. You can turn the tunes on but dude—" he pauses before rubbing his towel aggressively between his ass cheeks, "don't mess with my bass settings."

We keep the same daily practice routine through the end of the week. Johan Chang, the other hotel dweller, and I make quick friends. Johan, a twenty-seven-year-old forward from Stockholm, has a Swedish mother and his father is half-Chinese and half-Italian. Stocky and wide, Johan has a prototypical hockey butt and legs which accounts for his waddling gait. He has spent some time in the second highest Swedish league, Allsvenskan and, most recently, played in the top French league. Between his family background and hockey travels, he knows Italian, French, and a little Chinese, in addition to being fluent in Swedish and English.

* * *

"Merry Christmas, bitch." Dean barges through my door, his toothbrush lodged in the side of his mouth.

"Heard of knocking?" I close my laptop.

"Wanted to make sure you didn't kill yourself stranglebaiting. My bad." He sits at the foot of my bed and rummages through some papers as he brushes his teeth. "Belgium . . . Germany part one . . . Juniors . . . What is this shit?"

"Want to rifle through my underwear drawer too?"

"Don't have to. Your shit is still in your suitcase." He puts the papers down and switches on my television. "Blohan's at the grocery store getting food. Said he's gonna make us a Swedish Christmas dinner. Probably gonna have the shits all night but figured when in Sweden."

"Great, now go take the toothbrush tour back to your room."

Crammed in the fourth floor hotel kitchen, Johan, Dean, and I set up a makeshift table complete with the desk chairs from each of our rooms. Johan slips on an oven mitt and serves up a meal of herring, crayfish, potato balls, and lingon-berries.

"Try this too." Johan retrieves a long blue tube from the refrigerator labeled Kalle's Kaviar. "Hope you boys enjoy. Close as I could get to the Swedish *julbord*."

"What's this white shit?" Dean pokes at his food with a plastic fork.

"Grilled herring," says Johan. "It's Swedish tradition on Christmas."

"We got a tradition in Tampa too that says eat pizza if the food smells like ass. No offense Blohan, but this ain't my thing." Dean stands up, removes a pizza from the freezer, and puts it in the microwave.

"More for me." Johan scrapes Dean's food onto his plate and places a paper napkin on his lap. "Saw your Red Jacket girl on my way to Hemköp."

"Oh yeah?" Dean spins around.

"I think she was on her way to file restraining order against you." Dean shakes his head and removes his pizza from the microwave.

"You ever talk to her?" I ask Dean.

"Haven't gotten the chance, but I'm telling you, every time I pass her in town or at the rink, she smiles at me, like intentional shit."

"I guess there's hope," I say.

"So one night with Red Jacket or a full week with the counter girl at McDonald's in Sundsvall?" asks Johan.

"One night with Red Jacket."

"Okay. One night with Red Jacket or a full month with the counter girl at Mickey D's plus that other blonde who's always wiping down the tables?" I ask.

"RJ," says Dean without hesitation. I would've hesitated.

"You really have some issues, buddy," says Johan.

"You guys don't realize how good you got it here, Blohan." Dean turns to me. "Dude, you should see our coach's daughter. I hope they got that take your daughter to work thing here. She visited once like a month ago. She's a ten, Billy."

"She *is* ten, you sick bastard," says Johan shoveling crayfish covered in lingon-berries into his mouth.

"It's a projection, assbag. She's a ten-in-training. Seriously though, back when I was playing in the States, we were surrounded by broncos."

"Like the horses?" asks Johan.

"Nah. Broncos like the car. Broads there were like some beat-up Bronco you'd scoop up at a fire sale, take off-roading for the weekend when you're hammered, then ditch on Sunday."

"As much fun as it is talking about ten-year-olds and Ford Broncos, is there something to do after we're done eating that involves other people?"

"Club in town called Gladan," says Dean finishing his last bite of pizza. "But first, I gotta shower. We smell like dead fish dicks."

After we're all cleaned and changed, we hit Gladan, where Johan and Dean introduce me to the bouncer, a big hockey fan who ushers us to the front of the line and lets us in gratis.

"If you have any computer problems, that dude'll help. He's the manager at the electronics place, *Expert*. I think he also moonlights at this restaurant a couple miles away. It's boring as shit here. People like to keep busy," Dean says as we walk down the winding staircase.

"Hope there's some mistletoe down here," I say as we enter the underground club.

"Sounds good," Dean says. "You keep an eye out for the mistletoe, and I'll be on the prowl for camel toe."

Downstairs, I strike up a conversation with an excited Kramfors hockey groupie—tall, blond, skinny, everything a lonely newcomer could hope for. Unfortunately, his name is Lars; fortunately, there's no mistletoe. After ten minutes of him bombarding me with questions, I excuse myself. As I see Dean pounding his fist at the blackjack table in the corner, I decide to park it the bar, where I strike up a conversation with one of the bartenders. She serves me drink after drink and soon I fade into oblivion.

Stumbling to the bathroom finally away from the strobe light and steamy dancefloor, I'm dumbfounded and wonder if in my drunken stupor, I'm seeing an illusion. No sopping wet floor, no pee all over the seat, no nasty paper towels littered all over the floor. If I didn't know any better, this could be my own bathroom at home. I try to maintain my balance as I elevate my right leg to lift up the toilet seat. I stand there wobbling, my underpants around my ankles, taking aim. Hockey coaches always preach character—what you do when no one's looking, that's how you're defined. You can tell a lot about a place by the way the bathroom is maintained. Maybe it's socialism or maybe it's just a courtesy that is second nature to the Swedes, but it's a nice change to see a public restroom, at a nightclub to boot, kept spotless.

I wake up the next morning on the floor next to my bed, naked. My sheets are a tangled mess. I call out, "Hello?" Nobody answers. The room is empty.

I scour the room for signs of what happened last night: nothing on the floor by the bed, nothing in the bed, nothing in the toilet. Opening the shower curtain, I find an earring and a shoe that's not mine. My head is pounding and my mouth is dry.

I stumble across the hall to Dean's room which is propped open.

"Got any gum?" I ask as Dean lies in his bed, his computer resting on his chest.

"Should be a pile on the desk over there." He points across the room, his eyes fixed on his computer screen.

Despite having an empty dresser, Dean's clothes are folded in his open suitcase with a laundry bag next to it. It's the same way I keep my wardrobe, a way of making things feel temporary, so that at any moment we could get the call we're wanted by a new team, at a higher level, one step closer.

In the back, Dean has set up his own hockey equipment storage unit complete with seven new sticks, some extra skate blades, two new visors, and a few tubs of protein powder. Next to his bed is a box of tissues and two poker magazines.

I walk to his desk and see a pile of small square pieces of gum. I pop in three, start chewing to get saliva back in my mouth, then inspect his huge flat screen TV. "She's a beaut, huh?" Dean tilts his computer screen down. "That dude from Gladan who works at the electronic store—I hook him up with tickets to our games and he lets me use this while I'm here."

"Good deal," I say.

"How'd your night turn out?"

"Okay. I think."

"You think?"

"Last thing I remember is that bartender telling me about the tattoo that wrapped around her waist to her lower back—something to do with a tribute to her grandma. Didn't quite understand."

"Yeah, you were bundled, huh? Shoulda mixed in a water at the end. Sorry about your bathroom by the way. Bartender was a fuckin' nut. Grandma probably was too back in her day. Not sure why we ended up in there but whatever."

"We got a lift today?"

"Nah."

"Why you wearing team warmups and have your workout bag hanging on the door handle?"

"The chick wouldn't leave this morning so I had to put on a whole dog and pony show. Really had to sell it—said we had a mandatory practice this morning, got all dressed up. Then she said she wanted to watch practice so I had to change it and say we had a team meeting. Even had to walk down with her and get in the van. Took me five minutes to open the door 'cause the lock was frozen shut."

"I'm guessing she liked the Modano then?"

"Yeah. Handled it pretty good." Dean cups his crotch and smiles. "Heard from a couple guys on the team that she likes to go Nordic style. You coulda joined us but you were tits up in your bed when we got back."

"Nordic style?"

"Two cocks. Like ski poles." He makes a double jerk off motion. "By the way, that vibrator thing in your bathroom—"

"Yeah, it's my face washer. What about it?"

"Might want to wipe it down with one of those Clorox things you got all over your room or at least run it under some hot water."

"You're buying me a new one."

"I'll see if the Gladan guy can get you a deal on one. Anyway, you get the apple on my kill."

"Why's that?"

"I told the chick I went to Harvard. Barely made it through high school so I couldn't help myself. Felt good being a college grad for the night. The people here love that shit, huh? Anything about famous US shit and they go nuts."

"I hear ya."

"You know what an *au pair* is?"

"It's like a nanny."

"Yeah, this chick was saying how her dream is to go to the US and be an *au pair*. I think she meant her dream is to pull what Tiger Woods's ex-wife did."

"Where do you do your laundry? They got a machine at the hotel we can use?"

"I usually throw my boxers and socks in the laundry at the rink, but for the other shit, I go down to the basement of the hotel. They got a machine there. Door's usually locked, but I got a key. You can use it whenever. It's just in that drawer, next to my lotion."

I hear my phone ring in my room. It's Niklas Gulliksson, the team manager, summoning me to the lobby. I drag my sorry ass to the elevator, hoping I don't look as bad as I feel.

I sit next to Niklas on a couch as a hotel staff member enters through the revolving door holding a shovel and stamping his feet to remove the snow. A rush of arctic breeze bites my skin. Being outside here is like stepping into a freezer. I turn to Niklas.

He smiles. "Lucky we have only a mild winter so far. Maybe 25 at worst," he says referring to the degrees in Celsius, with the negative implicit." Let's keep fingers crossed it doesn't get bad."

After I sign what needs to be signed, making my trade to Kramfors official, Niklas hands me an envelope with "S-F-I" written on it.

"Inside is information on the Swedish for Immigrants program. I know you said you were interested in taking Swedish classes so I have talked with the teachers and we can fix you a spot in this. It's mostly refugees from Iraq, Somalia, and those places, but the class times work with our practice schedule. Fill it out if you want to go."

I open the envelope, but the letters swirl on the page as a wave of nausea suddenly hits me and another frigid wind gust swirls through the lobby. I stand up, the dizziness intensifying, and stumble to the elevator, feeling my heart pound faster.

When I reach the hockey annex on the fourth floor using the walls as support, I return to Dean's room.

"I'm struggling. Just hit me hard."

Dean, standing in front of his bathroom mirror, a towel wrapped around his waist, is playing with his right pectoral muscle. "Maybe you got Stockholm Syndrome." He pokes his head out, smiling at me. "Seriously, that's a thing. Maybe you caught it. Wasn't your last team near Stockholm?"

I lie down on his bed.

Dean struts out of the bathroom, inspects his hair in the mirror above his desk, then opens his computer, and slaps at the keyboard. "Jesus, you look like ass. Do me a favor, if you're gonna pull the trigger, do it in your room."

"After what you did in my bathroom last night, if I gotta puke, I'm doing it in here." Dean shrugs, accepting my logic.

"How many pieces of gum you have?"

"I don't know, three or four. The flavor sucks by the way." I swipe the sweat from my forehead.

"Well, it's Nicorette. I ain't chewing it for the flavor," he responds plopping onto his bed. I remove the gum from my mouth, but before

I can throw a hissy fit, there's a gentle knock on the door. "Yep, door's open," says Dean.

A large man with a large head and an even larger grin slowly enters—it's Peter, the team's coach. I sit up, feeling slightly better now as the nicotine buzz subsides, and we shake hands.

Peter looks to be in his fifties, and his large bifocals have lenses so thick they distort the size of his eyes; the screws holding the rims to the frame look moments away from popping out. His accent is thick and his English isn't perfect, but he speaks with a booming confidence, grammatical errors be damned. "My son, Tobias, he are playing in USA with team in Louisiana—the Ice Gators. He like Louisiana great. You resemble like him," he says placing a hand on my shoulder. "I'm comfortable liking you."

"Likewise."

He slaps me on the back. "Is terrific news! See you on the ice. I go unpack now."

"Dude's a trip, right?" says Dean after Peter leaves. "Sometimes he doesn't make any sense. One minute he'll tell me to rush the puck whenever I get a chance then five minutes later he pulls a complete 360 and tells me to make the outlet pass and stay back. Dumbass sometimes. Alright, man. I gotta focus on this tourney—no limit, hold 'em. Gonna be a long day."

* * *

The day before New Year's, Peter runs an intense two-hour practice, which ends with a twenty-five minute bag skate, the type that makes you question how much you love the game. I'm fried, ready to slow down, or quit, or make a Christmas dinner, but I think of Ragge's mantra—"Go maximum"—and I push on. Then Ragge's voice is replaced by one in Swedish: "*Du kan inte göra det! Sluta nu! Du orkar inte, tjockis!*" (You can't do it. Stop now. You don't have the energy, you jackass!) I call the Swedish voice a *jävla idiot* (fucking idiot), realize I'm also a *jävla idiot* for cursing at myself in Swedish, and finish the drill in maximum style.

Because I'm in new territory, I haven't had time to scout out each player's work habits to pick a corner when it comes to the bag skate. You see, on every team during bag skates, there are a few different groups. You have the go-hards (usually led by the guy who wears a heart monitor during off-ice workouts); I stay away from these guys. They go all out, all the time. If I do end up in their corner, odds are I'm so far behind these heroes that I trip on their capes. On the opposite end, there's the group that prays the Zamboni driver is about to kick the team off the ice, guys who have no clue what a heart monitor is but are familiar with all the local ice cream shops. If hockey doesn't work out for these guys, acting is a solid backup plan because their ability to pump the shit out of their arms and make it appear as though they're skating hard as a group is downright inspiring. As for me, I'm usually in one of the groups somewhere in between, seeing as I can't keep up with the go-hards and I'm not a good enough actor to join the never-go-hards.

After practice, players do a number of things: centers practice faceoffs; wingers practice receiving passes in their skates; scorers play three-bar; go-hards perform self-imposed wind sprints to impress the coaches; never-go-hards try to flick pucks into the bucket or on top of the net; and some guys get right off the ice because they want to play video games or online poker. As I survey the scene, Peter skates up to me.

"How did it feel out there?" he asks.

"Felt good. Seems like everyone has a lot of energy."

"Yes. You suck a lot."

"Pardon?"

"You suck. You do lots of sucking today." He takes deep breaths, in and out, in and out. "You suck."

"Ahhh. *Sucka* you mean?"

"Yes! *Sucka.*"

"It was a hard skate," I admit.

"I like how you look today. Look better tomorrow. How are it in Kramfors for you?"

"Been good so far. *Jag kan svenska lite om du inte vill prata engelska.*" (I can speak some Swedish if you don't want to speak English.)

"That are okay. My English need work," he says.

"I don't know, you sound okay to me."

"That's good. You help me with the English, and I will learn you some Swedish. Peel your eyeballs. Funny things happen in this city and team. They could write a book about things which happens here. Crazy sometimes." I nod as Peter watches a group of players sprinting down the ice, looking over their shoulders to see if they're being monitored. He returns his attention to me, and the group of sprinting players then darts off the ice.

"I have played once with American guy, Dino Ciccarelli. You know him? Many years on Detroit Red Wings."

"Yeah, big goal-scorer in the '90s. Tough guy."

"Yes, this is Dino Ciccarelli. He were great player." Peter whacks me on the ass with his stick. "Time for my coffee!"

I skate two wind sprints as Peter skates one final lap on the ice then shortly after he leaves the ice, I head to the locker room.

Dean's holding court by his stall, four guys with their bottom equipment and skates still on, listen closely, "So she thinks I'm turning the ringer off, but I'm snapping pics—" He reaches into the pocket of his pants that hang behind him to retrieve his phone.

Matty Dahlberg waves me over. "Buddy, come have dinner with me and my family tonight. We have a camping area where we grill sausages, take some beers, and skate on the pond with my son. You ever go camping?"

"I set up a tent in my living room once when I was five."

I accept the invite.

On the pond, as Matty and his son pass the puck back and forth, I take in the stark beauty of the vast expanse of idyllic countryside surrounding me, and I feel at ease. Iron gray clouds hang in the cobalt blue sky as if painted.

"This is awesome," I tell Matty, stickhandling through his son's legs as I stand stationary.

He nods. "*Lagom.*"

"What's that mean?"

"*Lagom är bäst.*"

"So *lagom* means best?"

"Yes. But, no. It means . . . You could say it means 'just right.'"

"You're right. This is *lagom*." I breathe in the frigid air, before Matty's son sticks me in the balls in an attempt to restart our game of pass. In the horizon, the sun plays its daily peekaboo game, as its rays glimmer off the glistening, frozen pond. I can never tell whether it's rising or setting.

*　*　*

On January 3, two days after breaking my New Year's resolution, I wake with my stomach full of butterflies, this time not a result of a Nicorette overdose.

Game day is here.

This is my fourth first game with a European team—not exactly finding a groove. Before heading to the lobby for breakfast, I open my email and see a message from Lin, the Lilliputian waitress in Neuwied. Written entirely in English, she wishes me a Happy New Year and asks when I'll be returning to Neuwied. Enclosed in the email is a picture of her wearing my Neuwied jersey that was auctioned off at the end of the season. The last time I saw someone wear a jersey of mine was a homeless guy sleeping on Fifth Avenue a couple weeks after Mom donated some old clothes to the Salvation Army. As much as I wanted to bring the Neuwied jersey home with me, it's a good feeling to see someone else proud to show it off. I can only hope her mom washed it in boiling water.

"Ready to roll?" I poke my head into Johan's room where he lies on his bed wearing a headset and playing video games with the television muted. He raises his index finger as he speaks Swedish into the headset. After another minute, he shuts off the console and tosses his headset on the desk.

"*Dags att dra*," I say.

"Getting better, buddy. Still sound like stupid Norwegian guy trying to talk Swedish but not bad."

"You playing Xbox live against little kids?" I point to the headset.

"No, no. I have part-time work, selling some shit. I make twenty calls a day, and people hang up on me. But I get paid. I forget the word in English."

"Telemarketer," I say as we head to the lobby where Dean is waiting in the van.

Two hours prior to the opening faceoff, Dean, Johan, and I arrive at the rink.

Jonas, one of the younger players, strolls into the locker room, a St. Louis Cardinals baseball hat perched on his head, turned slightly to the side in a gangsta fashion. As I fiddle with my stick, Dean taps me on my knee. "Check this out." He calls to Jonas, "Dude, how about some of those offseason moves by the Cards?"

Jonas smiles, nods, then curses Dean in Swedish calling him a *hora*[40] and *jävla tjockis*.[41]

"What's he saying to me?"

"He wants you watch a Cards game with him."

"That's cool. Good kid."

Peter walks in and posts the something on the board.

"He give you the Dino Ciccarelli bullshit yet?" Dean says as he tightens his skate laces.

"He mentioned him the other day."

"You get him going on that and cancel whatever you got planned for the rest of the day. First night I was here, I had to withdraw from a seven-card stud tourney I'd entered—lost my buy-in."

After lacing up my skates, I pass by Jonas's stall.

"Every day Dean asks about Cards. What the fuck is that?" he asks.

"The baseball team on your hat. Just ask him why the Devil Rays have sucked for the past five years."

Once dressed, guys shuffle out of the locker room to the ice surface for warmups.

"*Fan också!*" I turn around and see Johan dripping in water, two small cups on the ground. He looks at me. "Fucking Dean. Always

---

40 Whore.

41 Fuckin' fatass.

with the hidden water cups. I get him back," Johan says strapping on his helmet. "I get him back soon, Billy."

As both teams take the ice, Dean skates up behind me. "You like those little leaners I set up in Blohan's gloves? Fuckin' nailed him. Too easy." We make one loop in our zone before the zebras take the ice. "Fuck me," says Dean. "It's Skoglund. He hates us. Or maybe just hates me. Yeah, he's not a big fan of me."

Tonight, I'm on a line with Johan and Emil, our team captain. Emil, who's also built like Johan, is a bulldog on the ice, relentlessly pursuing pucks, finishing checks, and generally causing mayhem. Although not as skilled as Johan, Emil compensates with a tireless work ethic and that effort results in the first goal of the game.

Seconds before the first period ends, a slapshot by a Sollefteå defenseman gets blocked in front, leading to a scrum in which the puck takes a fortuitous bounce for the bad guys and ends up in the back of our net. Surrendering a goal in the last minute of any period is unacceptable and, to make matters worse, the initial slapshot knocks out some of Adrian's teeth.

Adrian (a.k.a. the Bizarro Anders), who's just recovered from shoulder surgery, searches furiously on the ice for his missing jibs. Thanks to some help from a useful referee—yes, a useful ref!—he tracks down two large tooth fragments. Returning to the bench with his mouth filled with blood, Adrian hands the tooth chips to the team trainer and takes a seat next to me. He curses in Swedish as he squirts water into his mouth and spits it back out onto the bench floor.

"How many you lose?" I say.

"I think one and a half," he says still trying to stop the bleeding.

"I'm sure the dentist can put those back in or maybe fit you with some new ones," I say, as if I know anything about dentistry.

"Maybe. It's just that I must go to my parents' home tomorrow for dinner." He shakes his head. "My mom, you don't know her. She's going to kill me. I lost a tooth last season and promised to wear a mouthguard from then on."

In the second period, scoring chances are hard to come by, as both teams tighten up on defense. But two minutes into the third period, I have an opportunity to make a mark.

Johan, who plays on the opposite wing from me, sends a beautiful cross-ice pass which, like a billiard shot, banks off the boards behind me before careening onto the tape of my stick. The pass leaves the Sollefteå defender who is covering me tangled in his jockstrap. As he unwinds himself and dives out in desperation, his stick clips the back of my skates, tripping me up before I'm able to get off a shot.

Skoglund the ref immediately raises his arms in an "X" formation, signifying a penalty shot, and I skate by him acknowledging his call with a few words in Swedish. As I glide to the bench to wipe off my visor, I hear someone shouting my number. Skoglund.

"Sixteen! Sixteen! Come here!" Skating to center ice, I see the ref glowering at me.

"What's up? I know the deal. I wait for your whistle then go."

"Yes. But you said something in Swedish to me?" I nod. "If you think the Swedish language is funny, keep it to yourself. Your American teammate, number 9, already causes me enough problems. If you make fun again, I give you an unsportsmanlike conduct and put your team on penalty kill!"

"But Skoglund," I plead, "I'm trying to learn the language. That's the truth. Quiz me. I'm not trying to mock you. Quiz me on something. Nothing too hard, though."

"*Hur är det,*" says Skoglund.

"That's like, 'how is it,' or 'how's it going.' Kinda informal."

"Too easy, even number 9 on your team knows that one . . . *Jag hatar alla Amerikaner som skriker åt mig under matchen.*"

"Can you say that again?"

"*Jag . . . hatar . . . alla . . . Amerikaner . . . som . . . skriker . . . åt . . . mig . . . under . . . matchen.*"

"Ah. Okay. You said, 'I hate all Americans who yell at me during the game.'"

"Correct. Got it?"

"Got it."

As he skates backwards and blows his whistle, I focus on the task at hand. Picking the puck up on my backhand and sliding it to my forehand, I become aware of the weight of my equipment. The seconds grow longer the closer I skate to the goal. I can see the headline in Swedish, '*Keenan Visar Vägen*,' (or would it be '*Visade?*'). *Jesus, who gives a shit? What's wrong with me?* I throw a series of head and shoulder fakes, hoping to force the goalie to make the first move. I hone in on his every twitch, gathering information and processing it. Just as I see him begin to slide his stick out for the poke check, I pull the trigger and snap a shot through his legs.

Well, not quite. That's the way it will happen when I tell my parents. What actually happens is because I'm so busy trying to figure out what the hell the newspaper headline will be, I lose control of the puck and it slides harmlessly into the boards. Didn't even get a shot off. On the lonely skate to the bench, I turn my stick around and futz with my blade, knowing full well it's not broken and the tape job is fine. On the bench, I continue to sell my stick routine, finally breaking it on the third attempt. Our equipment manager wanders over, shaking his head. That'll be coming out of my paycheck.

Despite my penalty shot gaffe, I score the game-winner on a backhander in the third period. On that note, coaches often preach shooting backhanders as apparently goalies aren't able to pick up where they're aimed. But how could they? I don't have the damndest clue where the puck's going when I release a backhander. Anyway, that doesn't matter. What matters is we win the game tonight.

After the postgame handshake (and subsequent hand swipe on the ice), I seek out Skoglund to ensure our misunderstanding has been fully squashed. By nature, referees are a defensive group, understandable since they spend the majority of every game being hollered at by coaches, fans, players, dogs, and cats. While they wear uniforms that are black and white, their job is all about the gray area, and no matter what calls they make, one team will disagree. It really must be a miserable profession. They never get to experience winning or losing—just yelling.

Whenever a ref has stood facing me, arms akimbo, it tells me I just received a ten-minute misconduct. However, today, Skoglund, with arms akimbo in a much more relaxed setting, invites me over for a chat.

"The other American on your team always bothers me about making sure he gets credit for his points after the game," says Skoglund.

"Kinda sucks we have to hound you guys, but unfortunately, the points matter, especially for us imports if we want to keep moving up."

"I understand. We don't have stats as referees, but we usually count how many times coaches tell us to fuck off—the less times, the more good we did."

"You like reffing? I mean, it can't be much fun knowing one team is always screaming and cursing at you when you call a penalty."

"Of course that part sucks. But you must remember, that means the other team loves us. And yes, it's not so fun when they play that song—you know, the one from the American movie, with the girl who has red shoes?"

"Yeah, from the *Wizard of Oz*." "If I Only Had a Brain" plays over the loudspeakers when the refs call a penalty on Kramfors.

"If I was good enough player, I would have kept playing, but I wasn't." He shifts his weight from his right leg to his left. "I love the game, always have, so I decided to become a referee." The Zamboni door opens as the driver honks for us to get off the ice.

"By the way," I say as we skate slowly off the ice. "That roughing call you made on me was a horseshit call." I open the gate and let him off first.

"It was a great call."

In the locker room, noticing his coffee cup is empty and clearly in need of a refill, Peter's post game speech is short: "Good match today. We need to make sure we don't do stupid things though," he says in Swedish. Facing me and Dean, he says in English, "We must do this with mouth," then makes a zipper-like motion across his lips.

"Skoglund and I are best friends," I say.

"You make friends with him too." He eyes Dean. "No fucks. No shits. Just hello, goodbye, and thank you. We must quit this," Peter uses his hands to demonstrate yapping mouths, "if we want to keep winning."

After showering, I find Peter lingering around my stall. He pats me on the shoulder then lifts his right leg and props his foot on the bench, his junk inches from my head. "I think it works well with you and Johan on same line. He are good with the technique, and Emil are also hard worker who can get you guys the puck. Good first game. You continue to look good to me."

Peter drops his leg and takes a step back as Dean returns to his stall from the shower. "Right now, are we in top three of standings."

"Yeah, we are," Dean responds.

"Right now, are we second place."

"Yeah, Peter, we're second," says Dean. Peter walks away as Dean turns to me. "Everything is a fuckin' question with that guy: Are we top three? Are we in second? No shit. You're the coach, figure it out."

"Thing is, in Swedish when you start a sentence with any adverbial phrase, you have to invert the subject and verb in the main clause." Dean's face scrunches up like he smells something that stinks. "So when Peter says, 'right now, are we in top three of standings,' he really means 'right now, we *are* in—"

"Alright, relax Shakespeare. All I know is that guy's gotta figure his shit out and quit saying everything like it's a question."

As I dry off from my rink shower, Niklas Gulliksson walks into the locker room with his two young sons, Eliot and Oliver. The three of them make the rounds, congratulating each player on the win. Before exiting, Eliot and Oliver run to my stall. First, eight-year-old Oliver recites a few lines from Eminem's "Shake That Ass."

Then it's six-year-old Eliot's turn. "He wants to show you how he can count in English," says Niklas.

"One, two, tree, four, five, *sex, sju, åtta, nio, tio!*" Eliot then swipes his crotch before raising his hand and offering me a high five. I decline.

Before exiting the locker room, I notice a small addition to my nameplate penned in by someone: An umlaut. I never thought two small dots could make me feel so good. I'm *Keenän*, now and forever.

Back at the hotel, after I take a real shower, I hear a loud slam in Dean's room, followed by a barrage of curses; it's like he's just been assessed a retroactive game misconduct from Skoglund. (I also hear the television blaring next door in Peter's room. I knew his eyesight was bad but apparently he's on the verge of losing his hearing.) I knock on Dean's door, which swings wide open.

"Everything alright in here?"

"Goddamn computer froze and cost me 500 bucks!"

Who knew online poker could be so dangerous? "That's brutal. Right in the middle of a hand?"

"Yeah, damn thing froze and the hand was *mine*. Got the flush on the kicker, then that fucking thing froze. Goddamn hand was mine!" As the steam pours from his ears, I see the monitor of his computer lying face down on the floor. A few feet away is the keyboard. It's probably not the most opportune time to enlighten Dean that his computer spike probably doubled his losses. Not the brightest move, but I respect the guy's passion. "Now I gotta fuckin' win it back in live poker in Sundsvall," he continues. A door in the hallway creaks open. "Is that Peter that just walked out, or Blohan?"

I pop my head into the hall. "Peter."

Dean pulls on some sweatpants. "Hey, Peter," he calls, then hobbles after the coach with an exaggerated limp.

"Dean! Are you injury? What happens with the walk?" asks Peter hunched over, peering at Dean's right leg.

"Yeah, yanked something in the game, think I tweaked my hammy," he says, pointing to the back of his right leg.

"Back leg injury? This is no good. Dean, you must play next game. Very important match. Maybe you must rest tomorrow. No practice," Peter says.

"Fuck, that might be a good idea. I'd fight through it, but I don't wanna aggravate it. I guess I'll see how it feels tomorrow, and if it still hurts then I'll rest it to make sure I'm good to go for the game. I'll let you know tomorrow morning." Peter turns around as Dean gives the universal "suck it" sign in Peter's direction. Once Peter is out of sight, Dean jogs back to his room.

I can't help but admire his performance. "That shit is way harder back in the States," he says. "Barely gotta sell it here. If I leave now," Dean eyes himself in the bathroom mirror and styles his hair, "I can make the late table in Sundsvall—Omaha, I think, no limit—and play all night. Be back to watch you suckers practice tomorrow afternoon." He pops three pieces of Nicorette in his mouth.

"How long ago you quit smoking?"

"Never smoked. Take this shit to stop dipping. I've quit like six times, but this time it's for good." He buttons his jeans and slips on his loafers then grabs the van keys off his desk. "Peace out."

Just as Dean disappears around the corner of the hallway, I hear Johan. I turn around as he pokes his head out of his room. "Dean gone?" I nod. Johan disappears into his room then a few seconds later reemerges in the hallway. "He thinks his pranks are so funny . . . Blohan this, Blohan that." Johan holds up a tube of IcyHot. "We see how he likes this."

"How you getting in his room?"

Johan reaches into his pocket with his other hand, removing a key card like a magician revealing a rabbit. He dips the key in and the little green light illuminates. Johan chuckles before entering Dean's room and exacting his revenge. "Now want to get your ass kicked in some *NHL?*"

"I'd love to."

Johan sprawls on his bed and signs into his Xbox account, Mr. Miyagi1984. "I hate when they clean our rooms . . . can never find my controllers. Wait, I think I feel something." He wiggles his ass then rips a booming fart. "Here you go." He removes the second video game controller from under his ass and chucks it to me.

"Might've soiled your thong." I hook my shirt over my nose and sit at the foot of his bed. "Since I can't breathe now, I get to play up screen the entire series."

"As long as I don't have to hear any bitching about no offside or icing."

Johan's phone rings. He checks the screen and silences it before the opening faceoff. "Girlfriend is pissed. Must wait till she cools down." Johan scores in the first minute of play. "You still suck, buddy. I thought I told you to practice." He tosses a pillow at my head.

"I have been practicing—been playing against the computer and winning a lot actually."

"On dumb-dumb level?"

"'*A*,' '*A*' . . . Hit '*A*,' idiot. We don't need to see the replay of every garbage goal you score."

"That's good ice hockey from me." Johan points at the screen and then finally taps '*A*' on his controller.

"Your girlfriend visiting this weekend?"

"Not sure."

"You guys in a *sambo*?"

He pauses the game and beams at me. "She wants us to have that. Me too, but I don't think it's possible until I quit hockey. She doesn't want to be living with me here in a hotel room that smells like shit."

"Understandable. There some reason people here don't really get married?"

"You know the word for 'marriage' in Swedish?"

"*Gift.*"

"Right. How about the word for 'poison?'"

"Not sure. Why?"

"Look it up. It's *gift* too."

"We talked about *Jante* law the other day in class. You know about that?"

"Of course. Everyone in Scandinavia knows."

"So it's about everyone being equal, right?"

"More than that. We are humble people, no showing off." He pumps his fist as his video game team, the team he always picks when we play, Team USA, scores. "It's part of our history."

I nod. Now one might consider it ironic that a consensus-driven, self-restrained, egalitarian society that emphasizes humility and modesty have so many of its citizens obsessed with the United States, a capitalist country riddled with ostentatious displays of wealth and defined by massive inequality and indulgence. Luckily for both of us, I'm not conducting some anthropological study. Just a kid trying to figure shit out.

"How's the Swedish for Idiots class going?" Johan asks as he scores again. "Fun game!" He nudges me in the back with his foot.

"I thought it was hard learning Swedish coming from the US. All the other people in the class from Africa and the Middle East, they don't even have the same alphabet."

"No chance for them. Can't learn the language so they can't work. Our system is getting fucked up."

"It's a place to start. Better than staying where they're from I guess."

I dump the puck into Johan's zone and his defenseman puts the puck in his own net. "Lucky bastard with the glitch goal," he says popping a snus under his lip.

"Now that's a replay worth watching," I say.

"You know that shit Dean likes to chew—some nicotine gum?" I nod. "So weird guy. I tried a few pieces—doesn't even do anything."

His phone rings again. "I got to take this now."

"I'm heading to Hemköp." I toss the controller to him. "You want anything?"

"Get me some of that syrup, cranberry flavor—the stuff Dean drinks straight."

In my room, I throw on my long-sleeve shirt, long underwear, sweater, fleece, second sweater, and overcoat then begin the half-mile trek to Hemköp. As is the case most weekday nights, the town center is deserted as candles light up the windows in the apartments above the stores. Nearly everything visible, the branches and parked cars that line the street, is coated in a fresh layer of snow except for the ground which is coated in sixty layers. An icy wind howls from my back, the type that freezes car doors locked.

As I make the second and final turn before reaching the supermarket, I notice a silhouette coming my way. Wrapped in a large, puffy, massive green jacket, his face is barely visible with his hood up, cinched tightly around his head exposing only his eyes, nose, and mouth. As he nears me, he smiles.

He's in my SFI class, and while I never got his name, I know he's one of four students from Somalia. He always sits in the first row and carries a briefcase in which he stashes his meticulous notes.

"*Tjena!* How are you?" I ask.

"Hello, Bill!" he responds, his eyelashes like mini-icicles shooting from his eyes. I didn't realize he knew my name. "How is the hockey?"

"Going well." Earlier in the week, our teacher had us describe our dream job. I said playing on the New York Rangers; his was being a cashier.

"Time for studies at the library. Have a good night, my friend."

I watch the man, briefcase in hand, walk into the dark, snowy night.

I don't get my Nutella and bread. I don't even make it to Hemköp. I walk back to the hotel, up to my room, and get into bed.

CHAPTER THIRTEEN

Northern Lights

OVER THE NEXT three weeks, the on-ice chemistry with my linemates, Johan and Emil, amps up—there's nothing like playing on a good line, with everybody clicking, putting forth the same effort. We topple Njurunda in a home and home series, before edging Ånge in a come from behind victory. I know the names of these teams mean absolutely nothing to you, but it's fun trying to pronounce them.

Dean's gambling prowess isn't limited to poker; he doubles his month's salary on bets he's placed on our games. With his winnings, Dean seeks out Magnus, the Gladan bouncer/Kramfors hockey fan/ *Expert* electronics manager, who hooks him up with a new computer and even replaces my electronic face washer.

I receive a box one morning with some belated Christmas gifts all of which demonstrate that my parents can still read my mind: two sweatshirts, a UV fluorescent light lamp, and a book, *What's a Nice Harvard Boy Like You Doing in the Bushes?* Eager to try out the lamp—which claims to help provide the skin with vitamin D—I neglect to read the manual per usual, thus not taking into account the required voltage conversion. I not only blow out the lamp but also set off the fire alarm. The book, it turns out, is just as helpful as the cold weather repellants. Written by Rick Wolff, it's a memoir of his year playing minor league baseball while on hiatus from attending Harvard. Although it takes place decades earlier and thousands of miles away, and is about a completely different sport, the characters he encounters and the experiences he goes through resonate deeply. I guess everywhere you play, there's a version of Dean, a version of Chara, and even a version of Röös. You get lost, you get found. You win, you lose. You get laid, you get lonely. But you stick with it because that's what you do with something you love.

On the first Wednesday of February as I prepare to hop into my newly changed bed sheets and pen in my diary entry for the day, my fire alarm inexplicably bursts on. I grab a broom and piñata it, until it shuts up.

As I slip into my pre-sleep drooling state, a pounding at my door forces me to my feet. I open the door, and am greeted by two firemen, axes in hand. They ask me about the fire, and I assure them it must have been a false alarm.

"How did you turn the alarm off?" one of them asks.

I point to the mess that was once my alarm. The firemen shake their heads, sigh, and retreat to the truck. One returns with a new alarm, then, after installing it, says, "Beat Härnösand on Friday. Also, tell Dean Moore #9 to move his fucking van out of the fire truck spot."

In our locker room as we pack our bags to load on the bus, a couple of the younger players stand, arms crossed, Yankees flat brims on backwards, in front of the dry erase board. Usually, Peter writes the line combinations here, to avoid any awkward confrontation with the guys not dressing for the game.

"What's up, boys?" I say to the two players.

"Perfect," says one of them, slapping the other guy on the shoulder with the back of his hand. "Harvard guy can help us. We stole our final test for Math class," he says waving a few sheets of paper in his right hand. "But we can't figure out this one." He points to the board which is covered in algebraic equations. I study the board, trying to act like some math genius and solve the problem in my head.

"What are you bitches doing?" Dean says from behind us, nudging the two younger guys out of the way. "Jesus, could they make their fuckin' language more complicated?" he says eyeing the board.

"This is algebra," I say.

"Where's Blohan? He's half-Chinese—probably get hard looking at this."

"Already on the bus," says one of the Swedes.

"Well what are we trying to solve?" asks Dean.

"Need to find X and Y. I think you need two equations to solve for two unknown variables, but it looks like the—"

"Yeah, blah, blah . . . move over." Dean picks up the blue marker and motions us to back up. He stares at the board, his eyes darting down from one equation to another. "X and Y, right?"

As Dean gets to work, one of the younger guys turns to me. "Billy, I wanted to ask you something. Is it true all the girls at Hooters in US are having big boobs?"

"Yeah, pretty big."

"This is awesome." He turns to the other young guy and they high-five as we return our attention to the equation.

With all the poker he plays, maybe Dean is some math idiot savant. Not making a single mark on the board, Dean performs silent, private calculations on his fingers. The two younger guys glance at him then me, and I feel the pressure to come up with the correct answer first.

"Boom. Got it," Dean says smiling at me and then the two Swedes.

"X and Y." He circles the two letters. "Hard to believe I barely passed the SATs, eh?" He winks at me and flips the marker up before catching it. "Now that I solved this Einstein shit, let's play some hockey."

Härnösand, located a short distance due south, is viewed by Kramfors much the way Lindlöven views Arboga. And I love these sorts of rivalries. Not only do they get the blood boiling, but they're a measuring stick; they tell you exactly where you rank. They help define you and your team.

While only 40 km south as the crow flies, the large lakes scattered throughout Norrland make it a winding, snakelike bus trip down E4 that lasts over an hour. The herd of moose loitering in the highway doesn't help.

"Check this out." Dean removes an earbud and leans across the aisle, phone in hand.

"You planning on a pregame pump in the bathroom?"

"Just recreational. Wi-Fi is ten times faster on the bus than hotel. Gotta take advantage of it." He taps the screen. "It's like Swedish Brazzers—one of the boys gave me the password. Look at this." He pauses the scene and pinches his fingers together, zooming in on the lone male actor who, standing on his tippy toes with an American flag draped over his shoulders, is mid-thrust on one of his female counterparts.

"I gotta start locking my door at night."

"Check the dude out. Looks probably forty, forty-five, and his goddamn hairline is flawless. Every one of these sons of bitches here— same deal." He shakes his head in admiration. "Something in the water. That's what I've heard."

"Could be."

"No actually something in the water—copper or iron or some shit." Dean tilts the phone in his hand. "Looks like he's got a Modano curve too." He flashes the screen in my direction, looking for confirmation.

"More of an Yzerman, I'd say."

Dean taps the hardcover book in my lap. "You're really into this shit, huh?"

"What? Reading?"

He nods.

"Lotsa down time. Can't lose money doing it."

"Can't win it either."

"True. This one is actually about a guy playing minor league base-ball. Some stuff is a lot like the shit here." I flip open Rick Wolff's memoir and search for a passage. "There's this one part where—"

"Yeah yeah, I get it. Books." Dean waves his fingers at me and puts his earbud back in.

In the last twenty minutes, I finish the book and scribble some calculations on my bookmark as we pull into Högslätten Ishall, home of AIK Härnösand.

"X is 13 and Y is 3," I whisper to one of the young guys as we file off the bus.

Eager to impress their home fans—or possibly jacked up on amphetamines—Härnösand comes out hard and storms to a 2–0 lead after the first stanza. In between periods, Peter treats us to an unusual screaming tirade.

"Fuck! *Helvete! Faaaan!* Fuck, what we do out there tonight? Fuck! *Helvete!* Shit! *Fy Faaaan!* We, everyone, shit fuckin' play. This *jävla* team fuck us, and we play like pussy in first period! We just lie there like girl and let them fuck us *i röven.*"[42] Across the room, Dean leans over, towel draped over his head, hands covering his face, shoulders bobbing. Peter picks up a folding chair and throws it against the back wall, then races towards the table in the middle of the room, ready to flip it over before noticing the coffee pot. He pauses, pours himself a cup, takes a sip, and lets out a contented sigh. It's like somebody turned off a switch.

Over the next two periods, we claw our way back in the game, eventually tying it at two. Few chances are generated in the five minute 4-on-4 overtime, which means the game will come down to a shootout. Peter chooses Johan, Emil, and me as the three shooters. None of us convert our chances, but Crille, one of our dozens goaltenders (we have a new goalie every week it seems), makes three big saves to send the shootout into extra rounds, after which Niklas Gulliksson, as he often does in tight games, makes his way onto the bench.

Härnösand takes the first shot of the fourth round and is unable to score, giving us an opportunity to end the game with our next shooter. As Peter and Niklas decide who'll be given the opportunity to play hero, Dean, sitting next to me on the bench, mutters, "Enough of this shit," then jumps over the boards onto the ice.

---

42 We'll skip the translation here. There's only so much verbal I'm willing to fully relive.

He casually skates to center ice, informs the ref he's shooting and takes off with the puck. It isn't until he reaches the blue line that Niklas and Peter become aware of what's happening. Peter adjusts his spectacles while Niklas clasps his hands together and looks to the heavens.

Although a big, strong skater and great passer, Dean has not impressed in our weekly shootout competitions during practice. More than once he's worn the Yellow Helmet that goes to the loser of each week's shootout competition.[43] Displaying the poise of a seasoned poker player, Dean skates in towards the goalie, winds up at the ladies tees, and blasts a slapshot over the Härnösand goaltender's glove. Guess he had an ace up his sleeve after all.

After the game as the team stretches/dicks around in the hallway, I overhear Peter from where I'm eavesdropping on the local newspaper reporter interviewing him. When the question is posed about having Dean, a defenseman, go in the shootout, Peter explains he felt it was time to give him an opportunity—Dean had earned his chance.

* * *

Inspired by Dean's recent success with gambling—he's been on a poker hot streak, and he won a ton of money on our Härnösand victory—I accompany him to Sundsvall for his weekly night at the casino. (I always know when it's casino night, because that's the only time Dean trades his flip-flops and shorts for loafers and blue jeans.)

"What are you doing?" I ask as Dean kneels in front of the van.

"Layer of snow over the license plate. We gotta make tracks and I got priors."

On the hour long drive in the *Micke's Måleri* van, I ask Dean about his net earnings from gambling. He goes into a long-winded monologue, peppered with incomprehensible poker terminology. It reminds me of *Medieval Latin 110: Latin Literature of the Twelfth Century* had I been dumb (or smart, I guess) enough to take the class.

---

43 The Yellow Helmet isn't a helmet you can wear in a game, but rather a piss-colored, beat-to-shit Jofa helmet that has a bow pasted on top and the word "idiot" drawn on the side.

Not quite Vegas, the Sundsvall casino boasts a vast array of slots, table games, roulette wheels, and a few old guys in oversized suits looking around for someone to be impressed by the wad of bills they're flashing. As a neophyte to this world, I listen closely as Dean teaches me basic strategy at the blackjack table. I wonder why the team doesn't just pay him in casino chips.

Dean's Swedish may be nonexistent and his English slightly better, but he's fluent in Blackjack as he taps and swipes at the table with his right hand and fiddles with his ever-growing stack of chips with his left hand.

After thirty minutes of watching, I toss two chips into the betting area.

"One hundred krona minimum bet, sir," says the dealer pointing to the sign in front of me. I toss in another two chips.

"Dude, you don't have to shield your cards. It's blackjack, not poker," says Dean shaking his head and giving some hand signals to the dealer.

"Fifteen, sir," says the dealer eyeballing me skeptically, as if he knows I'm clueless and will be wasting his and everybody else's time.

"Uh, hit me." I feel the growing pressure from the other players. Dean smacks the table.

"Fuck, man. You stay, you gotta stay on fifteen there. Dealer's showing six. That's a great bust card. 42 percent chance he'll bust on that. They teach you anything at Harvard?"

The dealer slaps a Queen in front of me, then removes my cards and sweeps my chips down a small opening in the table.

"Split 'em." Dean points at his two aces with his index and pinky fingers.

Queen. "Blackjack." King. "And blackjack."

Dean turns to me. "Now *that's* how you play fuckin' blackjack."

A few hands later, Dean turns to me. "You don't need the sunglasses either. No one's trying to read your shit. Plus, you look like you drive a windowless van." The dealer tosses each of us a couple of cards.

"We do drive a windowless van. Actually, you're the one who drives it," I say. Dean taps the table and the dealer tosses him another card.

"Twenty-four. Too much," says the dealer.

"Fuck this noise. Table's cold. Let's bounce."

We cash in then wait for the valet to bring around our van (Dean's frequent customer status at the casino has its perks).

After a stop at the gas station where Dean buys a Red Bull and two scratch lottos, we start the trip home through the blizzard that seems to never end here.

"I'm done with blackjack. Not my game." He places one of the lotto tickets on the steering wheel and scratches it with a coin.

"Why?"

"You're playing the odds, playing the cards in blackjack. I got no advantage. Poker is where it's at."

"But you're playing the cards in poker too, aren't you?" I ask as Dean tosses the lotto ticket to his feet and pops open his energy drink.

"Nah, man. Not at all. Check it out." Dean taps his window. "Sundsvall's rink. Now that's a fuckin' hockey arena." The rink looks brand new, a towering blue structure that catches your eye every time you pass it. There's a huge parking lot in the front with the team's logo lit up above the main entrance. The Sundsvall Dragons play in Allsvenskan, the league above us. That means, compared to our team in Kramfors, biweekly paychecks for Sundsvall players have more zeroes to the left of the decimal point than the right. And die-hard Sundsvall fans don't just work at the local electronic store and wear team jerseys to home games; they show their loyalty with tattoos of the Dragons' logo on their forearms. But those facts are just incidental to what matters most—playing in Sundsvall is one step closer to the dream.

"That's where we need to be next year—they had a guy last season who signed an NHL deal," Dean says, his eyes transfixed on the arena and what it stands for.

"Just need to finish this year off strong. Heard they're going to dump their two Canadian imports." The rink fades to black in my rear-view mirror.

"Yeah, so anyway, here's the deal with poker. It's simple once you understand the secret to winning."

"Knowing how to play the cards you're dealt, right? What's the best hand again? Royal flush?"

"Fuck the cards you're dealt. You play the cards you're dealt and they'll buttfuck you."

"So how's it work?"

"It's simple. Even a dumbass from Harvard could understand this." He looks at me smiling and gets working on his second scratch lotto before rolling down the window and chucking it.

"So what is it?" I adjust my body towards him.

"Secret is," Dean says as turns down the radio. I lean closer. "Dude what the fuck is that?" He leans over the steering wheel, staring into the night. I look up and see a green glow blazing through the star-dotted sky.

"They slip something in our drinks at the casino? That doesn't look real."

"Maybe it's some sort of air pollution coming from those mills up north," Dean says as the spectacular, celestial glow brightens, swirling about, oily in texture.

"You know what? I think that's the *aurora borealis.*"

"What? In English, not Swedish, dipshit."

"The Northern Lights."

Dean shakes his head slowly. "But that Northern Light shit . . . I thought that was in Alaska."

"I think you can see them anywhere near the North Pole."

"Sure beats the lightshow at our games."

The green lights, dancing in the dark, winter sky intensify and scatter as we get closer to Kramfors. It's like God is putting on a light-show, giving us a peek of heaven—a sight that makes you search for some greater meaning.

The yellow lights of Kramfors become visible in the distance, like an oasis in the middle of the desolate, Swedish northern woods. The snow, perpetual darkness, and bright lights of the city have a way of covering up the bad stuff and making everything look like a scene out of a fairytale. "Looks like some fantasy land," Dean says. "Not the hole it really is."

* * *

It seems like the Northern Lights were the hockey gods' way of saying they still have their eyes on me. Over the next month, we win seven of eleven games and life in Kramfors is good. Taking each game, each shift, and each red gummy bear at a time, I put up a flurry of points, as do Johan, Emil, and Dean.

Following in Dean's footsteps (yeah, you read that correctly), I place bets on seven of our games, converting on six of them. As Warren Buffett preaches, it's all about identifying the fool, and in this case, the fool is the clueless guy in Stockholm whose job it is to calculate the odds of the Kramfors-Alliansen hockey games. Some might argue the bigger fool is the Kramfors player who's betting on his own games taking cues from Buffett. Matty Dahlberg, an avid gambler in his own right, also makes some winning bets on our games; he's so hot that one of the online betting sites suspends his account. Dean and I stick to placing all of our bets in person at the local kiosk next to Hemköp, where Dean always points out, "I know I'm crushing it when Butterfly Tattoo tells me they're out of money and I have to pick up my shit at the bank."

On the ice, Skoglund officiates a number of our home games, and we become closer. He even inspires me to become one of those suck up douches who picks up the puck and hands it to the ref after whistles:

ME: Skogs, I made that triple we talked about last time. Asplöven came through and won in OT. Made four times on my money.
SKOGLUND: *Snyggt.* I've been referee a couple times with Asplöven games—very good team this season, good technique and skill. I tell you also if you like the betting, look at Innebandy matches—tomorrow Falun play at home against Helsingborg. Falun never lose at home.
ME: Oh yeah? I don't know shit about Innebandy though. Looks kinda like fake hockey for guys who don't wanna get hit. Actually, sounds up my alley. Maybe I should try playing.
SKOGLUND: Interesting game. They don't have back in the States, right? I tell you that is easy money. Take Falun and you thank me later.

ME: Alright, Skogs. I'll give it a go.

SKOGLUND: Do that. I read you come from New York City, is that true?

ME: Yeah, you ever been there?

SKOGLUND: Not yet, but my wife wants very much to take a trip there—shopping, Times Square, and all that—but it's very expensive.

ME: I'll hook you up. You quit giving me penalties and I'll make sure you and your wife have a great time.

SKOGLUND: You fucking Americans are unbelievable, always trying to rig the system.

With three games remaining in the regular season, we're lying on the bubble of making the playoffs, so it's desperation time—some guys desperate to make the playoffs and other guys desperate to have the season end so they can head to Thailand where the entire Swedish population goes in the spring. March may signify the beginning of springtime back home, but in Kramfors, it's when winter kicks into sixth gear. Micke of *Micke's Måleri* even installs a snowplow on the front of our van to make sure we never have issues driving to and from practice.

Saturday morning, with snow falling in heaps as it does twenty-three-and-one-half hours a day, Dean and I, snowplow down, make our way to the rink. At practice, our equipment manager stumbles out of the skate sharpening room and hands me my skates, almost cutting my carotid artery in the process. When I tell Dean about my near-death experience, he hits me on the back of the head. "Dude, what'd I tell you about getting your skates sharpened Saturday morning? He's still fuckin' buckled from last night. I smelled the whiskey on him from the other side of the rink when we got here."

"Relax. I didn't have him sharpen them. He just changed the tuuk.[44] Matter of fact, this one looks great and he did it in like five minutes." I shake my left skate to demonstrate its stability.

"Check it out," Dean says as he flips the skate upside down, showing me the tuuk hadn't been changed. Instead, he superglued a nail under

---

44 Tuuk: The plastic holder that connects the skate boot to the skate blade.

the blade. "Might want to use your backup wheels." Dean walks to the stick rack as I remove my second pair of skates from my locker.

"I gotta change my stick routine." Dean flips his stick upside down and sandpapers the shaft. "Takes me legit an hour per stick. And this sandpaper is for shit. Barely gets any of the grip off."

"Why not just order the non-grip model?"

"How 'bout you shut up."

Next up is Östersund, and there's a buzz in the bus on the way to the game. The team is excited to redeem itself after the two prior defeats against them before I came aboard. The trip is long enough for Dean to go through four packs of Nicorette and 4,000 hands of online blackjack.

Located in the geographic middle of the country, Östersund is, not surprisingly, cold as shit. Although Peter insists the entire team warm up together outside, it seems like jogging through the snow in subartic weather is a shitty way to get the blood pumping. I wouldn't be surprised to see a fat bearded guy on a flying sleigh pulled by reindeers above me one of these nights. On my way out to join the rest of the guys for a "warmup" run, I see Dean, wearing his flip-flops and hoody, in the stands of the rink, windmilling his arms before kneeling down, lunging his left leg forward, and bobbing his body forwards and back.

"Good idea, man. Probably easier to get a warmup staying inside than jogging around outside," I say to Dean as I walk up to the top of the stands to join him. "Tight hip flexors?"

"What's that?" he says without taking his eyes off the rink's lobby just below us.

"My hip flexors get crazy tight especially 'cause of my back issues. You wanna do a partner stretch, get my hamstrings?"

"Hip flexors? The hell you talking about?"

"The stretch you're doing . . . for your hip flexors."

"Dude, I'm just here for the view." Dean directs me with a nod of his head to the young blonde girls getting the rink's concession stand set up. "I sure ain't going outside runnin' around with those other morons."

And this is how professionals warm up. But Dean probably does have a point. I'd have a better chance breaking a sweat trying to work up the courage to go talk to one of the girls down there than I would jogging around the rink for fifteen minutes.

But while whoever staffed the rink's cafeteria gets an A+, whoever designed the rink's visiting locker room gets a D. The room is like a maze and half of Peter's pregame speech is lost on me since he can't figure out how to equally distribute his time between each of the room's hallways.

Östersund is one of the larger cities in which we play, thus it's not surprising that their team has a sizable budget, ensuring they always have top tier players. They also have a solid fan base and a nice rink, where they put on a good light show before each home game. After presenting some community service award to one of the players, the lights in Z-hallen are dimmed in preparation for the home team's starting lineup introductions. As each player is announced, the spotlight shines brightly on him. Most of the Östersund players sport the same coif—long blond hair slicked back and tucked behind their ears. With a palpable arrogance, each guy lifts his stick to the crowd before lining up on his team's blue line with his back facing us. After all the players are announced, the lights remain dimmed, a carpet is rolled out, and the spotlight turns to a young Swedish girl as she begins belting out the Swedish national anthem. After the noise stops, we slowly skate back to our bench while the Östersund players, still on a high from their ego-stroking introductions, begin wheeling around their zone. As I lean against the boards, squirt some water in my mouth, and spit, the Östersund-ians pick up speed around their own net, then each player, one by one, trips over the carpet, sending them catapulting through center ice on their stomachs. They scramble back to their skates and raise their sticks, as if it was planned. Maybe it was. We erupt in laughter, but this is where the fun ends for us tonight. Östersund playing at Z-hallen is like Nadal playing on clay, and they demolish us 9–1.

The bus ride home is quiet—no movies, just a few computer screens lit up as guys check scores around the league and send a variety of emoticons to their girlfriends on Facebook chat.

"Scooch over," Dean says as he folds his online poker hand and takes a seat next to me. "Last time I lost a game by that much was when I played peewee football." He shakes his head and pulls down the hood from his sweatshirt. "Some of the guys here—it's like they're happy to just stay in this league forever. Look at this shit. I'm sick of it." Dean tosses his plastic fork in the rectangular tin container which holds our dinner; the same as usual, cold meatballs and colder potato balls. "I don't know about you but I want to move the fuck up next season. I talked to my agent the other day and he said that no matter what sort of points I put up, it's going to hurt my stock next season if we don't make it to the playoffs."

"I hear you. It's like these guys don't really care when we lose. They're more worried about their girlfriends. Look." I point at the computer screen between the seats in front of us, where one of our defensemen is in the middle of an emoticon war with his girlfriend.

"If he put as much time working on his outlet passes as he does deciding between a smiley face or a winky face, he wouldn't have been a dash six tonight." Dean shakes his head. "I got friends in my summer mixed slo-pitch league who take it more seriously." He reclines his seat and turns his head to the window, gazing into the vast, snowy darkness. "Sometimes, I wonder, man. Like is there something better, not better, but different I should be doing? I mean this ain't exactly the life of a pro hockey player I envisioned as a kid." He pauses, not for me to respond but to collect his thoughts. "You ever think about what would happen if you were better?"

"What do you mean?"

"Better at hockey. Whether we like it or not, the hard work shit only gets you so far. Bottom line is there's shit we can't control. I just wish I was better." Players rarely will admit this to anyone, especially themselves.

"I know what you mean."

Dean tosses his hood over his head. "Guess I got to look at the bright side of our loss tonight." He removes a piece of paper from his pocket. "Got me the triple on my bet."

* * *

We need to win our final game, a home matchup against Kovland, to make the playoffs but our fate doesn't lie entirely in our hands. All we can do is win our game, then hope that this team beats that team, and that team loses to the other team. It doesn't look good.

With the game knotted at one a piece in the third period, we receive word that this team lost to that team, and that that team beat the other team, so we're mathematically eliminated from contention. Everyone on the bench is deflated, but after Dean yells, "*Fuck that shit! Let's not go out like bitches*," we put the foot to the accelerator and take Kovland to OT.

Twenty seconds into the extra stanza, with the faceoff in the left side of our offensive zone, Johan and I skate out. As a centerman in this situation, there are options—push the puck forward and try to hit the other forward on a backdoor pass for a tap in, tie up the opposing center and have your forward partner come in for the loose puck, or try to win the puck back to the defenseman and rush to the net. There are also a few tricks. Sometimes, right before I glide in for the faceoff, I'll turn my head back to the defenseman and point with my stick where I want him, hoping that'll fool my opponent into thinking I'm trying to win the faceoff back, leaving me free to push it through his legs and attack the net. While it sounds like a wily move, I have yet to pull this off successfully.

As I survey Kovland's faceoff formation and get in a few spits, Dean yells, "Billy!"

My buddy Skoglund, fortuitously reffing our season closer, allows me to skate over to Dean, delaying the drop of the puck. The situation is similar to a group of infielders in baseball consulting with the pitcher before a dangerous batter steps to the plate, something that never happens in hockey.

"You want me to go back with it?" I say.

"Dean!" yells Peter from our beach. Dean takes a few strides towards Peter who leans over the boards to tell him something.

"Yeah, yeah, I got it!" Deans yells, his back now towards Peter as he circles around.

"What'd he want?" I ask.

"Told me we should do the Ciccarelli faceoff play."

"What the hell's that?"

"Not a fuckin' clue."

"You want me to win it back to you, then tie up my guy and you get it to the net?"

"Yeah, sure." He motions to the stands with a nod of his head. "Top row. Look."

I do a 180-degree turn while Dean yells at Adrian, the other defenseman.

"The guy from Gladan?" I ask as Magnus, camcorder in hand, rises and waves at us.

"I wish he'd quit wearing my jersey every game. If we win, I'm definitely getting a late-night Facebook message from him with all sorts of fuckin' winky faces. I'm talking about the broad next to him. It's her. Red Jacket."

Adrian skates over. "What's up? Should we try the Ciccarelli play?"

"The chick with the red jacket," says Dean. I can't understand how he's just now spotted her. I saw her back in the first period while sitting on the bench.

Fuckin' Americans, I think to myself.

Adrian smiles. "Fuckin' Americans. Unbelievable."

Skoglund blows the whistle, and I return to the faceoff dot.

Miraculously, I win the faceoff back to Dean, who dekes out an opposing forward, then slides the puck over to me. I drop my shoulder, get the goalie on his knees, and roof the puck past his neck. Maybe it's a muffin that trickles through his legs—I forget the details. Either way, it's a goal. Game over.

There's not much of a celebration. The crowd, what's left of them, gives a subdued cheer which seems equal parts relief that the game's over as it is excitement that we won. We shake hands with our opponents, go to the locker room, change, and head back to the hotel.

In my room, as I sit at my desk dicking around on the Internet seeing how many different ways I can Google my statistics from this season, I get a call on Skype. It's Munch, one of my college roommates, who was a soccer player at Harvard.

"Yo, Munch. What's going on?"

"Holy shit, Keenan. You're alive."

"Yeah, yeah."

"You fell off the map the second you got your diploma and rocketed back home after graduation. Where the hell are you these days? Germany?"

"Sweden. How 'bout you?"

"Nice. Actually moving to New York City next month. That's why I'm calling. I was wondering if you were done with the hockey shit and wanted to be roomies again. I figured you're clean as fuck, and I know if we ever have girls back, well . . ." There's a pause and I hear him gently laugh. "Remember that time you asked Annabel Goldstein what she was doing for Easter? Classic Negative Game."

"I didn't know her last name at the time."

"How 'bout that time you refused to kiss that one girl 'cause you'd heard she had mono like three years ago."

"She had it six months prior and that shit can be dormant for a year. Gimme a break. So how's the real world treating you?"

"I thought the Harvard degree was supposed to make shit easier. Doesn't mean jack apparently. All I do is bang out models every day. It sucks."

"Banging out models doesn't sound too bad to me."

"On Excel, you idiot. So what's your plan?"

"Been thinking about it a little, but not really sure . . . maybe we should just start a cleaning business. I mean you like your stuff clean and so do I," I say, my voice picking up speed. "Or maybe we should open a pizza place here in Sweden. Their pizza is brutal and they love American shit. It could work!"

"Alright, relax. Listen, about the living situation. Here's the thing. The place I got needs us to sign a two-year lease. Can you handle that or you going to pack up one day and head to Kazakhstan with your fuckin' hockey gear?"

"Let me think about it."

"Alright, cool. I'll send you some of the info. Keep me posted."

* * *

They take it all off—the decals on the helmet, the patches velcroed to the hockey pants, everything. That's how you know the season is over in the European minor leagues. Guys pack their bags one last time; some say their goodbyes, others don't, and nearly everyone steals a bunch of extra gear from the equipment room.

Once back at the hotel, Niklas arrives while Peter, Johan, Dean, and I sit in the lobby discussing the games we should have won. After Niklas expresses his disappointment at the abrupt end of the season, he hands me and Dean our plane tickets home, then wishes us luck.

As I pack up my room, I can't help but wonder if next year at this time I'll be packing up another hotel room in some foreign city or sitting at a desk surrounded by computer monitors and guys in suits screaming at each other, or furiously taking notes in a lecture hall, or none of the above. Before I get too wound up about the future, I head across the hall into Dean's room.

"Hey, let's head back to the rink."

Dean's sitting at his desk, his face inches from his computer screen. "Why? I'm balls deep in a fifty-fifty tournament?"

"I forgot something." He clicks his mouse twice then shakes his head in disgust. "Fuckin' rags." He stands from his chair and closes his laptop. "Alright."

"So what's your plan this summer?" I say as we pull out of the hotel parking lot.

"Got free ice with my buddy who runs a rink in Tampa. Matter of fact—" Dean whips out his phone, swipes the screen a couple times, then hands it to me. "Our summer jerseys just got in."

I zoom in on the picture, reading the block letters stitched on the front. "DIXON CIDER. That some sort of drink? Never heard of it."

"Just say it a couple times, slowly." He snatches his phone from my hand. "So probably skate a few times a week and play some poker to keep my head above water for the summer. How 'bout you?"

"Not sure yet."

"I gotta cash this baby in." He pulls out a scratch lotto from his pocket as we turn into the lone gas station in Kramfors. Dean scampers through the snow into the convenience store, returning a minute later.

"So a couple years ago you were in school with that Facebook guy who's making billions now—"

"I told you—he dropped out the year before I got there."

"And now you're classmates with some guy working in the gas station in bumfuck, Sweden. Come a long way, huh?" He whacks me on the shoulder as he swerves the van out of the station.

"What're you talking about?"

Dean points into the convenience store. "That African dude in your class, right?"

Through the glass window of the store, I spot my SFI classmate, the guy in the green jacket, now wearing a suit, tie, and vest as he stands behind the cash register accepting money from an outstretched hand.

"Hey, you never told me the secret to poker. I'm thinking I might open an online account and give it a shot."

"Do me a favor. If you do, send me your username. I could use the extra scratch."

"Sure thing, dickhead. So what is it?"

Dean pops in some Nicorette. "Want some?" he smiles offering me a piece.

I knock it out of his hand.

"First, you need to tell me about all those papers in your room. You writing a book or something?"

"Figured there's some weird shit that happens here and didn't want to forget it."

"No one's gonna read your life story."

"Probably true."

"Maybe your mom."

"Harder part would be finding a publisher to give it a shot."

"You shitting me? That's easy. Slap 'Harvard' in the title. People'll think you're some sort of genius then they could read about what a dipshit you are. You gotta make sure you put that in." He smiles and slaps me on the shoulder with his hand. "And write a shit ton about me. Make me look cool." Dean gives me a serious look. "And smart."

"I guess I could make it fiction."

Dean smacks me in the stomach. "You gonna use real names and shit?"

"Probably."

"What if people were dickheads?"

"Then they should've been nicer."

"I'm not a big reader, but if your shit ever makes it out, I'm gonna attempt to read the whole thing. Maybe put some pop-out pictures or something in there."

"Alright, now tell me how to win at poker?"

We pull down the road to the rink, towering pine trees coated in snow lining both sides of the road. "See, I don't care if I have deuces offsuit or pocket aces. All that matters is the cards I see up here," he says raising his middle finger and gently tapping his temple. "I need to convince myself I'm holding the best cards. If I can't do that then I won't get anyone else to believe it."

"Like bluffing?"

"Not really. Kind of. It's not just about deception. You got to know your shit is better than everyone else's no matter what the cards say. If you can do that, you're golden." I stare at him, my brow furrowed. "What I'm saying is I can win a hand without ever looking at my cards. I don't care what I'm holding and I don't give a shit what anyone else has."

"So that's it? Trick yourself into thinking you've got the best hand, and you'll win?"

"That's part of it. Look, no one wins every hand. You're gonna lose eventually. That's how shit works. The key," he says taking his right hand off the steering wheel and pointing his index finger at me, "is knowing when to fold. The second you can't convince yourself you're sitting on the best hand, you're done. That's when you fold. When you figure that shit out, you're untouchable."

"Thanks, Kenny Rogers. You got any insight into *how* you know when to fold? What sort of stuff do I need to look for?"

"Christ, you know you can't always go around asking how shit works or trying to read about it in goddamn books and school."

"You got to have something helpful for me."

"If I knew it myself, I'd be at the final table of the World Series of Poker with Phil Ivey, not in this shitty van hauling your ass to a rink somewhere in Sweden. You want to know how to tell when it's time to fold? You play enough hands and figure it out yourself."

As we pull up to the rink, Dean swerves through the parking lot, jerking the emergency brake and sending us spinning on the ice.

"Almost had the 360 that time," he says as the car comes to a halt in a snow bank. "Ice's probably free. Wanna go for a quick skate? Play some three bar?"

"Nah, man. I'm good out here," I say as I peer out the window at the rink.

"Dude, you okay?"

"Just thinking." The snow falls harder. A lone hockey bag sitting outside the rink entrance quickly disappears.

"Don't get all gay on me." He unbuckles his seatbelt.

"Sit tight. I gotta go grab something from the locker room."

With the sun dropping behind the rink, I race into the locker room. Our game jerseys are packed up, probably somewhere rotting in a closet until next season. I kick the hockey bags out of my way, grab one of my practice jerseys in my stall, and tape my number on the back. Outside the locker room, the Zamboni makes its final lap around the rink, scraping off the ice, preparing a new sheet for the youngsters who wait eagerly at the gate, jockeying for position to see who'll be first on once the Zamboni doors close. The smallest of the bunch scurries to the bench, props himself on the boards, then hangs over them before tumbling to the ice. I bang on the glass as he scrambles to his feet before I return outside.

A fresh layer of snow has already filled in the footprints I made walking into the rink.

"Give me a hand with this," I say as I put the jersey on a hanger. Dean interlocks the fingers of his hands where I put my foot as he boosts me up so I can hook the jersey high on the outside of the rink.

"Not exactly a Madison Square Garden retirement ceremony, but it'll do." He helps me down and we take a step back.

"Here." I hand him my phone. "Snap a pic for me."

Dean opens the rear door of the van and removes a stick. "Sniped a few extra twigs from the equipment room after the last game," he says es the stick and tosses it to me. "Should last me through the Scooch to the right so I can get the jersey in the background."

ow's my salad look?" I ask.

"Money."

He raises the phone, and a moment is captured—

"Yo, your phone's ringing. Looks like an American number." Dean tosses it to me.

"Hello?" I say.

"Billy, it's Mario Amonte. What's going on?"

"Just packing my shit."

"Billy," Mario says. "Sundsvall wants you at their practice. Tonight."

I peer to the left. My jersey sways in the arctic breeze.

One step closer.

ACKNOWLEDGMENTS

I could write another book filled with the names of the people who contributed to making this book happen, but I won't. A special thanks to Deb Placey, Stan Fischler, Adam Graves, Arnold Gosewich, Alan Goldsher, Niels Aaboe, Joe Stopper, and Max Carter. Kudos to St. Bernard's School for giving me the audacity to think I could write a book about myself. Also, thanks to the doctors who put me back into one piece, the coaches who were always there to yell at me, and the teammates who were always there to make fun of those coaches with me. And like most of the stuff I do in life, the scoring line for this book should read: B. Keenan, unassisted . . . just kidding—assists go to P. Keenan and H. Keenan.